THE
ARCHAEOLOGY
OF ROMAN
BRITAIN

THE
ARCHAEOLOGY
OF ROMAN
BRITAIN

R. G. COLLINGWOOD

BRACKEN BOOKS
LONDON

The Archaeology of Roman Britain

First published in 1930 by Methuen & Co. Ltd, London

This edition first published in 1996 by Bracken Books,
an imprint of Random House UK Ltd, Random House,
20 Vauxhall Bridge Road, London SW1V 2SA

Copyright © R. G. Collingwood 1930

ISBN 0 09 185045 2

Printed and bound in Guernsey by
The Guernsey Press Co. Ltd

PREFACE

THE purpose of this book can be best explained by explaining the situation out of which it has arisen. Romano-British studies have for generations been among the usual interests of educated Englishmen ; but it is only lately that they have become a branch of scientific archaeology, demanding for its prosecution a special training and the thorough mastery of a special literature. Year by year, as this movement gathers force, the special literature grows in bulk. For the most part, it consists of monographs on particular sites, or rather, on particular pieces of work carried out at particular sites. They are highly technical, repulsively unintelligible to the general reader, and usually published (for that reason) only in the journals of societies, whence they never emerge into the general book-market except at the death of these societies' members. It is therefore impossible for the inquiring amateur, impossible for the beginner in archaeological studies, impossible for the foreign scholar, and all but impossible even for the best-equipped expert in this country, to work with the necessary books round him, or even to consult them at all.

The longer this situation is allowed to last, the worse it inevitably becomes. Owing to the inaccessibility of our technical literature, our amateur antiquaries become more and more amateurish, foreign archaeologists lose touch with our work more and more completely, and even the best archaeologists in this country show signs of not knowing what each other has done. The time seems ripe for some one to make a first attempt to digest the mass of technical detail into a manageable form ; and that is the attempt which is represented by this book. It is strictly, as the title of the series implies, a handbook of archaeology, not an history. It is deliberately elementary, because the people who need it most are the beginners ; what I have tried to do is to write the book that every one needs when he is first feeling his way in the subject, the book from which he can " learn the ropes" about the strictly archaeological aspect of the material which he comes across.

So elementary a book ought to have been easy to write ; but it has not proved so, because, on some of the subjects with which I felt obliged to deal, elementary and simple ideas were just what no one seemed previously to have worked out. No one, so far as I know, has reviewed the types of Romano-British forts, villas, or town-houses, as a whole, with attention to their varieties ; still less has anyone tried to draw up a list of the easily recognisable and certainly datable forms of coarse pottery or of the varieties of brooch. I have tried to do these things, and I cannot hope to have done them otherwise than rather badly ; the wonder is (to adapt a saying of Dr. Johnson's) that it should be necessary to do them at all. I shall be well satisfied if the defects of my treatment stimulate others to do them better.

However imperfect this book may be, it would have been far worse but for the generous help which other archaeologists have lavished upon it. Where I felt more than usually incompetent to deal with a subject, I sent my chapter on it to some friend who could help me ; and in this way Sir George Macdonald revised my pages on the Antonine Wall, Mr. H. Mattingly the chapter on coins, and Dr. T. Davies Pryce that on Samian ware. Mr. F. G. Simpson has helped me with the section on Hadrian's frontier; and the whole, or the bulk, of the proofs have been read by my father, Miss M. V. Taylor, Dr. R. E. M. Wheeler, and Messrs. E. B. Birley and C. E. Stevens.

The illustrations, except for the photographs and four or five others, have been drawn by myself; detailed acknowledgment of their sources will be found in the List of Illustrations. My warmest thanks are tendered to all the societies, museums, individuals, and firms upon whom I have depended for such materials. There is one whom my thanks cannot now reach: the late Mrs. Isobel Clayton of Chesters, with whom I discussed the project of this book several years ago, and in whose museum many of the drawings were made from which these illustrations have been chosen.

R. G. C.

Oxford
January 14th, 1930

CONTENTS

LIST OF ILLUSTRATIONS

(*Figs. 40, 43, 44, 49 are from a work in preparation on the Roman Inscriptions of Britain, and are here used by kind permission of the Haverfield Bequest Committee.*)

LIST OF ABBREVIATIONS

A. = *Archaeologia.*
A.A. = *Archaeologia Aeliana*, series 1-4.
A.C. = *Archaeologia Cambrensis.*
A.C.R. = Fox, *Archaeology of the Cambridge Region.*
Agr. = *Agricola* (Tacitus).
A.J. = *Archaeological Journal.*
Ann. = *Annals* (Tacitus).
Ant. J. = *Antiquaries Journal.*
Appletree Turret = *C.W.*[2], xiii, 351 *seqq.*
A.W.R. = *Antonine Wall Report.*
A.U.H.V. = Lindenschmit, *Altertümer unserer heidnischen Vorzeit.*
Balmuildy = Miller, *The Roman Fort at Balmuildy,* 1922.
Birdoswald = Birley, *The Pottery*, in report of excavations at Birdoswald, *C.W.*[2], xxx (forthcoming).
Birdoswald Turret = *C.W.*[2], xiii, 346 *seqq.*
B.J. = *Bonner Jahrbücher.*
B.M. = British Museum.
Brecon = Wheeler, *The Roman Fort near Brecon,* 1926.
Bushe-Fox = Bushe-Fox, " Mortaria," in *Wrox.,* 1912, pp. 76-80.
Caerleon = Wheeler, *The Roman Amphitheatre at Caerleon, Monmouthshire,* in *A.,* lxxviii.
C.I.L. = *Corpus Inscriptionum Latinarum.*
Coll. Ant. = C. Roach Smith, *Collectanea Antiqua.*
Corbridge = Reports on Corbridge excavations in A.A.[3]
C.W. = *Transactions* of the Cumberland and Westmorland Antiquarian and Archaeological Society, series 1, 2.
Devizes Mus. = *Catalogue of the Devizes Museum.*
Drag. = Dragendorff, *Terra Sigillata,* in *B.J.,* xcvi, xcvii.
E.A.S.T. = *Transactions* of the East Anglian Antiquarian Society.
E.E. or *Eph. Epigr.* = *Ephemeris Epigraphica.*
Gellygaer = Ward, *The Roman Fort of Gellygaer,* 1903.
Glastonbury = Bulleid and Gray, *The Lake Village of Glastonbury.*
Haltwhistle Burn = *A.A.*[3], v, 213.
Hardknot = *C.W.*[2], xxi, 31 *seqq.*
High House Turret = *C.W.*[2], xiii, 350 *seqq.*
Hofheim = Ritterling, *Das frührömische Lager bei Hofheim im Taunus,* 1913.
Huntcliff = *J.R.S.,* ii, 215 *seqq.*
Isca = Lee, *Isca Silurum,* 1862.
J. = *Journal.*
J.R.S. = *Journal of Roman Studies.*

Lowbury = Atkinson, *The Romano-British Site on Lowbury Hill in Berkshire*, 1916.

New Forest = Heywood Sumner, *Excavations at New Forest Roman Pottery Sites*, 1927.

Newstead = Curle, *A Roman Frontier Post*, 1911 (Maclehose ; now Jackson Wylie & Co.).

O. and P. = Oswald and Pryce, *An Introduction to the Study of Terra Sigillata*, 1920.

Old Kilpatrick = Miller, *The Roman Fort at Old Kilpatrick*, 1928.

O.R.L. = *Das obergermanisch-rätische Limes des Römerreichs.*

Pevensey = *Sussex Archaeological Collections*, li, lii.

Poltross Burn = *C.W.*², xi, 390 *seqq.*

P.S.A. = *Proceedings* of the Society of Antiquaries of London.

P.S.A.N. = *Proceedings* of the Society of Antiquaries of Newcastle-on-Tyne, series 1-4.

P.S.A. Scot. = *Proceedings* of the Society of Antiquaries of Scotland.

P.W. = Pauly-Wissowa's *Realencyclopädie.*

R. = Roman.

R.B. = Roman Britain, Romano-British.

R.B.B.E. = Ward, *Romano-British Buildings and Earthworks*, 1911.

R.E.B. = Ward, *Roman Era in Britain*, 1911.

R.F.H. = *Römische Funde aus Heddernheim.*

Rich., Richborough = Bushe-Fox, *First (Second) Report on the Excavation of the Roman Fort at Richborough, Kent*, 1926, 1928.

R.O.B. = Haverfield and Macdonald, *The Roman Occupation of Britain*, 1924.

Romanization = Haverfield, *The Romanization of Roman Britain*, ed. 4 by Macdonald, 1923.

Roman London = Royal Commission on Historical Monuments (England), *London (Roman)*, 1928.

Rotherley = Pitt-Rivers, *Excavations in Cranborne Chase*, vol. II.

R.W.S. = Macdonald, *The Roman Wall in Scotland*, 1911.

Segontium = Wheeler, *Segontium and the Roman Occupation of Wales* (= Y Cymmrodor, vol. xxxiii, 1923).

S. Ferriby = Hull Museum Publications, pamphlet on South Ferriby.

Slack = *Y.A.J.*, xxvi.

Swarling = Bushe-Fox, *Excavation of the Late Celtic Urnfield at Swarling, Kent*, 1925.

Throp = *C.W.*², xiii, 374 *seqq.*

Trans. = *Transactions.*

Traprain = Reports on the excavation of Traprain Law, Haddington-shire, in *P.S.A. Scot.*

V.C.H. = *Victoria County History.*

W.A.M. = *Wiltshire Archaeological Magazine.*

Woodcuts = Pitt-Rivers, *Excavations in Cranborne Chase*, vol. I, 1887.

Wroxeter, Wrox. = Bushe-Fox, *Excavations on the Site of the Roman Town at Wroxeter, Shropshire in* 1912, 1913, 1914.

Y.A.J. = *Yorkshire Archaeological Journal.*

York = *J.R.S.*, xv, 176 *seqq.*, xviii, 62 *seqq.*

THE
ARCHAEOLOGY
OF ROMAN
BRITAIN

CHAPTER I

ROADS

" TRANSPORTATION is civilisation " ; and no one ever knew this better than the Romans. Of all the remains that they have left behind them, their roads are the most familiar and the most impressive. But Roman roads are not so uniform in character as we are apt to think. It is a mistake to suppose that a Roman road always has the same features and the same structure. Some were elaborately metalled highways laid out in straight lines ; others were more simply made and less rigidly laid out ; others, again, were mere tracks with little or no metal and little or no definite design. Of the last class, which were probably the most numerous, it is naturally difficult to quote instances ; but the disposition of farms and villages is clear enough proof of their existence. It is only the most elaborate that can now be traced with any certainty, and they alone will be discussed in this chapter.

These first-class Roman roads are normally made of rammed gravel on a foundation of large stones. Sometimes many distinct layers can be traced when a section is cut through such a road ; but these are often due not to the original construction but to successive repairs. This system of covering a heavy bottoming with a stratum of closely-packed small stones is identical with modern practice, except that Roman metal is generally a natural gravel, not artificially-broken material ; and a Roman road thus made is often difficult to distinguish from a nineteenth-century macadamised road, unless other facts than construction are taken into account. Two others are especially significant : lay-out and evidence of age.

The lay-out of a first-class Roman road is, when the ground permits, rectilinear. This does not mean that the road looks straight on a small-scale map, but that it looks straight on the ground itself, because it has been laid out in straight sections from one point of view to the next. A Roman road does not often run really straight for long together ; but its changes of direction are angular, not curved, and occur normally on hill-tops, even quite slight hill-tops, where a new length of the line comes into sight. Hence, when one is walking along the road, it seems straight, even when on a small-scale map it may seem to be almost constantly changing direction. These facts, carefully observed, may enable the archaeologist to identify a Roman road which is structurally concealed by a wider modern road that exactly covers it.

Evidence of age is important in trying to distinguish a Roman road from a disused modern road. It may take two forms, documentary and topographical. Documentary evidence of age may come from old maps, or charters, or the like, or from parish boundaries ; for Roman roads have often been used as landmarks, and wherever a parish boundary runs along a road, or follows a straight line across country for a mile or so together, it gives rise to the suspicion of a Roman road. Topographical evidence of age depends on the time required by certain changes in the landscape, notably changes in the exact position of water-courses. This cannot be accurately estimated, but accurate estimate is not necessary for the present purpose. A metalled road, for instance, is found crossing a stream, and the stream has eaten into its bank so deeply that the road now ends in mid-air ten feet above the water-level. By its construction, as tested by eye and probing, it is either Roman or modern ; the question then is whether the erosion in question could have taken place since (say) 1750. If it could not, the road is Roman. Or again, a choked culvert in a metalled road has resulted in a wash-out, scouring away metal and bottoming alike. Could all this have happened in the last century or two, or is it necessary to allow much more time ? In the latter case, the road is Roman. In order to form judgments on points of this kind it is useful to study modern roads which have been abandoned and allowed to fall into decay. When this has been done, it is often possible to distinguish their condition from that of Roman roads similarly constructed in similar country, in which the same

processes have gone perhaps fifteen times as far. Where
excavation is possible, the character of the metalling may
be decisive ; and in this case special care should be taken
to look for kerbstones, which are normal in Roman work and
almost always absent in modern macadam ; but much can
be done even without excavation by a careful and practised
observer.

It is also necessary to distinguish Roman roads from the
pack-horse roads of the Middle Ages. These are normally
much narrower, and are commonly paved with large stones
laid transversely so as to give the horses a hold on the road ;
they are not aligned like Roman roads, and in lay-out they
are more like cross-country footpaths.

A Roman road is often, though not always, raised up in
the form of a causeway between ditches ; the width of the
road may be anything from 8 to 25 feet (16 feet is a common
width), and the ditches, which in the absence of a marked
causeway are close to the road—20 to 25 feet centre to centre
is a usual distance—are generally set well back when there
is a large causeway, and may be 50 or even 60 feet apart.
But a ditched causeway, though characteristically Roman,
is also characteristically modern ; and a well-cambered 16-foot
road with ditches 25 apart might easily be either Roman or
modern, apart from other evidences.

So far, the commonest structural type of recognisable
Roman road in this country has been described. Others
vary in respect of foundation, being built on piles or timber
corduroy ; or there may be no foundation at all ; nothing but
a layer of gravel. Or they may vary in surface. Here and
there, especially in the south of England, a paving of large
stones, as found on the Continent, has been discovered ; and
sometimes these paved roads are remarkably elaborate, as
in the case of the road over Blackstone Edge, with its central
track for skid-pans and its periodical transverse ribs, and—
most curious of all—the fact that it is constructed floating
upon a bed of peat. But these pavements are exceptional ;
normally the surface is of rammed gravel, though in many
cases this has disappeared either as the result of fair wear
and tear or because the modern excavator has unwittingly
removed it ; in these cases the road is reported as having a

surface of boulders or cobbles, but it does not follow that
this is the Roman surface as originally planned.

The normal lay-out is often interfered with by topographical
facts.   In hilly country a Roman road may be nearly as sinuous
as a modern ; though even here an attempt is almost always
made to reassert the principle of the straight line in short
sections where a modern engineer would not think of doing
so ; and the principle of angular changes of direction is in such
districts often abandoned in favour of curves so laid out as
to follow the contours or to obtain a constant gradient.   In
general, Roman roads admit of far steeper gradients than
modern roads ; and they often traverse hilly country by
climbing to the tops of the hills and staying there, when a
modern engineer would search for the lowest available pass ;
but this characteristic is partly due to military considerations
—a plateau country like the English Pennines being safer
to traverse along the summits than in the wooded and blind
valleys—and partly, perhaps, to haste, for the later Romans
often put in loops to ease a gradient which the earlier builders
had approached at right angles.   These mountain roads
sometimes show decided curves, the road swinging from side
to side of a summit-ridge in order to get a tolerably level
course and avoid peaks.   But among really rough mountains
the natural passes are used by the Romans no less than by
modern road-makers.

There is little doubt that most of the main roads were
first made for strategic purposes in the course of the conquest.
Hence, though it is a mistake to suppose that they were chiefly
used by troops—there were never any troops permanently
quartered in central and south-eastern England, except in
the late forts of the Saxon shore—the original planning of the
roads often bears traces of a military design.   One such trace
is the commonness of ridgeways, or roads built along the summits of ridges, like the Fosse between Leicester and Newark.
But though originally military, most of the British roads
soon became primarily means of peaceful communication,
including the passage of imperial messengers.   These employed
a system, organised by Augustus, of relays of posting-carriages,
travelling between *mansiones*, or stations on average about
twenty-five miles apart, and covering about fifty miles in

an ordinary day's journey. On occasions of emergency and
in favourable circumstances greater distances could be accomplished. The Emperor Tiberius once rode 200 miles in
a day ; but this seems to have been a record. The inhabitants
of the country through which a road passed were compelled
to act in this postal service, and roads of local importance
were maintained by local money and labour, the emperor
making himself responsible for military roads and those
definitely required for the service of the State. In practice,
most roads in northern and western Britain and, probably,
several main roads in the south-east were in the hands of
the emperor, to judge by imperial milestones recording their
construction and repair.

The posting-stations along the main roads tended to develop
into villages or small towns provided with hotels, baths, shops,
etc. ; and these form a definite class of Roman settlements,
distinct on the one hand from the agricultural villages and
on the other from the true towns, the centres of cantonal
life and local administration. They seldom seem to have
attained any considerable size, and in the military north
they are unknown, their place being taken by forts. Police
posts, which might be fortified, often occurred along the roads,
but in Britain these are hitherto almost unknown.

Bridges were built by Roman road-makers in great numbers,
and some, such as the famous bridges of Alcantara in Spain
and Saint-Chamas near Marseilles, are still in use to-day.
In Britain very few have been discovered, and the various
old bridges now standing that have been called Roman seem
in no case able seriously to claim such antiquity. All the
Roman bridges of which we have certain knowledge in this
country were wooden structures on stone piers ; instances
are those over the Tyne at Newcastle and Corbridge, those
which carried Hadrian's Wall over the North Tyne at Chesters
and over the Irthing at Willowford, and that crossing the
Nene at Caistor. It is difficult to decide how far a bridge or
a ford is to be expected at any given river-crossing ; for on
the one hand large rivers like the Trent at Littleborough
were crossed by stone-built fords, and on the other hand quite
small streams, at first forded, were later provided with bridges.
It is fairly certain that the majority were of timber throughout,

and of such nothing could now remain except piles, to be found sunk in the river-bed. Cases are not infrequent in which piles of this kind, probably Roman, have been removed to assist navigation, *e.g.* from the Lune at Lancaster.

It is sometimes said that most of the main Roman roads are based on British tracks of earlier date. While it is certain that there were such tracks, and that they had developed into a fairly complex system before the Roman conquest, we know very little of their details, and no general account of them can be given that is not mostly imaginary. There is no reason to suppose that the Roman roads were generally based on them. On the contrary, most of the main Roman roads seem to have been designed as instruments of conquest ; their course is dictated by the needs of strategy and not by those of normal communications, and the probability is that they were seldom at all closely guided by earlier roads. Nor is there any mystery about the means by which Roman engineers laid out their straight lines ; where direct sighting from point to point was impossible, the degree of straightness actually achieved is no greater than could easily be secured by the use of the most obvious methods.

REFERENCES.—Practical hints on finding and following Roman roads : O. G. S. Crawford, *Man and His Past*, chs. xv, xvi. Their construction : Ward, *R.E.B.*, ch. ii. Bridges : Gündel in *Germania*, vi (1922), 68 *seqq.* ; Ward, *R.B.B.E.*, 230 (not wholly reliable). Inns : Wolf in *ix Bericht der röm.-germ. Kommission*, 1916, 76 *seqq.* Police stations : Domaszewski in *Westd. Zeitschr.*, xxi (1902), 158 *seqq.* ; *O.R.L. Stockstadt*, 66 *seqq.* ; Behrens, *Germania*, iv (1920), 12 *seqq.* ; one in Britain, *C.W.*², xxvii, 170. Posting system : *J.R.S.*, xv, 60-74. The Roman road system in Britain is described in detail by Codrington, *R. Roads in Britain*, but with lack of accurate detail in the northern regions. The *Ordnance Map of Roman Britain* supersedes all other maps and has a far higher standard of accuracy than any other publication on the road system.

CHAPTER II

CAMPS

ROMAN remains of several kinds, as well as several not Roman, are popularly known as " Roman camps " ; but it is best to restrict the name to Roman works for the temporary accommodation of troops. Places in which troops were to be permanently quartered, though in certain respects resembling camps, are better called forts, if small in size, or fortresses, if large ; and the word " camp " is even less appropriate when applied to the ramparts surrounding a town, village, or fortified house.

Camps properly so-called form a recognisable class of earthworks, due to the Roman practice of surrounding every camping-place in which an army pitched its leather tents for even a single night, with a ditch (*fossa*) and an earthen rampart (*agger*) supporting a palisade (*vallum*). Theoretically.[1] the camp (*castra*) was rectangular, and had rounded corners and a gate in each side ; in the middle was the commanding officer's tent (*praetorium*), and the rest of the tents were laid out according to invariable rules, the basis of the lay-out being a network of streets based on two axes, the *cardo* and *decumanus*, crossing one another at right angles at the entrance to the *praetorium*. In practice, however, we find these rules constantly broken. They are far better observed by the *mensores* who laid out the permanent forts than by those who laid out camps proper. Camps are sometimes roughly rectangular, but not always ; often they are extremely irregular in outline. Sometimes they have four gates, but often they

---

[1] Hyginus, *de munitionibus castrorum*, written at a date not precisely known but probably in the second century, is the text-book for the camps of the Imperial army. The standard edition is von Domaszewski, Leipzig, 1887.

have more or fewer. The shape of a camp and the number of its gates, therefore, cannot be used as criteria of Roman origin.

But though the shape varies, a Roman camp—here, as always, restricting the term " Roman " to the Roman occupation of Britain—is always bounded by straight lines. Whatever their number, and whatever the angles between them, the sides never show any appreciable curvature. The corners are always curved, the sides never. Even when a Roman camp departs widely from the normal rectangle and becomes an irregular polygon, its sides are still approximately straight. Curvilinear earthworks are non-Roman.

The gates, again, are safe indications of Roman or non-Roman origin. With rare exceptions (Raedykes, Fig. 1, no. vi, is one) they do not occur at the corners of the camps, but in its sides. Even Raedykes is more an apparent than a real exception to this rule ; it, like most Roman camps, is trying to be a rectangle, and the west side is distorted so as to conform to the ground ; the true north-west and south-west corners have no gates in them. In type, there are two main varieties of gate : those defended by traverses (*tituli ; cf.* Fig. 1, nos. v, vi) and those defended by curved projections (*claviculae ; ibid.,* nos. ii, iii). Hyginus prescribes an external *titulus* combined with an internal *clavicula*, but this is rare in practice, and the type of gateway most often found is that with a simple *titulus*, which is a detached length of rampart and ditch forming an isolated work in front of the gateway. Double *claviculae* are found (Fig. 1, viii, A and B), and an even more complicated type is shown, *ibid.,* no. vii.

The internal arrangements of a camp are elaborately described by Hyginus. In the centre was the commanding officer's tent (*praetorium*) ; this faced the *porta praetoria,* and gave on the *via principalis,* joining the *porta principalis dextra* and the *porta principalis sinistra.* Parallel to this street, and behind the *praetorium,* ran the *via quintana,* at whose ends gates might or might not be provided. At the back was the *porta decumana.*

So far, most camps probably conformed pretty well to the rules. We generally find that a Roman camp is rectangular or shows obvious traces of being based on the rectangular plan, and that it has either four gates—two central in the ends,

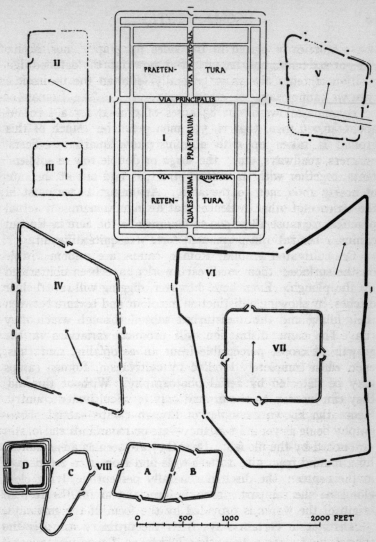

FIG. I.—CAMPS.

1000 feet to 1 inch = 1 : 12,000.

I, Hyginus's theoretical camp for three legions and auxiliaries (46,000 men).
II, Dargues (Northumberland).
III, Four Laws (Northumberland).
IV, Featherwood (Northumberland).
V, Reycross (Yorks).
VI, Raedykes (Aberdeenshire, showing distinction between large and small ditch).
VII, Dealginross (Perthshire).
VIII, Cawthorn (Yorks ; A, semi-permanent camp ; B, subsequent addition to A ; C, oblong camp ; D, unfinished fort).

two eccentrically placed in the sides (*cf.* Fig. 1, nos. ii, iii, vii)—or six (*ibid.*, nos. iv, vi). But how far the detailed disposition of tents always or generally followed the theoretical type we cannot say.

Hyginus allows about 83 acres of ground for a force of about 46,000 men, that is, 554 men per acre. Much of this ground is taken up with administrative quarters, officers' quarters, roadways, etc. ; the *striga* or double row of soldiers' tents, together with its central street, is laid out at the rate of nearly 1000 men to the acre. Assuming, as we must in the absence of other evidence, that his figures represent actual practice, we must allow 500 to 600 men to the acre in Roman camps. The ratio in permanent forts was quite different.

On cultivated ground, Roman camps are seldom visible on the surface ; their small earthworks have been obliterated by the plough. Even here, however, digging will reveal their ditches, by showing a distinction in colour and texture between their filling and the undisturbed subsoil through which they run. The same distinction will produce variations in the growth of crops, perceptible from an aeroplane ; and thus, even when completely levelled by cultivation, Roman camps may be detected by aerial photography. Without this aid, they can be seen on the ground only in uncultivated country. Hence the known examples of Roman camps—aerial photography being as yet in its infancy—are on moorlands and wastes untouched by the plough. Here they are seen as areas limited by a mound from 5 to 10 feet wide and from 1 to 2 feet high in the centre ; the ditch is generally perceptible, lying close alongside the rampart ; and the crucial test for the Roman origin of the works is provided by the form of the gateways.

Distinct in certain ways from the ordinary camp is the special kind known to archaeologists as " semi-permanent." Here the works are more massive ; the mound of the rampart may be 20 feet wide, or even more, and may stand to a height of 10 feet above the ditch bottom even before excavation. Apart from the gateways, which are of " camp " types with either *claviculae* or traverses, such remains are not easily distinguishable from permanent forts without digging ; and, theoretically, the temporary camp may shade off into the semi-permanent camp and that into the permanent fort by imperceptible gradations. In practice, however, the three types are generally distinct enough. The presence of *claviculae* or traverses at the gates generally indicates a camp and not a fort (a few forts have traverses, hardly any have *claviculae*) ; and the distinction between the massive rampart of a semi-permanent camp, and the slight rampart of a temporary, almost always jumps to the eye.

In a semi-permanent camp the rampart may (as at Cawthorn) be of turf, instead of earth ; it may (as at Burnswark) be reinforced by some kind of stone pitching on its surface ; it may (as at Cawthorn) expand at intervals into *ballistaria*, emplacements for artillery ; and it may (as at Inchtuthil and Cawthorn) contain remains of ovens. Inside a semi-permanent camp may be found " dug-outs," latrine-trenches, and mounds such as might serve to keep wind and water out from under the flies of tents—all structures suitable to a camp occupied for more than a night or two. A camp of this kind might serve as quarters for a force during an entire campaigning season, and might even be reoccupied another year, whereas the slender earthworks of a temporary camp were so easy to make that it would generally be more convenient to make a new camp, even for a single night, than to reoccupy an old. It must be borne in mind that a ditch 6 feet wide and 3 feet deep (a fair average size) surrounding a 20-acre camp to accommodate 10,000 men, would only hold about [1] 3000 cubic yards of earth ; so that even if only a third of the men were actually employed in digging, each would have only a cubic yard of earth to move.

The earthworks of a camp, whether temporary or semi-permanent, did not constitute its only defence. On the contrary, their main purpose was to serve as a basis for some kind of palisade. In the case of a temporary camp, this consisted merely of stakes driven into the *agger ;* the larger earthworks of a semi-permanent camp supported more elaborate palisades, which might amount to a vertical timber revetment in front of the rampart,[2] supported by posts and spurs, together with

[1] The exact amount depends, of course, on the shape of the camp.
[2] Dimensions in such a case might be roughly as follows : thickness of rampart, 10 feet ; height of same, 10 feet ; parapet, 3 feet ; battlements, 3 feet ; external height to top of battlements, therefore, 16 feet. *Cf. Germania Romana*[2], I, pl. viii, Fig. 1.

an embattled timber parapet, and a wooden " duck-board "
parapet-walk. When so elaborated, the earth-and-timber rampart of the semi-permanent camp becomes indistinguishable
from that of the earth-and-timber type of permanent fort.
The palisade of the temporary camp, on the other hand, was
a portable affair ; each soldier carried two stakes, and these
were used to make the palisade when camp was pitched.
It may be observed that, in the case taken above, there would
only be three or four running inches of rampart per man ;
in a camp for 3000 men there would be about 6 inches per
man.

The ditch of a temporary camp is normally single, 4 to 10
feet wide, and 2 to 6 feet deep. In a few cases, whether
because it is completely silted up or because there never was
one, no trace of a ditch is now visible (*e.g.* at Four Laws near
Risingham). Almost always the ditch is V-shaped or, as
Hyginus calls it, " fastigate " ; Hyginus describes another
type, the " Punic," which has its outer side vertical, but this
seems to have been seldom used, though an example (in a
fort, not a camp) has been found at Cawthorn. In a semi-
permanent camp the ditch is larger, and, on the Continent at
any rate, it may be double. Thus in a semi-permanent camp
at Cawthorn the rampart was found standing 7 feet high and
20 feet wide, and the ditch 15 feet wide and 8 feet deep when
cleared out (*Roman Camps at Cawthorn*, first interim summary,
1924, p. 2). The bottom of a fastigate ditch is normally cut
into a small square channel ; this makes it easier to clean
out with a shovel, and seems to increase its effectiveness as
an obstacle ; it is almost impossible for a man standing in
this channel, which compels him to have both feet parallel
to the axis of the ditch, to climb out.[1] In a camp, whether
temporary or semi-permanent, there is little or no berm, or
level space between the ditch and the rampart. A berm
becomes necessary only when the earthen rampart is replaced
or revetted by a heavy stone wall, which might crush the lip
of the ditch.

[1] This square channel is sometimes interpreted as a foundation for a
wooden palisade or barrier of some kind. It may in some cases have been
so used ; but in general no traces of such use are found, though they would
have been well preserved and easily found had they existed.

REFERENCES.—Useful (though second-hand and often inaccurate) general description of camps, Ward, *R.B.B.E.*, ch. i. Many plans of camps in Roy, *Military Antiquities*, and (more accurate) MacLauchlan's *Roman Remains in the North of England*. For semi-permanent camps, the British excavated instances are Inchtuthil (*P.S.A. Scot.*, xxxvi, 205 ; Burnswark, *P.S.A. Scot.*, 1898-99 ; *Trans. Dumfriesshire and Galloway Nat. Hist. and Ant. Soc.*, xvi ; *Royal Comm. Hist. Mon. Dumfriesshire*), and Cawthorn (interim reports in *Y.A.J.* ; full report promised in *A.J.*). Cawthorn alone of these has been excavated with a proper understanding of its character and the problems it offers. The *locus classicus* for a semi-permanent camp of the Empire is Haltern (*Mitteilungen der Altertumskommission für Westfalen, iii seqq.*). The planning of the internal arrangements in a semi-permanent camp is well seen, as revealed by air-photography, at Masada in Palestine (*Antiquity*, iii, 207 ; the whole article is highly instructive). Schulten's monumental work on *Numantia* (vols. i-iv) gives a detailed account of similar works of Republican date.

Although many temporary camps in Britain have been studied and planned, few have been excavated ; special interest, therefore, attaches to Macdonald, " The Roman Camps at Raedykes and Glenmailen," in *P.S.A. Scot.*, l, with report of excavations. The method of discovering camps by excavation, where surface traces have been obliterated, is described in Rice Holmes, *Caesar's Conquest of Gaul*, pp. xxv-xxvii.

CHAPTER III

FORTRESSES AND FORTS

§ 1. FORTRESSES

THIS chapter, like the last, is concerned with military as opposed to civil sites ; but, unlike that, it deals with sites which were, or at least were intended to be, permanently occupied. These permanent military strongholds fall into two classes according to size : the larger are conveniently called fortresses, the smaller, forts. The difference is not in size alone. The army of the early Empire was divided sharply into two classes of troops : legionary and auxiliary. The legions were units, each about 6000 strong, composed of Roman citizens. The *auxilia* consisted of cohorts (infantry) or *alae* (cavalry) with a nominal strength of 500 or 1000, composed as a rule of men from the recently-conquered tribes of the frontier provinces. The legions were therefore relatively civilised, highly trained, and expensive ; the auxiliaries relatively barbarous, rough, and cheap. The Romans, understanding that

> The captives of our bow and spear
> Are cheap, alas ! as we are dear,

preferred to put the auxiliaries in the forefront of the battle ; Agricola, at the Mons Graupius, deliberately kept his legions in reserve in order to have the credit of winning the battle " without shedding a drop of Roman blood " (Tac., *Agr.*, 35, § 2, *ingens victoriae decus citra Romanum sanguinem bellandi*), and in fixing permanent quarters for the various units it early became usual to station the auxiliaries forward on the frontier, the legions more towards the rear behind a screen of small auxiliary forts. Thus the small forts of the auxiliary cohorts and *alae* occupied a zone of territory along the edge of the Roman possessions ; the larger fortresses of the legions were disposed behind this zone, at once protected by it against the first shock of invasion and in a position to strike at an enemy who should break through it.

In Britain, when the first movement of conquest was over, the legions settled down into three fortresses, at York, Chester, and Caerleon-on-Usk. The steps by which this state of things was arrived at are not fully known ; but certain facts are established.

York was the successor of an earlier fortress at Lincoln. The Ninth Legion (Leg. IX, Hispana) established itself at Lincoln within a few years of the Claudian invasion, and remained there for about a quarter of a century. Of the plan and structure of its fortress we know nothing except by probable inference from the plan of the later town ; by analogy, we may assume a rectangular *enceinte* defended by an earthwork revetted with timber, and containing wooden barracks and administrative buildings. The stone walls at Lincoln, one gate of which, the Newport Arch, is still standing, must belong to a later period.

Chester, in the same way, may have been the successor of Wroxeter. Here the evidence is less satisfactory ; in place of the seven or eight legionary tombstones at Lincoln we have, at Wroxeter, only three ; and all attempts to find relics of an early fortress underlying the town have hitherto been vain. It is probable that there was such a fortress, but it is far from certain.

Caerleon must have had a predecessor ; but we do not know where it was. Gloucester is an obvious possibility, but no more ; the only point in its favour is the fact that an ancient *enceinte*, traceable there and ascribed to the Roman period, is the right size for a legionary fortress.[1] At the same time, if Caerleon was founded by Frontinus, we must look not very far away—conceivably at Gloucester—for the fortress

---

[1] See Baddeley in *A.J.*, 78, 264 *seqq.*, who traces a quadrangular lay-out implying a possible original settlement measuring about 1530 by 1300 feet (Caerleon is about 1600 by 1350) and apparently defended by a mound and ditch. But this, regarded as evidence of a fortress, is weakened by the fact that Glevum was a *colonia* (*C.I.L.*, vii, 54), and therefore more likely to be laid out after a military pattern than an ordinary town.

of Ostorius, twenty-five years earlier. For the whereabouts
of the legion before that date, the only positive evidence
which we possess might lead us to look in Devonshire; for
it consists of an early tile-stamp (*Eph. Epigr.*, ix, 1268) at
Seaton on the South Devon coast.

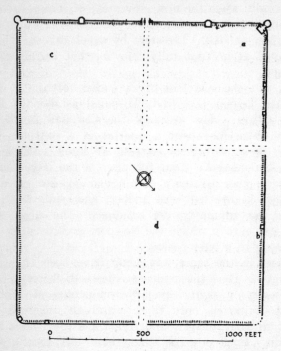

FIG. 2.—THE LEGIONARY FORTRESS AT YORK.

500 feet to 1 inch = 1 : 6000.

(*a*) Early timber buildings.
(*b*) Stone barrack-buildings demolished and covered by fourth-century ram-
            part-bank.
(*c*) Stone barrack-buildings with relics down to *c.* A.D. 250.
(*d*) Fourth-century occupation-deposits.

It would be out of place in this book to give a detailed
description either of a legionary fortress in general or of the
three British examples. For the general type, reference may
be made to Stuart Jones, *Companion to Roman History*,
pp. 232-243 ; *Germania Romana* [2], part i ; *Bonner Jahrbücher*,
cxi, cxii ; Cagnat, *L'armée romaine d'Afrique*, and " Les deux

camps de Lambaesis" in *Mémoires de l'Académie des Inscriptions*, xxxviii. We shall give a brief account of the British fortresses according to the present state of our knowledge, most of which is very recently acquired.

York (*Eburacum*, changing to *Eboracum* in the later imperial age).—The outline of the fortress, as shown on the plan, obviously lacks homogeneity. The south-west front, facing the Ouse, has the projecting towers of the late Empire. The "Multangular Tower" at the western angle, which is still standing to a considerable height, the similar tower of which traces have been found at the southern angle, and the two known intermediate bastions, breaking the line of the curtain-wall and projecting both before and behind it, recall work dated elsewhere to about A.D. 300 ; [1] but features of this kind are altogether absent from the rest of the *enceinte*. Search for a similar corner-tower has not yet been made on the north ; but on the east excavation has shown that no such tower ever existed ; and the interval-towers, so far as they are known, are all of the early internal type except on the south-west.

Excavation at once reinforces and modifies this *prima facie* appearance. The work of the York Excavation Committee, begun in 1925, has shown that the north-east and south-east walls are on the line of a Flavian earthen rampart, which has been followed by two successive stone walls, one about the beginning, the other about the end, of the second century. On these two sides it appears that the limits of the fortress never underwent any change. But on the other two sides this is not the case. On the north-west the existing wall is wholly of late date, contemporary with the Multangular Tower and the late south-west front ; and there is reason to think that the earlier fortress extended farther to the north-west, because at *b* on the plan the remains of a building have been found which appears to have been a first- and second-century barrack underlying the earthen bank of the late wall (*J.R.S.*, xviii, 90-92), and demolished when that wall was built.

On the south-west, similarly, the existing wall as shown on the plan fails to correspond with any earlier wall ; search

---

[1] *Cf.* the plans of fortifications of this period in Stähelin, *Die Schweiz in römischer Zeit.*

has been made for earlier ramparts and ditches on its line, but without success (*J.R.S.*, xviii, 83), and here, too, it is suspected that the earlier fortress extended farther, this time to the south-west. That it did not stop short of the later wall, is shown by the discovery (at *a* on the plan) of early wooden buildings not far inside its line, presumably belonging to the Flavian fortress (*J.R.S.*, xv, 186). Elsewhere (at *c* on the plan) what appears to be a second-century barrack-building has been found in a rather similar position (*J.R.S.*, xviii, 96). It may be observed that evidence of a fourth-century occupation has come to light within the fortress only at one place (*d* on the plan) ; a fact which suggests that at this time the garrison did not live inside the walls.

As a general summary of our present knowledge, Mr. S. N. Miller's conclusions (in *J.R.S.*, xviii, 98-99) may be quoted in full :—

" The first fortress at York, the headquarters of the Ninth Legion, was probably established by Petilius Cerialis between 71 and 74, and it must have served as one of the bases from which Agricola laid out his system of forts over the Brigantian territory in 79. It had a clay rampart and timber barracks. Its extent is unknown. In the early part of the second century stone gateways and towers were erected, linked up by a stone wall built, for a considerable part of its course at all events, along the outer margin of the original rampart. The timber buildings of the interior were rebuilt in stone at the same time. This translation of the early fortress into stone was begun at least as early as the middle of Trajan's reign (108-109), though it may not have been completed until the early years of the reign of Hadrian, when the Sixth Legion replaced the Ninth, or there may have been some reconstruction at that time. There was certainly an extensive restoration [now assigned to the reign of] Septimius Severus, following upon a serious disaster. . . . So far as we can tell, this restoration did not mean any change in the outline of the fortress, but that outline is known to us only along parts of the north-east and south-east sides. Of the other sides we know nothing, except that on the north-west the defences in the second and third centuries probably lay further out than in the fourth century.

" For nearly a hundred years after the death of Severus

no further changes can be recognised as due to external causes, but in the disorders that marked the closing years of the third century the defences of the fortress were again largely destroyed. Their reconstruction is probably to be connected with the activity of Constantius Chlorus in Britain in the early years of the fourth century. Along part at least of the south-east front, and along the north-east front as far as the gateway, the existing wall was in a condition to be re-used. Between the north-east gateway and the corner it had to be rebuilt. On the north-west side the fourth-century builders marked out a new line, and a new line was also probably followed along the river-front, where the defence now took the form of a curtain-wall connecting two large corner-bastions, with smaller projecting towers between. On the north-west side, if not on both, the change apparently meant a reduction in the size of the fortress, but the area enclosed was still fifty acres. That the large defensive force which such an area implies may not have lived in permanent quarters within the walls is suggested by certain evidence for barracks being demolished within the reduced *enceinte*, as well as by the rarity of fourth-century objects within that part of the area which adjoins the defences." [1]

Chester (Deva).—The fortress lies on the north bank of the Dee, and, like York, has its front towards the river. Its northern and eastern sides are fixed, the walls being explored for a considerable length on both sides ; the south-east corner is visible, and this fixes the north-south length of the fortress ; but the position of its east side is known only inferentially. The inference, however, is fairly secure, and the plan here reproduced [2] may be taken as correct, the width from east to west being fixed by the discovery of the *porta decumana* in 1809. This gives a rectangle measuring about 1950 feet by 1360 feet, or, allowing for the thickness of the defences, about 56 acres. The defences consisted of a massive stone wall and double ditch, with a bank of sandy clay behind the

---

[1] Reports of the recent excavations—which are not yet concluded—are in *J.R.S.*, xv, xviii. Of earlier books the most important are Drake, *Eboracum* (1736), and Wellbeloved, *Eburacum* (1842). Home, *Roman York* (1924), is a popular work written just before the recent excavations were begun.

[2] By Mr. P. H. Lawson, in *Chester Arch. Soc. Journal*, xxvii, part ii.

wall. In 1883 and subsequently a large number of inscribed and sculptured stones were found built into the north wall; and from the dates of these it became clear that the wall had not been built until some time after 150 (Haverfield, *Catalogue of the Roman Inscribed and Sculptured Stones in the Grosvenor*

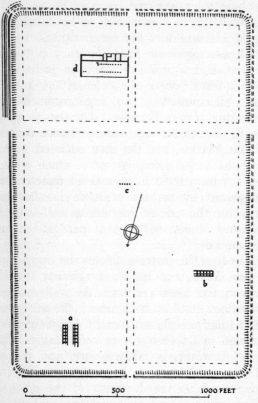

FIG. 3.—THE LEGIONARY FORTRESS AT CHESTER.

500 feet to 1 inch = 1 : 6000.

(*a*), (*b*), Barrack-buildings.
(*c*) Colonnade in praetorium.
(*d*) Building with two rows of columns; hypocausts adjoining on the south.

Museum, Chester, 1900, p. 7); "it would, therefore, seem probable that the wall which contained these stones was erected in the latter part of the second century or in the commencement of the third century " (*loc. cit.*). In other words, we find at Chester exactly what we find at York—an extensive rebuilding of the defences, after what must have been a serious disaster, about the year 200.

Many relics of internal buildings have come to light, but most are so fragmentary that little can be said about them. The largest and most important are shown on the plan. At *a*, in the Deanery Field, Professor Newstead has been exploring a group of barrack-buildings for some years past (cf. *Liverpool Annals of Archaeology and Anthropology*, xi, 59-86 ; *Chester Arch. Jour.*, xxvii, 144). These buildings go back to the late Flavian period, but no proof of an occupation earlier than that has yet been discovered. At *b*, in Hunter Street, another barrack-building has been excavated (*Chester Arch. Jour.*, xxvii, 61), and assigned to the same date. From these two sites it is clear that the barracks were arranged as at Novaesium, longitudinally at the decuman end of the fortress, transversely a little farther towards the front. At *c*, a row of bases would appear to indicate the position of a colonnade in the *praetorium ;* and at *d* considerable remains of a large colonnaded building have been found, which has been compared with the so-called *schola* at Novaesium (*Chester Arch. Jour.*, xxvii, 116). Adjoining this on the south are several rooms with hypocausts which have been explained as officers' baths (*ibid.*, xvi, 118).

Apart from the reconstruction already mentioned, little can be said about the history of the fortress. The fact that one tombstone has been found there which may have recorded a legionary with no *cognomen* points to an early date for its foundation ; but, although the possession of a *cognomen* becomes almost invariable after the middle of the first century A.D., this is too slender an argument on which to base any statement as to the date at which the fortress was first established. There is, however, more than a possibility that it may have been founded by Ostorius Scapula when, about A.D. 50, he invaded the territory of the Decangi, as Tacitus calls them, or Degeangli, as they are called on the lead pigs that come from their territory (Tac., *Ann.*, 12, 31-32 ; for the name, *J.R.S.*, xii, 284). The water supply of the fortress was reorganised by Agricola (*Eph. Epigr.*, ix, 1039) in A.D. 79 ; after that we have no further archaeological data except in connection with the reconstruction which probably took place under Severus.[1]

Caerleon-on-Usk (Isca Silurum).—In spite of the existence of a large number of inscriptions derived from this site, accurate

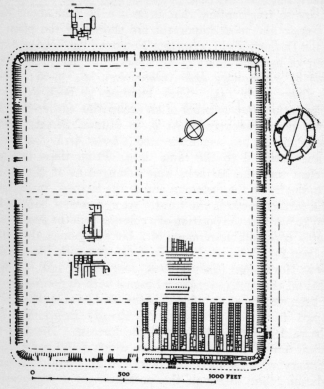

FIG. 4.—THE LEGIONARY FORTRESS AT CAERLEON-ON-USK.

500 feet to 1 inch = 1 : 6000.

knowledge of the site itself only dates from the end of 1925, when systematic excavations were begun. These were partly in the fortress and partly in the amphitheatre. The work in the fortress is still in progress and no report has appeared

[1] Lawson, "Schedule of the Roman Remains of Chester, with Maps and Plans," in *Chester Arch. J.*, xxvii (1928), is the latest summary of the material. Of the older works, Watkin, *Roman Cheshire*, is the most important. Publications quoted in the text need not be referred to here.

except the brief annual notes[1] contributed by Mr. V. E. Nash-Williams to *J.R.S.*; that in the amphitheatre is complete and has been reported on in *A.* (vol. lxxviii). This report will be used, for its bearing on the history of the fortress, in what follows.

The fortress measures about 1600 feet by 1350 feet, or 50 acres inside the defences. These consist of a composite rampart—a stone wall 5 to 5½ feet thick, backed by a clay bank—and a single ditch. Inside the fortress, a number of barrack-buildings have been excavated, as well as various other buildings shown on the plan, which records all discoveries down to December, 1929; outside, the bath-building and the amphitheatre have been explored, the former incompletely.

The history of the fortress, as determined by the recent excavations, is as follows. It was founded, in the shape of a clay and-timber structure with internal buildings mainly, at least, of wood, in the first century. The date of foundation appears to fall in the decade 70-80, and may well coincide with the campaigns of Frontinus in 74-75 (*J.R.S.*, xvii, 186); there is no evidence whatever that this was the fortress founded by Ostorius Scapula in the Silurian country a quarter of a century earlier (Tac., *Ann.*, xiii, 32), traces of which, had it been at Caerleon, could hardly have escaped the excavators, although (as Dr. Wheeler reminds us in *A.*, lxxviii, 152) that possibility cannot yet be absolutely excluded. The building of the amphitheatre followed, apparently, a few years later —about A.D. 80 or soon after (*loc. cit.*).

At the close of the century—the date seems definitely fixed at A.D. 99-100 by an inscription of Trajan (*J.R.S.*, xviii, 211)—the barracks began to be rebuilt in stone and a stone revetment was added to the rampart. During the years 140-200 the occupation was slight, and the legion was probably away in the north, or at any rate the greater part of its personnel was serving in the frontier area (*A.*, lxxviii, 153); but about 200 there was a reorganisation here as at the other fortresses, though we do not know that Caerleon had suffered any such disaster as they had. Throughout the third century this

---

[1] While this book was in the press, Mr. Nash-Williams's report on the excavations of 1926 appeared (*A.C.*, 1929).

revived occupation went on ; in 259 we have the record of barracks rebuilt (*C.I.L.*, vii, 107) ; but about 296 the coin-series abruptly stops, and it seems that when York was rebuilt at the end of the third century, Caerleon was abandoned. The existence of a Saxon Shore fort at Cardiff suggests that the legion was now moved thither from Caerleon (*Ant. J.*, ii, 370 ; *A.*, lxxviii, 155) ; the *Notitia Dignitatum*, placing the same unit at Richborough (*Oc.*, xxviii, 19), may refer to a later migration.[1]

§ 2. FORTS

The term " fort " is used as a translation of *castellum*, which strictly means a small camp. But in practice a Roman fort is something rather more than a small camp ; developed though it obviously is from the marching-camp, it has acquired certain features of its own, due to the fact that, whereas the marching-camp is essentially a slight and temporary work, the *castellum*, though small, is comparatively solid and permanent. Its purpose was to house a unit acting as a police force to patrol a small district. Such a force was too small to fight a pitched battle, and required strong defences against a sudden attack and comfortable quarters against inclement weather. These are the features, other than size, which commonly distinguished a fort from a camp.

A *castellum* is normally designed either for a *cohors quingenaria* or for a *cohors milliaria*.[2] In these permanent quarters, the crowded state of a marching-camp would have been intolerable ; and therefore we find that 200 to 250 men per acre is a normal ratio between garrison and area. The area of forts, throughout this book, means the extent of the ground contained inside the rampart and available for buildings,

---

[1] Lee, *Isca Silurum* (1862), is the most important of the earlier publications. H. G. Evelyn-White, *First Annual Report* (1908) of the Liverpool Committee for Excavation and Research in Wales, describes excavations before 1925. Wheeler, *Prehistoric and Roman Wales*, 222-228, summarised the state of knowledge in that year. Since then, see the annual notes in *J.R.S.*, xv seqq., and *A.*, lxxviii, 111-218, for the amphitheatre, and *A.C.*, 1929, for the fortress.

[2] Probably a *cohors quingenaria* had an actual paper strength of 480 men, a *cohors milliaria* of 800. Cheesman, *Auxilia of the Roman Army*, p. 28.

roads, etc.[1] Thus a fort with an area of about 2 to 3 acres would hold a *cohors quingenaria ;* one of 4 to 5 acres, a *cohors milliaria.* The presence or absence of a cavalry contingent would, of course, affect the ratio of garrison to area.

A generalised description of the main features of a Roman fort will show how closely its lay-out follows that of the traditional camp. Normally, a *castellum* is rectangular or approximately so, though its right angles are sometimes inaccurate. It is surrounded by a rampart (*vallum*) and one or more ditches (*fossae*), curving round its corners and interrupted (though the ditches are sometimes bridged, not broken) at the four gates. In the shorter sides these gates are central. In the longer sides they are out of centre, being pushed somewhat towards the front end of the fort. In the middle of the fort stands the headquarters building (*principia*),[2] whose gateway faces the front gate of the fort (*porta praetoria*) and is connected with it by a road, the *via praetoria.* At right angles to this road runs another, the *via principalis*, which runs along the front of the headquarters and connects the two side gates, the *porta principalis dextra* and *porta principalis sinistra.* To right and left of the headquarters are generally other official buildings, including a house, doubtless the residence of the commanding officer (*praetorium*), and one or more granaries (*horrea*), recognisable by their massive construction, buttressed walls, and raised damp-proof floors. This block of central buildings divides the *praetentura* or front area from the *retentura* or back area : in these areas are the long narrow barrack blocks in which the garrison is housed. The *via*

---

[1] In other books the area of forts is often differently calculated : sometimes it is based on measurements to the outer face of the ramparts, sometimes it even includes the ditches. The reader is warned against apparent contradictions between statements based on such different senses of the same term.

[2] In a fort, this administrative building occupies the central position which, in a camp, is occupied by the *praetorium.* But inscriptions show that in a fort there was a building called *principia* (a word which does not appear in Hyginus's account of the camp) and distinct from another building called *praetorium.* There has been controversy about the precise meaning of these terms, but the view taken in the text is based on the phrase *praetor(ium) quod erat humo copert(um) et in labe conl(apsum) et principia et bal(listaria ?) rest(ituit)* in an inscription found at Birdoswald in 1929. These words show (i) that the two names are not synonymous, (ii) that neither includes the other. Each therefore denotes a distinct building.

quintana, running parallel to the *via principalis* and dividing the central block from the *retentura*, may have a postern gate at each end, but this is rare. From the back of the head-quarters the *via decumana* runs, prolonging the line of the *via praetoria*, to the back gate or *porta decumana*. And a road runs all round the buildings in the *intervallum* immediately behind the rampart.

The history of the Roman fort in Britain covers a period of over 350 years. In that time its construction and design underwent considerable changes, which may be summed up under five heads :—

(1) In *size* there was a tendency to increase. The standard fort of the first and second century is about 2½ acres in extent, being designed for a garrison of 500. The standard fort of the fourth century, as we find it on the Saxon Shore, runs from about 5 to about 9 acres. On the other hand, these " standard " sizes must not be taken too seriously ; forts of the early period vary a great deal in size, and small forts were built in the Saxon Shore period.

(2) In *shape*, the earliest forts are apt to be irregular. Examples of this are rare in Britain, because in the second half of the first century A.D. the standard " playing-card " shape was establishing itself. This shape is practically universal in the second century. The latest forts, however, sometimes depart from it and adopt an irregular plan.

(3) In *materials*, the earliest forts in Britain were earthworks revetted with timber. About A.D. 100 or soon after, it became usual to replace the timber by stone. As time goes on, the stone work becomes increasingly important, and in some of the latest forts the earth bank was omitted altogether.

(4) In the *internal buildings* there is a marked change. The earlier forts exist primarily to house a garrison, and their barrack-buildings, whether of wood or of stone, are an essential feature. In the latest forts the barrack-buildings disappear altogether. The garrison, it would seem, no longer lives in the fort.

(5) In *tactical purpose* there is a change which is bound up with the preceding. The early forts housed a garrison trained to fight in the open ; they are therefore supplied with plenty of broad gateways, and the problem of turning their

rampart-walk into a defensible fighting platform is not taken
at all seriously. As time goes on, walls become higher, gates
become fewer and narrower, bastions are added to enfilade
attacking parties, and *ballistaria* or gun-platforms are multiplied.
The word *castellum*, from its original sense of " little camp,"
is moving towards its medieval sense of " castle."

To illustrate this history, we shall describe examples of
forts belonging to various periods.

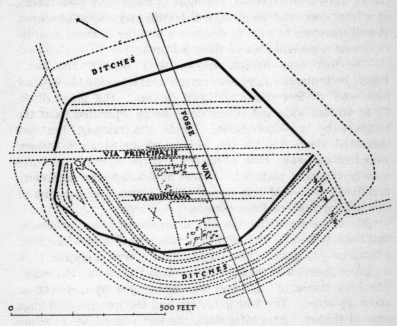

FIG. 5.—THE FORT AT MARGIDUNUM.

300 feet to 1 inch = 1 : 3600.
The earliest (Claudian) Fort in broken lines : fourth-century wall in black.

Claudian Period : Margidunum (Fig. 5).—This is a site on
the Fosse, 8 miles east of Nottingham. It is the only example
hitherto explored of the *castella* which Ostorius Scapula built
along that road in A.D. 47. The fort is irregular in shape
and measures about 200 yards by 250 yards inside the ditches,
which are very elaborate ; there are six ditches, altogether
50 or 60 yards across, with traces of timber entanglements

on the intervening ridges. The rampart was of timber backed by earth, and the chief buildings seem to have been originally wooden, but to have been rebuilt in stone after a destruction probably at the rebellion of Boudicca (A.D. 61). Several "dug-outs" have been found, suggesting that in the earliest period there were no wooden barracks. The space inside the rampart must have been about 6½ acres.[1]

Flavian Period.—Many forts of the Flavian period (A.D. 69-96) have been explored, but most of them have been rebuilt at a later date, and their original features somewhat obscured. It will therefore be best to describe a number of them in order to obtain a general idea of their features.

The fort near Brecon known as *Y Gaer* ("The fort," Fig. 6) built about A.D. 75, was surrounded by a clay bank, 5 feet high and 18 feet wide, and two ditches; the inner ditch, 15 to 16 feet wide and 6 feet deep, being separated from the rampart by a 5-foot berm. Inside the rampart the fort measured about 615 by 460 feet, or about 6½ acres. There were four gateways, built of timber, and the internal structures were of the same material. Traces of headquarters and commandant's house of this period were found, and remains of wooden barrack buildings (*Brecon*, pp. 6 *seqq.*).

About the same time the fort at *Segontium* (now *Carnarvon*) was built (Fig. 6). It had a clay rampart 18 feet wide, then a berm of 3 to 7 feet, then a 17-foot ditch with a midrib, then a 15-foot space, and then an outer ditch resembling the inner. The area inside the defences was about 510 by 415 feet or about 4½ acres. The four gateways and the internal buildings were of timber. At a later date, the fort was rebuilt in stone (*Segontium*, 20).

Another Welsh site of the same period is *Kanovium* (*Caerhun*). This is a square fort, 410 feet each way inside the defences (*i.e.* 3¾ acres), which consist of a clay bank 20 feet wide and a double ditch. The gateways and the internal buildings are of wood.[2]

In the north of England are numerous *castella* of Flavian date. We shall describe a few of these whose dimensions and general character are known.

---

[1] Exploration by Dr. F. Oswald, in progress; *Trans. Thoroton Soc.*, vol. xxxi, 1927.

[2] *A.C.*, 1925 and following years.

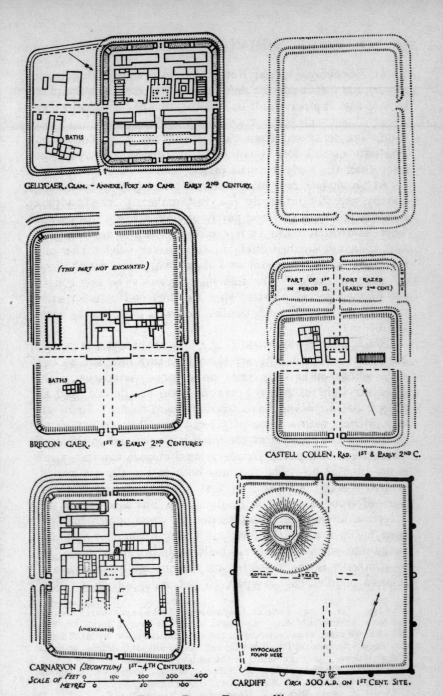

GELLYGAER, Glam. – Annexe, Fort and Camp. Early 2ND Century.

BATHS

(THIS PART NOT EXCAVATED)

BRECON GAER. 1ST & EARLY 2ND CENTURIES.

BATHS

PART OF 1ST FORT RAZED IN PERIOD II. (EARLY 2ND CENT.)

FILLED-UP DITCH

FILLED DITCH

CASTELL COLLEN, Rad. 1ST & EARLY 2ND C.

CARNARVON (SEGONTIUM) 1ST–4TH CENTURIES.

(UNEXCAVATED)

SCALE OF FEET 0   100   200   300   400
METRES 0   50   100

MOTTE

ROMAN — STREET

HYPOCAUST FOUND HERE

CARDIFF   Circa 300 A.D. ON 1ST CENT. SITE.

Fig. 6.—Roman Forts in Wales.

At *Templebrough*, near Rotherham, a fort measuring about 495 by 490 feet inside the defences (*i.e.* 5¼ acres) was found to have a turf rampart built on a foundation of gravel and clay about 18 feet wide on average (Fig. 7). A single ditch, 18 feet wide, was separated from the rampart by a 13-foot berm. The date of this fort is not perfectly certain ; it cannot be later than the early Flavian period, and it may be earlier.[1]

At *Castleshaw*, near Manchester, is a fort (Fig. 7) measuring 360 by 300 feet internally (*i.e.* just under 2½ acres), with a rampart partly of turf and partly of clay, about 18 feet wide. There is a ditch about 15 feet wide close up to the rampart, and a second smaller ditch on the weaker sides. The east and west gates (*praetoria* and *decumana*) were double, and all were of timber. The fort may probably be ascribed to the Flavian period. Later, when this fort had been for some time abandoned, a much smaller fort was built on the same site.[2]

Slack, near Huddersfield (Fig. 7), is about 256 feet square internally (*i.e.* about 3⅔ acres) with a turf rampart 20 feet wide whose outer edge rests on a stone foundation. The gates are built of timber ; two of them are double, and all except the *decumana* have wooden guard-rooms. There are two ditches, with a berm of 5 feet ; but they do not go all round the fort ; in places the ditch is single, and to the east, where there is a paved parade ground outside the fort, there is no ditch at all. The fort was built in the Flavian period, probably about A.D. 80 ; at first all the internal buildings were of wood except the headquarters, but later there was a certain amount of reconstruction in stone, which had not been finished when the fort was finally abandoned, perhaps at the time when the Wall was built, perhaps rather later.[3]

Ribchester is about 550 by 410 feet internally, or 5¼ acres. It has a puddled clay rampart 20 feet wide, laid on a raft of

[1] May, *The Roman Forts at Templebrough*, Rotherham, 1922. The site was never scientifically dug ; steelworks were built over it during the war, and what we know about it is due to the observations made by Mr. Thomas May during the preparation of the ground. Naturally, it is difficult to speak with confidence about the dating of the various structures.

[2] Bruton, *The Roman Forts at Castleshaw*, first and second interim reports. Richmond, *Huddersfield in Roman Times*, Huddersfield, 1925.

[3] *Y.A.J.*, xxvi ; Richmond, *Huddersfield in Roman Times*.

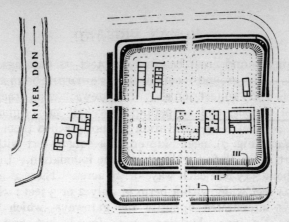

Templebrough

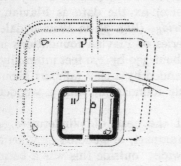

Castleshaw

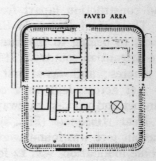

PAVED AREA

Slack

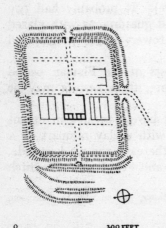

0   300 FEET

Brough-by-Bainbridge

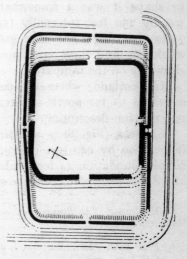

Elslack

FIG. 7.—FORTS.

oak shingles and cross beams to protect its base against the wetness of the ground ; outside it was a narrow berm and then a double ditch 20 feet across. The gateways and corner towers were of timber, and so perhaps were all the original inner buildings ; but if so, excavation has not reached them.[1]

Elslack (Fig. 7), near Skipton, is a square fort with a clay rampart, 16 to 18 feet wide, on a stone foundation. Internally it is about 345 feet each way, or 2¾ acres. There is a double ditch 24 feet wide, with a berm of only 2 or 3 feet ; the inner ditch is interrupted opposite the gateways, which were of timber. No inner buildings were found, but first-century pottery and the close resemblance to Ribchester in lay-out and construction (apart from size) fix the date as Flavian.[2]

The fort of *Brough-by-Bainbridge* (Fig. 7), in Wensleydale, seems to belong to the same series of Flavian foundations in the Brigantian country. It is about 330 by 270 feet internally, or 2 acres ; and was at first defended by a clay rampart about 20 feet across, laid on a cobble foundation, with a wooden parapet and wooden gateways.[3]

Near *Ambleside* (Fig. 8), at the head of Windermere, a Flavian fort was found whose rampart, of puddled clay, on a cobble foundation, was 12 feet wide ; outside this was a berm of 5 feet or less, and then a double ditch 25 to 30 feet wide. In shape it was a somewhat irregular quadrilateral about 300 by 250 feet internally (1¾ acre). It probably had two gates of timber ; the chief gate had guardrooms with glazed windows ; and there were wooden towers at the corners and elsewhere on the rampart.[4]

In Scotland, where the conquests of the Flavian period extended as far north as Strathmore, three *castella* may be selected for description.

Cappuck (Fig. 8) is a little fort barely an acre in extent (about 200 by 240 feet internally) with a clay rampart on a cobble foundation 24 feet wide on the east, the weakest side, and 8 feet elsewhere. On the north and west is a double ditch

---

[1] Hopkinson, *The Roman Fort at Ribchester*, 3rd ed., by D. Atkinson, Manchester, 1928.
[2] *Y.A.J.*, xxi.
[3] *Proc. Leeds Philos. Soc.*, vol. i, part vi ; vol. ii, part ii.
[4] *C.W.*², xvi, xxi.

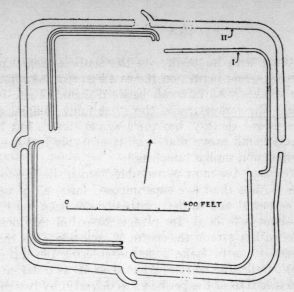

Newstead I and II (Ditches only)

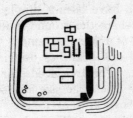

Cappuck

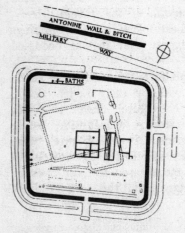

Bar Hill

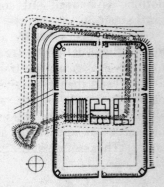

Ambleside

FIG. 8.—FORTS.

24 feet wide with no berm ; on the south a single 18-foot
ditch with a 9-foot berm ; on the east a 22-foot berm followed
by three ditches with intervals between them. There is only
one gate. The rampart, and the stone inner buildings, date
from the second century, but there was a Flavian fort here—
the objects found prove that—and it probably had the same
ditch system and similar ramparts.[1]

At *Newstead*, the most remarkable Roman site in Scotland,
there are no less than five superimposed forts, all of unusual
size. The lowest and earliest of these dates from the Flavian
period, about A.D. 80. Its plan is based on the idea of a
rectangle, with a gate in the centre of each side ; but the plan
is distorted so as to make a person entering the fort travel
on a line parallel to the rampart instead of, as usual, at right
angles to it. Half of the perimeter is defended by two ditches,
half by one ; they are 9 or 10 feet wide and 4 or 5 feet deep.
The rampart seems to have been a simple earthwork on three
sides ; on the west, where the ground is wet, it was laid on a
foundation consisting of a stone pavement $5\frac{1}{2}$ feet wide, behind
which was a layer of oak branches bringing up the width of
the whole to $22\frac{1}{2}$ feet. The area inside the rampart was probably about 10 acres. The large size and comparatively slight
ditches of this fort suggest that it was intended as winter
quarters for a number of auxiliary units, these units being
grouped together at a strategic point instead of being scattered
over a wide area (Cheesman, *Auxilia of the Roman Army*,
1914, pp. 105-106). Of this earliest fort's internal buildings
nothing is known, but coins suggest that it was occupied
until about 86.

It was superseded by a second fort defended by a single
ditch of unusual depth ($12\frac{1}{2}$ feet wide by 12 to 14 feet deep),
forming a *clavicula* in front of each gate ; inside this was
a berm, and then a massive clay rampart 38 feet wide resting
on stone foundations at either side. The four gates were
almost central to the sides, and the size of the fort inside the
ramparts was apparently about 750 by 700 feet, or over 13
acres. The position of the gates suggest that the main buildings
faced west.

[1] *P.S.A. Scot.*, xlvi. In so small a fort, the ratio 200 to 250 men per acre
no longer holds good, for obvious reasons.

The third fort at Newstead probably takes us beyond the limits of the Flavian period ; we shall therefore return to it later.[1]

Our last Flavian site shall be *Bar Hill*. Here, on the line of the Antonine Wall, the ditches of an earlier fort were found while digging was going forward in a second-century *castellum ;* and as it was clear that these earlier ditches had silted up naturally and become overgrown with brushwood before the later fort was built, it was inferred that they belonged to one of the *castella* which Agricola built on a line between Forth and Clyde (Tac., *Agr.*, 23 ; Anderson's ed., pp. lx *seqq.*). The fact that no objects of any kind (except one shoe) were discovered, was regarded less as invalidating this conclusion than as showing that the occupation was a very short one. The ditches were from 8 to 11 feet wide and on average about 4 feet deep. Their ground-plan was somewhat complicated ; but it appeared certain that the fort had occupied a rectangular space measuring 180 by 145 feet, with an annexe on the west. Some traces of an earthen rampart were found, but no stone foundation ; if the rampart was 10 feet wide, the internal dimensions would be 160 by 125 feet, or nearly half an acre. Nothing is known of its internal buildings, but a gap about 15 feet wide in the ditch indicates the position of a single gateway.[2]

General Features of Flavian Castella.—Flavian forts in Britain show certain constant features. Their ramparts are never of stone, but always of earth (puddled clay, as a rule) or, more rarely, of turf. Their shape is always more or less rectangular ; even Ambleside, the least regular in outline, approximates to a rectangle. Their internal buildings, so far as we know, were always of wood, except that their bath-houses, being heated with hypocausts, were necessarily of stone ; but these were nearly always outside the ramparts. When they were more than two acres in extent, they always had four gates.

Other generalisations are less binding. Their ramparts are as a rule about 18 to 20 feet across ; but at Ambleside I the

---

[1] *Newstead*, pp. 22 *seqq.* *Cf. P.S.A. Scot.*, 1923-24, pp. 309-321.

[2] Macdonald and Park, *The Roman Forts on the Bar Hill, Dumbartonshire ;* Glasgow, 1906 ; reprinted from *P.S.A. Scot.*, xl. For the Flavian period in Scotland as a whole, Macdonald, " The Agricolan Occupation of North Britain," in *J.R.S.*, ix, is fundamental.

width is 12 feet, at Newstead II, 38 ; and at Cappuck and
Bar Hill I, it must have been much less than 18. There is,
therefore, a variation in rampart-width according to area.
Forts of 2 to 10 acres seem to have a standard 18 to 20-foot
rampart.

The berm is either absent or quite narrow, from 2 to 7 feet.
To this the only exception is Templebrough (13 feet), and,
bearing in mind the conditions of excavation, one may doubt
whether this exception is a real one.

The ratio of length to breadth varies from Cappuck (·83),
which is broader than it is long, to Brough-by-Bainbridge
and Ribchester (1·34), which are markedly oblong. Large
forts like Templebrough and small ones like Elslack I may
be square ; large forts like Segontium and small ones like
Brough-by-Bainbridge may be definitely oblong. There is
no connection between size and length-breadth ratio.

Lastly, in area there is great variation from Newstead II
(13 acres) to Bar Hill ($< \frac{1}{2}$ acre) ; and it is not easy to classify
the intermediate forts into groups of approximately the same
area in at all a convincing manner. And, knowing so little
as we do about their internal buildings, we cannot, as a rule,
prove that a given fort was designed to house a garrison of
any particular size.

Trajan and Hadrian (A.D. 98-138).—About the beginning
of the second century this type underwent a simple but
important change : the substitution of stone for timber. The
rampart, instead of being an earthwork with wooden revetment
and wooden parapet and gateways, now becomes an earthwork
with a stone revetment and stone parapet and gateways.
The internal buildings, formerly of timber, are henceforth,
either partly or wholly, of stone.

This change makes itself felt early in the reign of Trajan,
and that in two ways : first, in the remodelling of Flavian
forts according to the new formula ; and secondly, in the
building of new forts. We shall examine some typical cases
of these in turn.

Flavian Earthworks Remodelled in Stone.—We shall mention
half-a-dozen examples.

At *Y Gaer* (Brecon ; Fig. 6), " in the early years of the
second century, the original rampart was raised in height and

faced with a stone wall, the west and south gateways and the principal buildings were rebuilt in stone, and corner turrets of stone were soon afterwards added to the defences " (*Brecon*, 71). This work is shown by tile-stamps to have been carried out by the legionary masons of Leg. II Augusta, quartered near-by at Caerleon-on-Usk. " The work of the builders, however, was never finished. The space left in the plan for the usual second granary remained unoccupied . . . again, neither in the praetentura nor in the retentura were the barrack-blocks ever rebuilt in stone " (*ibid.*, 72). It has been suggested, not without probability, that the rebuilding of this fort in stone was interrupted by the removal both of the legionary workmen and of the auxiliary garrison to the north of England, in connection with the new frontier policy of Hadrian's reign. The *porta praetoria*, with its projecting towers, is abnormal. Projecting gate-towers, though common enough in the town fortifications of the early Empire, do not appear as a rule in *castella* until a later date (*ibid.*, pp. 20 *seqq.*).

At *Caerhun* additions in stone were made, in the first quarter of the second century, and early rather than late in that period (*A.C.*, 1926, 321). The outer margin of the clay rampart was cut off to a width of 2 feet, and a stone wall 6 feet thick at its base built between the rampart and the ditch (*ibid.*, 286). The inner half of the double ditch was filled up soon afterwards in order to strengthen the foundation of this wall (*ibid.*, 289). The gateways also were rebuilt in stone. The east gate (*porta praetoria*) was a double opening with guard-rooms, singular in having its two arches of different widths (15 feet and 5 feet respectively). The new south gate was a double opening with no guard-rooms ; but one of the arches seems to have been blocked up during construction for use as a guard-room (*A.C.*, 1927, 318-321). At the same time the internal buildings were all reconstructed in stone.

Slack (Fig. 7) seems to have undergone a partial reconstruction in stone at about the same period, but this was confined to the internal buildings. No stone revetment was added to the rampart. And (as at the Brecon Gaer) the reconstruction was incomplete when, perhaps about A.D. 125 or somewhat later, the fort was abandoned (*Y.A.J.*, xxvi, 85).

Ribchester was at some time provided with a 6-foot stone

revetment founded on a timber raft, for which the outer
margin of the clay rampart was cut away as at Caerhun ; and
as the bath-house dates from the early second century the
revetment (with which may be reasonably associated the
stone internal buildings) is probably of the same date (Hopkinson, *op. cit.*, ed. 3, pp. 12, 23).

Brough-by-Bainbridge has an added stone revetment very
like those of the forts mentioned above (*Leeds Phil. Soc.*, I, 264).

Newstead III is related to Newstead II in a slightly
different way. The *claviculae* at the gates were disused and
filled up ; two new ditches were added ; the position of
the *via principalis* was changed, and the *portae principales*
were therefore moved, the other gates remaining in their
original place. A stone wall over 7 feet thick was built all
round the fort, and the excavator noticed that this was an
independent structure, not of one build with the clay rampart
(*Newstead*, 33). Stone central buildings facing east, and stone
barracks, were built at the same time, and Richmond (*P.S.A.
Scot.*, 1923-24) has argued that this time was the early years
of the second century. The case for this view is, however,
not quite conclusive ; in particular, there seems to be a lack
at Newstead of the Trajanic pottery which, on this view,
ought to abound there.

Flavian Earthworks Altered in Plan.—Some *castella*, in this
process of stone rebuilding, underwent a change of plan more
drastic than that which we have seen at Newstead.

At *Castell Collen* (Fig. 6) the length of the fort (originally,
it would seem, a Flavian fort of ordinary type) was reduced
by 40 feet. A cross-wall was built cutting off most of the
retentura, and forming the back wall of a square *castellum*
measuring 410 feet externally each way (*i.e.* probably 360
to 370 feet square internally, or 3 acres. Wheeler, *Prehist.
and Rom. Wales*, 230.)

The same state of things appears to exist at *Tomen-y-Mur*,
where the medieval motte stands on the centre of the Roman
cross-wall (Wheeler, *op. cit.*, 230.)

At *Templebrough* (Fig. 7) the same thing has happened,
though we have no evidence when it happened. The *retentura*
of the early turf fort has been cut down, and a new fort built,
surrounded by a stone wall about 9 feet thick with a clay

bank behind it and a single 18-foot ditch outside. The internal dimensions of Templeborough II were probably about 380 by 440 feet, giving an area of 3¾ acres (May, *op. cit.*).

Flavian Earthworks Superseded by New Structures on the Same Site.—When the second-century builders wanted a fort larger than the pre-existing work, they might level its ramparts and build a new *castellum* on the site. Of this *Ambleside* (Fig. 8) may be taken as an example. The site of the early fort was converted into a platform raised above flood level; on this was built an entirely new fort, conforming in type to the ordinary Trajan-Hadrianic pattern, with a 10-foot clay rampart revetted by a 4-foot stone wall (*C.W.*², xv, 5). The *porta praetoria* is double, with guard-rooms (*ibid.*, xxi, 7); the other gates are single, without guard-rooms. Outside the *porta praetoria* a paved area represents the parade ground (*ibid.*, xiv, 448). The central buildings are of stone, the barracks of wood. The internal dimensions are 395 by 270 feet, or close upon 2½ acres.

Elslack (Fig. 7) is another possible case. Here an oblong fort 603 by 406 feet externally, with a stone wall 8 feet 6 inches thick, revetting a clay bank, has been superimposed on the smaller Flavian earthwork described above; but, apart from the manner of its construction, it has yielded no evidence of date (*Y.A.J.*, xxi, 125-133).

On the other hand, at *Castleshaw* (Fig. 7) a new fort has been built for the opposite reason—because the old one was far too large. Castleshaw II is a tiny fort 160 by 190 feet externally, with a turf rampart 13 feet broad (internally just half an acre), a double gate in each of the longer sides, built of timber, and at least one stone building inside. Relics suggest a date of about 100-120, and the fort is obviously a mere block-house for a handful of men policing the road (*Castleshaw Reports, cit.;* Richmond, *Huddersfield, cit.*).

Trajan-Hadrianic Forts on Virgin Sites.—A brand new Trajanic or Hadrianic fort has, as a rule, certain definite characteristics. It is rectangular (oblong or square), though the accuracy of its right angles is often defective. It has a composite rampart of earth and stone. Its gates and corner towers are of stone, and it may have intermediate stone towers as well. Its central buildings are of stone, and its barracks are generally, though not always, of stone likewise. Forts of this pattern may always (in Britain at any rate) be provisionally assigned to the reigns of Trajan and Hadrian ; and nothing in plan or construction permits us to discriminate between the reigns of these two emperors. On the other hand, there are cases in which some of these characteristics fail to appear. We shall describe, first, some typical *castella* known to belong to this period ; then some whose construction, in the absence of other evidence, suggests this date ; and lastly some belonging to the period but showing abnormal features.

Normal Trajan-Hadrianic Forts.—*Gellygaer* (Glamorganshire ; Fig. 6) is 404 by 385 feet externally, with a 20-foot composite rampart composed of a 4-foot revetment, 13 feet of clay, and a 3-foot inner revetment—the last an unusual detail. Its internal area is rather over 2¾ acres. It has four double gates, with guard-rooms, centrally placed in the sides ; each passage-way is 11 feet wide. There is a single 20-foot ditch with a 5-foot berm. Inside, the buildings are all of stone. They include (beside the usual headquarters, commandant's house, and granaries) six L-shaped barrack-blocks for the six centuries of a *cohors quingenaria*, and five other buildings for various other purposes. It was built between A.D. 103 and 112 and not occupied later than Hadrian's reign. Outside the fort are a temporary camp, a gravelled parade ground, and an entrenched annexe containing a bath-house (Ward, *The Roman Fort of Gellygaer*, 1903 : Haverfield, *Military Aspects of Roman Wales*, § xix).

Hardknot Castle (Cumberland ; Fig. 9) is 375 feet square ; internally it was rather less than 2¾ acres. The stone rampart-wall is 5 feet 6 inches thick and the total thickness of the rampart must have been about 20 feet. None of the gates have guard-rooms, but all except the *porta decumana* are double ; the two archways of the *porta praetoria* were each about 10 feet wide and those of the *portae principales* about 8 feet. Two ditches are visible on the weak uphill side. Inside, the central buildings were of stone ; the barracks of wood ; but a heated building in the *retentura* must have been of stone. Outside, there is a bath-house, and an interesting parade ground, artificially levelled against the mountain side. It was occupied from A.D. 100-110 to A.D. 125-135 (*C.W.*², xxviii).

Housesteads (Hadrian's Wall; Fig. 9; built about A.D. 120-125) measures internally 570 by 330 feet (4¼ acres), and has a stone rampart-wall about 5 feet thick with a clay bank behind it bringing the total thickness of the rampart up to about 20 feet. Its four gates are all double, and have guard-

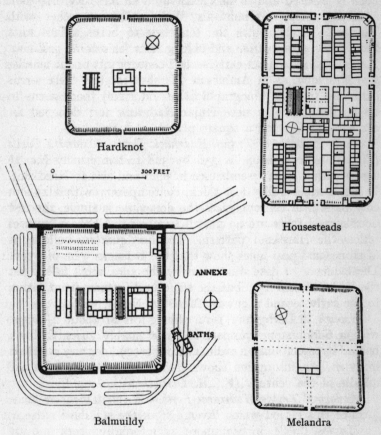

Hardknot

300 FEET

ANNEXE

BATHS

Balmuildy

Housesteads

Melandra

Fig. 9.—Forts.

rooms entered from the archways; and the *via principalis* and *via quintana* divide its internal area into three equal portions, all occupied by stone buildings. Six long blocks occupy the *praetentura* and six the *retentura*; in the centre are the headquarters, granaries, commandant's house, and other buildings. The garrison (*Coh. i. Tungrorum*) was a milliary cohort ; the ten barrack-blocks of its ten centuries can be easily distinguished from among the other buildings. Its ditches have not been explored. Outside, a bath-house and traces of an extensive civil settlement with temples, etc., have been recognised and in part excavated (*A.A.*[2], xxv, 193-300).

Great Chesters (Hadrian's Wall), taken together with Housesteads, illustrates the tendency to build square forts for *cohortes quingenariae* and oblong forts for *cohortes milliaria*. Sometimes, indeed, an early second-century fort of the smaller size is oblong, as at Ambleside II ; but for this there seems generally to be a topographical reason ; and there seems to be no instance of a new Trajan-Hadrianic fort designed for a *cohors milliaria* on a square plan (*A.A.*[2], xvi).

Forts Probably of Trajan-Hadrianic Date.—*Melandra Castle* (Fig. 9), near Glossop, is 358 by 328 feet internally (*i.e.* 2⅔ acres) with a close resemblance in plan and size to Hardknot. It has a stone wall 5 feet thick, contemporary with a 15-foot clay bank ; of its four gates the *decumana* is single, the rest double, and there are no guard-chambers. All these features follow the Hardknot pattern. The headquarters building is of stone, and post-holes show that the barracks were of wood. The evidence of date was taken by the excavators to suggest the late first century ; but the structural features point rather to the early second (Conway, *Melandra Castle*, 1906).[1]

Brough, in Derbyshire, is an oblong fort of about 2¼ acres, with a 6-foot stone rampart and presumably an earth bank behind it, resembling an ordinary early second-century *castellum* in type. An inscription shows that it was rebuilt about the middle of the century (*V.C.H. Derbyshire*).

Abnormal Trajan-Hadrianic Forts.—We shall mention three forts of this period which diverge from the standard pattern.

Maiden Castle, in Stainmore, is internally about 130 by 100 feet (¼ to ⅓ acre). In plan and in area it closely resembles Castleshaw II, which, as we saw, belongs to this period. The main York-Carlisle road passed right through it from gate to gate, so that the road could be blocked by merely shutting the gates. The fort had a stone (presumably a stone and earth)

---

[1] The excavations hitherto carried out do not enable us to assert positively that there was not an earlier fort on the site.

rampart and internal barrack-buildings in stone ; these facts, and some objects found, suggest a second-century date for it. Obviously it was a police post guarding the road in a lonely place (*C.W.*², xxvii. For a larger fort astride of a road, *cf.* Castle Flemish in Pembrokeshire ; *A.C.*, 1923).

South Shields is a *castellum* at the mouth of the Tyne, belonging to the Hadrianic frontier system. But it shows features that differentiate it from the ordinary frontier fort. It measures 624 by 370 feet, and therefore contains about 4⅔ acres, which gives it the appearance of being designed for a milliary cohort ; but an anomalous feature is the fact that the *via principalis* runs along the back, instead of the front, of the *principia*, producing " the curious anomaly of a (*principia*) turning its back on the praetorian gate " (*A.A.*², xxv, 245) ; and still more striking is the fact that, except for the headquarters, all the buildings explored within the fort belong to the well-known granary type. Evidently South Shields was designed not to house a garrison but to act as a depôt for military stores brought by sea to the mouth of the Tyne (*A.A.*², xxv, 244-245).

Birrens,[1] in Dumfriesshire, is about 530 by 330 feet inside the defences, or just 4 acres. The buildings were all in stone and very massive. In the centre was a headquarters, and on either side of this, groups of buildings including the usual granaries and commandant's house. In the *praetentura* were six buildings about 160 by 45 feet, which have been explained as stables, and other buildings which might be harness rooms and hay barns. In the *retentura* were barracks for the men. Its defences are the only unusual feature about it ; but in view of the special interest attaching to its ditch system it deserves to be mentioned here. A general note on the ditch system is added in the following paragraphs.

Its rampart is a massive mound constructed of alternate layers of earth and puddled clay, with layers of brushwood used as bonding-courses and a sheathing of clay over all. It stood upon a stone foundation, and appears to have been about 35 feet wide. The gates (apart from the *porta praetoria*, of

[1] Mr. E. B. Birley, since the above paragraphs were written, tells me that further study of the pottery leads him to regard Birrens as an Antonine fort. This would suit well with its structural peculiarities.

which nothing is known), are single and without guard chambers. On the north, the tactically weak side, there are six ditches with an aggregate width of 130 feet, a formidable entanglement in which assailants would be brought almost to a standstill under fire from the rampart. The absence of a stone revetment connects Birrens on the one hand with the Flavian tradition and, on the other, with the revival of that tradition (see below) in the reign of Antoninus Pius (J. Macdonald and Barbour, *Birrens and its Antiquities*, Dumfries, 1897 ; G. Macdonald, "The Romans in Dumfriesshire," in *Trans. Dumfr. and Gall. N.H. and Ant. Soc.*, 1920 ; Royal Comm. on Hist. Mon., Scotland, *Dumfriesshire*).

Multiple Ditches.—Temporary and semi-permanent camps normally have a single ditch ; permanent works normally have two, but occasionally three. Four ditches are sometimes found, *e.g.* in the Hadrianic fort of Great Chesters. But there is a well-marked group of *castella* with more than four ditches, which occur in northern Britain. They are anticipated by such examples as the Claudian fort of Margidunum, showing that Roman engineers were not unprepared to construct elaborate ditch-systems if occasion should arise. The group in question consists of the following :—

(*a*) *Whitley Castle* near Alston. A fort of about 2½ acres, unexcavated ; in shape a parallelogram with angles of about 60° and 120° ; stone (? composite) rampart, ruins of stone buildings visible. Seven ditches, altogether 150 feet across, on the uphill side, fewer on the other sides (*P.S.A.N.*, ser. 4, i (1924), 249-255).

(*b*) *Birrens*, described above. Six ditches on uphill side. On the east, the ditches have been destroyed by erosion ; on the west, by cultivation.

(*c*) *Risingham*. A squarish oblong fort of about 3½ acres ; composite rampart, stone inner buildings ; on the east, the weakest side, are seven or possibly eight ditches, 24 feet centre to centre ; elsewhere four ditches except on the north where the site is defended by the river (personal observation ; no description of the ditches in print).

(*d*) *High Rochester*. A squarish oblong fort of 4 acres ; very thick stone rampart with clay core, stone inner buildings ; on the north, remains of as many as thirteen ditches ;

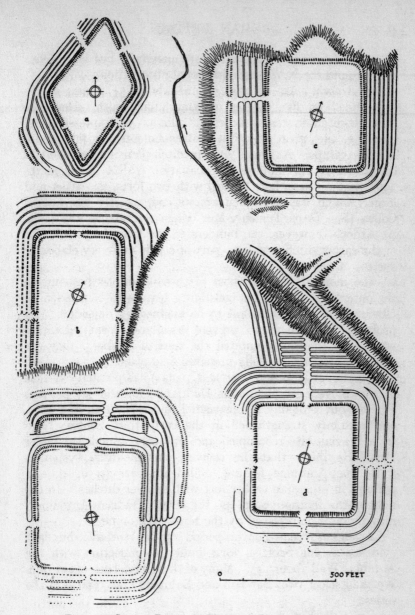

FIG. 10.—SKETCH-PLANS OF MULTIPLE-DITCH SYSTEMS.

400 feet to 1 inch = 1 : 4800.

(a) Whitley Castle, Northumberland.
(b) Birrens, Dumfriesshire.
(c) Risingham, Northumberland.

(d) High Rochester, Northumberland.
(e) Ardoch, Stirlingshire.

on east and south, four ; on west, uncertain, but six ditches curve round the N.W. angle (personal observation).

(e) *Ardoch.* An oblong fort of about 5¼ acres, partly surrounded by five ditches of remarkable depth. Here the multiple-ditch system reaches its climax of impressiveness, recalling the great multiple entrenchments of prehistoric hill-top camps. A glance at the ditch-plan shows, what is confirmed by the findings of excavation (*P.S.A. Scot.*, xxxii, 399), that we have here to deal with two forts, an earlier and larger, which was shortened at one end, exactly like Castell Collen (Fig. 6) or Tomen-y-Mur, when the second was built. At Ardoch, however, the builders of the later fort made use of the earlier ditches to form part of a new and very elaborate system of defence.

The mound which in most of these examples lies outside the outermost ditch is too constant a feature to be accidental. Obviously it was not meant to be manned by defenders. Its probable function is to prevent assailants from retreating when once they have entered the zone of ditches ; they are thus trapped in a carefully prepared field of fire.

Bosanquet (*P.S.A.N.*, ser. 4, i, p. 251) has pointed out that of the above examples (b) is Hadrianic, (c) and (d) perhaps Flavian but probably reconstructed under Hadrian and Pius, and certainly strengthened in the early third century, and (e) a Flavian site reoccupied and probably remodelled under Pius. He infers that the revived multiple-ditch system is a Hadrian-Antonine feature, added in cases (c, d, e), and perhaps in (a), to an earlier fort with simpler ditches. In the light of the footnote on p. 43, the term " Hadrian-Antonine " may perhaps be replaced by the term " Antonine."

Antoninus Pius.—For this period (138-161) we have abundant evidence in the Scottish forts built in connection with the Antonine Wall about 143. Many of these have been excavated. We shall select two, Bar Hill and Balmuildy, as typical of the series.

Bar Hill (Fig. 8) is a squarish fort of 3 acres, lying close to the Antonine Wall. It has a single ditch towards the Wall, double on the other three sides. The berm measured from 6 to 8 feet ; the rampart was of turf and was built on a 12-foot stone foundation. The four gates were about 12 to 14 feet wide, single, and built of timber. The two most exposed to attack were protected by *tituli* (*cf.* Brough-by-Bainbridge, Fig. 7). At the corners were traces of towers or artillery platforms in the thickness of the rampart. Inside were found the usual headquarters and granary and another building in stone, and a stone bath-house laid close against the north rampart. There were no certain traces of other stone buildings, and the barracks were of wood. The underlying Flavian fort has been described above (G. Macdonald and Park, *The Roman Forts on the Bar Hill*, Glasgow, 1906).

Balmuildy (Fig. 9) is a squarish oblong fort of nearly 3¼ acres, attached to the Antonine Wall. It has three ditches on the south and west, two on the east, where there is an annexe ; a berm of 20 to 30 feet ; and a composite rampart consisting of a stone revetment 7½ feet thick at the base and an earth bank, perhaps 20 feet wide. At the north-east and north-west corners expansions 4 to 5 feet wide have been added to the stone revetment, evidently platforms for artillery ; at the free southern corners were ordinary stone corner towers. The four gates were single, about 12 feet wide, with guard-chambers. In the middle was a range of stone buildings : headquarters, two granaries, commandant's house ; and to north and south were wooden barracks, thought to have been designed for a *cohors quingenaria equitata*. A bath-building was crowded up close inside the eastern rampart ; there was another in the annexe (*Balmuildy*, 1922).

A further examination of Antonine *castella* would support the general impression created by these examples, that this period saw a certain revival of Flavian methods in construction. Bar Hill resembles Slack far more than it does any ordinary Trajan-Hadrianic fort. Balmuildy has the composite rampart of the early second century, but not the stone barracks ; indeed, stone barracks are as conspicuous by their absence on the Antonine Wall as they are by their presence on the Hadrianic. The gradual increase in solidity and comfort between about 80 and 120 seems to have reached a climax at about the latter date, and soon after this it was evidently decided that the stone-built *castellum* was too expensive and perhaps too luxurious a thing to become normal for the future. A return was therefore made to simpler methods of construction.

This involved a loss in comfort for the rank and file ; but the central offices, the commandant's house, and the granaries were still built in stone. There may also have been some slight loss in tactical strength, but this was compensated for by narrower gateways [1] and, where necessary, more elaborate ditches. The more expensive methods could still be used when it was thought desirable. Thus, on the Antonine Wall, though most of the forts have earth or turf ramparts, we have seen a stone revetment at Balmuildy ; and, though stone barracks are normally absent in Antonine forts, they are present —together with a stone rampart-wall—at Newstead IV and V, the two Antonine forts on that site. We have seen above that the date of Newstead III is not certain.

The Early Third Century.—Of the late second century we can say very little, because we have no new forts of that period and no important remodelling of old ones. But in the early third century we see a tendency to an increase of defensive strength.

Artillery platforms were added at High Rochester by Caracalla and Severus Alexander (*C.I.L.*, vii, 1045, 1046) ; similar features elsewhere, *e.g.* at Housesteads, may well belong to the same period ; at Risingham a narrow gateway with projecting polygonal towers was built under Severus (A.D. 205-208 ; *C.I.L.*, vii, 1003) to replace the earlier, less defensive, gate, and alterations of a similar kind were carried out, perhaps simultaneously, on the gateways of High Rochester. The fact is that at the beginning of the third century the tactical idea of a fort was changing profoundly. But we have no new *castella* dating from this period ; our knowledge of the fortification of the early third century in Britain depends on the alterations made at that date in earlier structures.

The Late Third and Fourth Centuries.—About the end of the century it became necessary to build a number of new forts, and these reveal the changes in military architecture that had taken place since the middle of the second century. They were built not in the north but on the coasts of the east and south, and, in part, the west also. It is convenient, but not strictly accurate, to group all these new works together as

---

[1] One of the earliest modifications of the Trajan-Hadrianic pattern was in the direction of narrower gates. On Hadrian's Wall, some fort gates were built up immediately after their original construction ; others at later times after varying periods of use.

forts of the Saxon Shore ; the Saxon Shore being the Roman name for the south-east coast where the Saxon raids fell thickest from the late third century onwards, and where fortifications of this type most abound.

A rapid survey of these works will give a general idea of their character. We shall begin from the north, on the east coast, and work round clockwise.

Horncastle, in Lincolnshire, may have been a Saxon Shore fort. Stukeley in the early eighteenth century describes its walls as " three or four yards high, and four yards thick. . . . It is a perfect parallelogram . . . at the corners have been square towers, as they report ; the gates were in the middle of three sides, and I suppose a postern " in the fourth. His plan shows the area as about $3\frac{1}{2}$ acres (Stukeley, *It. curiosum*, p. 30). In point of fact the towers were probably round, and the plan is not quite a parallelogram.

Brancaster (Norfolk), dug in 1846, was found to have walls 11 feet thick, at the base, faced and bonded with sandstone. No bastions were recognised, with the exception of projecting towers at the east gate ; and in the north-east angle an internal corner-tower, like those of second-century forts, was found. There were two gates, and the fort measured 570 feet each way, which would imply an area of between 6 and 7 acres (*V.C.H. Norfolk*).

Burgh Castle (Suffolk ; Fig. 11*b*) is about 6 acres in extent. It is a quadrilateral whose longer sides are parallel, while the shorter sides are not ; the west or longest side has been destroyed by the river, but its foundations have been located. The walls still stand 15 to 16 feet high, and this seems to have been their original height apart from a parapet ; for the bastions have at this height a flat top with a circular sinking in the middle, showing where a ballista has been mounted. The walls, above all offsets, are 8 feet thick, and faced with flint, with triple bonding-courses of tile ; there may have been an earth bank behind them. The corners are rounded, and there is a gate in the middle of each remaining wall—the east gate 11 feet 8 inches wide, the other two mere posterns. The bastions only begin to be bonded into the walls 7 or 8 feet above the ground ; conceivably they may have been added to the plan after building was begun.

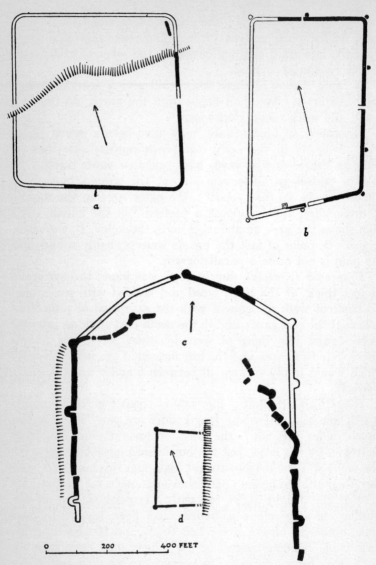

FIG. 11.—DIFFERENT TYPES OF SAXON SHORE FORTS.

300 feet to 1 inch = 1 : 3600.

(a) Reculver ; rounded corners, no bastions.
(b) Burgh Castle ; rounded corners, bastions added during construction.
(c) Lympne ; angular polygonal plan, with bastions.
(d) Caer Gybi, Holyhead ; small fort of late Roman type.

Walton Castle now lies in ruins under the sea off Felixstowe, and for its features we must rely on various old descriptions, which give the landward wall variously as 100 or 187 yards long, and 12 or 9 feet thick. A seventeenth-century drawing shows cylindrical bastions at the corners.

Bradwell-juxta-Mare, at the mouth of the Blackwater, has lost its seaward wall ; the west wall is 522 feet long, the north and south, both ending in the air, are respectively 290 and 150 feet. The area must have been larger than 4 acres, but one cannot say how much larger. The walls are 12 feet thick at the base and now stand at most about 4 feet high. They have triple bonding-courses of tiles. The corners are rounded, but the cylindrical bastions seem contemporary with them. There was a gate in the west side, and traces of a ditch are still visible.

Reculver (Fig. 11 *a*) was a square fort with walls 10 feet thick at the base, 8 feet thick above offsets ; the corners were rounded and no bastions are known, nor are there any bonding-courses. One gate is known, in the centre of the west wall. There is said to have been a ditch once visible. The internal area seems to have been about $7\frac{1}{2}$ acres.

Richborough (Fig. 12 *a*) seems to have been originally planned as a square fort about 500 feet each way externally, or about $5\frac{1}{8}$ acres if (as seems to be the case) there was no earth bank inside the walls. But before completion it was elongated to between 550 and 580 feet, making it over 6 acres. The walls are 11 feet thick, and in places still stand 25 feet high. The corners are angular, not rounded ; and there was probably a gate in each end and a postern concealed in a bastion in each side. The corner bastions are cylindrical, the others rectangular ; the existing gate, 11 feet wide, was flanked by projecting towers. Excavation shows that there were two ditches, reinforced near the gateway by a third ; and the date of construction is in the last quarter of the third century (*Richborough Excavation Reports*, i and ii ; Society of Antiquaries).

Dover was defended by a Saxon Shore fort, but nothing is known of its plan and details (Mothersole, *The Saxon Shore*, 103 *seqq.*).[1]

---

[1] While this book was in the press a fresh study of the evidence by Dr. Wheeler led to some tentative conclusions which will appear in *V.C.H. Kent*, and *A.J.*, lxxxvi.

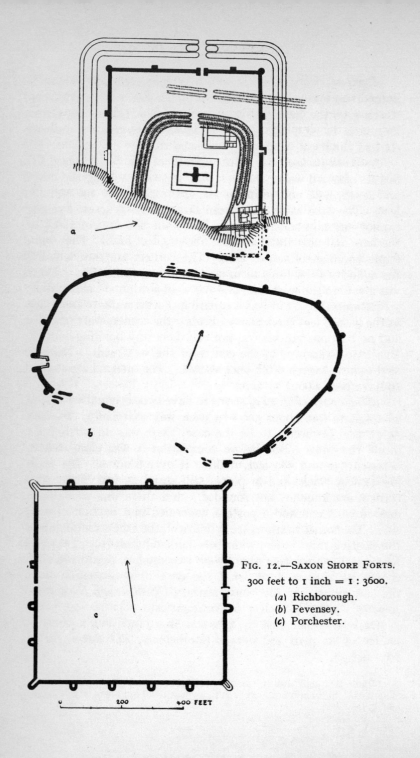

FIG. 12.—SAXON SHORE FORTS.

300 feet to 1 inch = 1 : 3600.

(a) Richborough.
(b) Fevensey.
(c) Porchester.

0   200   400 FEET

Lympne (Fig. 11 *c*) is to-day chiefly remarkable for its ruined condition ; huge fragments of its walls lie scattered at various angles, many yards away from their original positions, owing to the slipping of the wet clayey ground. The walls are 14 feet thick and stand in places 23 feet high ; they have tile bonding-courses and cylindrical bastions with chambers inside them. The main gate is 11 feet wide, with projecting towers, and there are several posterns. The shape is an irregular pentagon and the area between 9 and 10 acres.

Pevensey (Fig. 12 *b*) is oval in shape, with an area of over 8 acres. Its walls are 12 feet thick and stand 28 feet high ; they are built on a framework of timber sleepers embedded in the surface of a chalk and stone foundation, and have U-shaped bastions and tile bonding-courses. The gates, flanked by towers, are 10 feet wide, and there is a postern curved in such a way that a person entering cannot see into the fort.

Porchester (620 by 610 feet ; Fig. 12 *c*) has gates to east and west, defended by projecting towers. The corners are angular and the bastions, which are U-shaped, are hollow. The walls are 10 feet thick and provided with bonding-courses ; they stand in places over 20 feet high. The enclosed area is about 8 acres (*V.C.H. Hants*).

Bitterne is a spit of land projecting into the river Itchen ; across its base is an ancient fortification consisting of a ditch, earthwork and wall ; on its tip is a triangular walled enclosure with a ditch to landward. The outer wall was 9 feet thick, with bonding-courses, an earthen mound behind it, and towers at its ends. The walls of the triangular enclosure, which was about 5½ acres in extent, seem to be Roman work of the late third or fourth century, and may represent a citadel built for a seaport town at a period when Saxon raids began to make such towns unsafe (*Roman London*, pp. 77-78 ; *V.C.H. Hants*).

At *Carisbrooke*, in the Isle of Wight, the remains of a Saxon Shore fort have recently been discovered, consisting of walls 10 feet thick, with bastions, embedded in the Norman earthworks (*J.R.S.*, xvi, 235 ; *Antiquity*, i, 476).

On *Alderney* a small fort of the same series, resembling that known as Caer Gybi on Holyhead (see below), has lately been recognised to exist.

Cardiff (Fig. 6) is a rectangular, almost square, fort with angular corners and polygonal bastions. Its walls are 10 feet thick at the base, reduced by offsets to 8 feet 6 inches, and have an earthen bank behind them. The fort measures about 650 by 600 feet (7¾ acres internally) and has a single gate, with projecting towers, at each end, and perhaps a postern in the middle of each side. The Roman walls have been restored recently, and it is therefore possible at Cardiff to see what a Saxon Shore fort looked like in the fourth century (Wheeler, *Prehist. and Rom. Wales*, 234 *seqq.*).

At *Carnarvon*, the lower fort, 150 yards west of the earlier fort, has its east wall complete, about 230 feet long; of the north and south walls about 120 and 180 feet remain. The walls are 5½ feet thick and up to 12 feet high; bastions were once visible. There are bonding-courses of flat stones and regular rows of putlog holes. The area was something over an acre, and the fort was probably a small Saxon Shore *castellum* (*Segontium*, 95).

Caer Gybi, on Holyhead, is an oblong enclosure of under an acre, with cylindrical bastions at the corners. It measures 230 by 150 feet; its walls are 5½ feet thick, partly in herring-bone masonry with putlog holes and bonding-courses of flat stones; they stand 13 feet high to the rampart-walk, above which are the remains of a parapet. The entrance was in the south wall (*Segontium*, 97-101).

General Remarks on Saxon Shore Forts.—Thick and high walls, together with few and narrow entrances, are constant features. But apart from these, the divergence of types is remarkable.

(*a*) There is a type with rounded corners and no bastions, closely connected with the second-century *castellum* in design. Brancaster and Reculver (Fig. 11) belong to this class. What distinguishes them from normal second-century forts is their thick walls and narrow and few entrances.

(*b*) The next type adds bastions; but the corners are still rounded. Burgh Castle (Fig. 11) and Bradwell-juxta-Mare are the examples.

(*c*) Next, the rounded corners vanish and are replaced by angles. This gives the type of Richborough (Fig. 12), Porchester (Fig. 12), and Cardiff (Fig. 6), which are closely akin in plan and represent the most highly-developed pattern of Saxon Shore fort.

(d) Irregular ground plans occur at Lympne (Fig. 11), which, however, is in effect a variant of type (c), and at Pevensey (Fig. 12).

(e) There is also a miniature type, with thinner walls, as at Alderney, Carnarvon, and Caer Gybi (Fig. 11).

We have as yet no information as to the chronological relation between these types. Differences of type do not necessarily imply differences of date, but the men who designed group (a) and group (c) respectively had such very divergent ideas about the principles of fortification that it would be rash to assume, without definite evidence, that they were contemporaries co-operating in a single scheme. The chronology of the Saxon Shore is not yet fixed.[1]

There are other differences. Some (Cardiff, probably Burgh Castle, perhaps others) had an earthen bank behind the walls ; others, probably, did not. Whether they all had ditches we do not know, but the probability is that they had. Whether any of them had barracks inside is doubtful, but no traces have been found. The lean-to barracks built against the inner face of the wall at late forts such as Alzei (*Germania*, xiii (1929), 177-187) seem to belong to an altogether later phase of history ; no clear trace of them has been found in Britain.

---

[1] It may be noted that the Swiss fort of Tasgaetium (Stein) resembles type (c), but has bastions resembling those of York and not like anything on the Saxon Shore ; and epigraphic evidence makes it almost certain that it was built in A.D. 294 (*C.I.L.*, xiii, 5256, incomplete but apparently a duplicate *mutatis mutandis* of 5249. Stähelin, *Die Schweiz in römischer Zeit*, 245).

CHAPTER IV

SIGNAL–STATIONS AND LIGHT–HOUSES

§ 1. SIGNAL-STATIONS

THE ancients were well acquainted with the art of transmitting news by means of visible signals. As early as 458 B.C. Aeschylus, in the *Agamemnon*, could represent the news of the fall of Troy as having come to Greece by way of a chain of beacons ; and, in Rome, Polybius (x, 44 *seqq.*) describes methods of sending elaborate messages by light-signals as actually used in the second century B.C. The late military writer Vegetius (iii, 5) says that fire, smoke, and semaphore codes were in use in his time.

Archaeological evidence confirms the general sense of these statements. Early in the second century we find signal-stations depicted on Trajan's Column. They are wooden towers two storeys high, surrounded by palisades ; the upper storey has a balcony, and from its window projects a stick like a barber's pole, which must be a torch for sending fire-signals. Late in the same century we see them again on the Column of Marcus. They have undergone a certain development. They are now, sometimes at least, built of stone and provided with tiled, instead of thatched roofs ; the palisade round them has become stouter, and the opening in it is closed with a gate.

Outside Britain, excavation has revealed large numbers of such things along the German frontier. Here two kinds of tower are recognised. First, there is the wooden tower, with a post-hole at each corner, surrounded by a circular mound and ditch. In the mound, traces of the palisade are sometimes visible. Secondly, there is the stone tower, a building generally about 20 feet square externally. From their juxtaposition, it

56

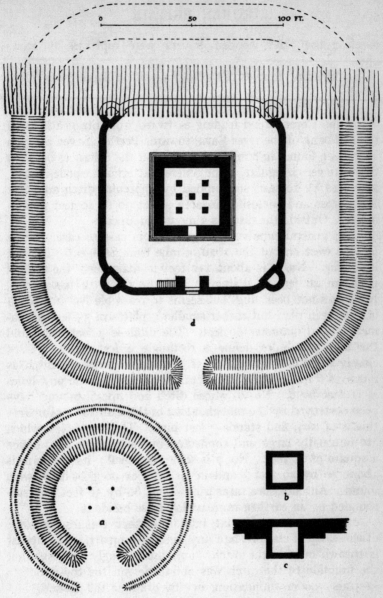

FIG. 13.—FOUR TYPES OF SIGNAL-STATION.

50 feet to 1 inch = 1 : 6000.

(a) Wooden signal-tower, Perthshire (presumed Flavian).
(b) Stone tower, Stanegate and Cumberland coast (Hadrian).
(c) Tower resembling (b) and contemporary with it, incorporated in Hadrian's
    Wall.
(d) Fourth-century signal-station on Yorkshire coast (Scarborough).

is clear that the wooden towers were replaced by stone
ones.[1]

In Britain, four types of signal-station have been identified.

(a) Wooden towers, surrounded by circular ditches, exist
along the Roman road leading eastward from Strageath down
the left bank of the river Earn, towards Perth. Seven of them
have been found, in 8 miles of road ; but the distances between
them are very irregular. The general pattern is a wooden tower,
about 10 by 10 feet, surrounded by a circular ditch about 12
feet across and enclosing an area about 30 to 40 feet in diameter. Outside the ditch is a mound of upcast.

This general type varies slightly from case to case. No. 1
(at the west end of the road, a mile from Strageath) has not
been dug. No. 2 is about 112 feet in diameter ; the central
platform 46 feet in diameter, and the ditch 12 feet across.
No. 3 has not been dug, but seems to resemble No. 2. No. 4
is similar in plan but rather smaller : platform 35 feet in diameter, total diameter 80 feet. The ditch is 3 feet deep, and
the four post-holes define a rectangle 9 feet by 7. No. 5
closely resembles No. 2, but is unusual in having a ditch as
much as 6 feet deep. The rectangle defined by the post-holes
is 11 feet by 9. No. 6, whose ditch and upcast-mound have
been destroyed by the plough, alone of them all has a rampart ;
this is of turf, and stands 3 feet high. The post-holes, which
are unusually large and connected by sleeper-trenches, define
a square of 11 feet. No. 7 is somewhat oval ; its platform is
about 50 by 40 feet ; and in its interior no post-holes were
found. An enclosure measuring about 80 by 50 feet and surrounded by an earthen rampart lay close beside it.

It will be observed that, in spite of their ditches, only one
of these signal-stations had any kind of rampart. The upcast
is thrown outside the ditch ; and this strongly suggests that
the function of the ditch was not to defend the tower but to
keep its wooden foundations dry by draining the ground.[2]

---

[1] *Germania Romana* [2], part i, plates x, xi ; for details, *O.R.L.*, Lieferung
xl, xliii, xliv, xlv.   The signal-station reliefs on the two columns are reproduced
in *R.W.S.*, plate iii.

[2] I owe this point to Professor Fabricius, in connection with the similar
German examples.

When these sites were dug, no evidence of date was found. But Roman remains in Scotland belong, broadly speaking, either to the Flavian period or to the Antonine ; and the simi-larity of these little wooden towers to the earliest towers on the German *limes* makes it reasonably certain that their date is the first century rather than the second.   Their function is obviously to maintain communication by signal between Ardoch and Inchtuthil, both Flavian forts ; and it is at least possible that they were established by Agricola in the campaigns that led up to the battle of Mons Graupius.

(*b*) Stone towers about 20 feet square externally, with walls 2 feet 6 inches to 3 feet thick, and very closely resembling

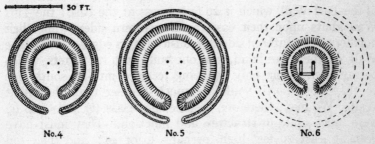

No.4   No. 5   No. 6

FIG. 14.—SIGNAL-STATIONS ON THE ROAD EAST OF STRAGEATH, PERTHSHIRE.

80 feet to 1 inch = 1 : 960.

No. 4 : diagram-sketch from measurements in *P.S.A. Scot.* xxxv, 27.   No. 5 : from plan *ibid.*, p. 27.   No. 6: from plan *ibid.*, p. 30.

the stone towers of the German *limes*, have been found in connection with the Hadrianic frontier and are attributable to about A.D. 120.

On the Stanegate, the road which runs some distance south of Hadrian's Wall and parallel to it (see p. 71), a signal-station of this type, with a ditch round it, was explored at Mains Rigg, south of Birdoswald, in 1928.   Though no dated objects were found, this signal-station must belong to the period during which the Hadrianic frontier was developing towards its final shape, that is, the early years of Hadrian's reign.[1]   It is 21 feet square externally, and its walls are 3 feet 6 inches thick.[2]

[1] *P.S.A. Scot.*, 1900-1901, p. 25 *seqq.*   [2] *C.W.*[2], xxix, 314.

Similar towers exist on the Cumberland coast, beginning where Hadrian's Wall ends and continuing, in all probability, as far as St. Bees Head.[1] They were so placed as to command a good view of the sea, and be in touch with each other ; and they were doubtless manned by detachments from the coastal forts, probably housed in special fortlets placed at intermediate points.

(c) Essentially the same as the preceding class are the turrets of Hadrian's Wall. These may be conceived as stone towers, 20 feet square externally, incorporated in a thick stone wall. The intermediate stage between the free-standing tower and the mural turret is provided by the turrets of the Turf Wall. These are 20-foot stone towers placed in the thickness of the Turf Wall, which is 20 feet across at the base ; the Turf Wall abuts upon their eastern and western sides, while their northern and southern sides are flush with its edges. The Stone Wall, on the other hand, is of one build with its turrets, which betray their origin only by being recessed into its south side so that their north walls are much thinner than the Great Wall. We may, therefore, assume that class (b) and class (c) were much alike in structure and function. They must have been at least 20 feet high, perhaps 30 or 40 ; and their top storey must have been designed for use as a look-out place from which signals could be sent.

(d) In the later empire the signal-station undergoes the same architectural development as the *castellum*. It grows larger and stronger, more massive in construction and more defensible in character. The tower increases in size to 45 or 50 feet square ; its walls are now 8 feet thick at the base, stepped back by offsets to 5 feet ; its height must have increased proportionally to about 100 feet. The palisade round it is replaced by a stone wall enclosing a space about 100 feet square, with a bastion at each corner ; outside this is a ditch, separated from the wall by a wide berm according to the tactical ideas of the age. Examples of this pattern have been identified at various points on the Yorkshire coast : at Huntcliff, Goldsborough, Ravenscar, Scarborough, and Filey. One has been found on the Bristol Channel, on the Exmoor

[1] *C.W.*[1], v, 124-130 ; *C.W.*[2], xxix, 138-165.

coast. These stations belong to the latter half of the fourth century.[1]

§ 2. Light-Houses

Light-houses, consisting of towers on whose summit a fire could be lit, were in use among the ancients from the Hellenistic period onwards ; the famous Pharos of Alexandria was built in the third century B.C. They served not to mark headlands and dangerous rocks, but to show the entrance to a harbour.[2] There may have been many Roman light-houses in Britain ; but we have certain knowledge only of two, one on each side of the harbour at Dover. That on the east side, on Castle Hill, is still standing to a height of 62 feet, of which only 43 feet are Roman work, the rest, together with most of the external face, being medieval. It is octagonal in plan, each side 15 feet long at the base ; internally it is 13 feet 10 inches square. The sides rose vertically and were stepped back at each storey, giving the tower a profile like that of an open telescope. Judging by the known dimensions, the original height must have been about 80 feet ; for at that height the walls, 12 feet thick at the bottom, would have been diminished by the successive offsets to between 3 and 4 feet. The core of the walls is concrete, the faces ashlar, and at every seven courses there is a bonding-course of tile. The doorway, and the recesses and windows which occur at each storey, are mostly arched with blocks of tufa alternating with pairs of tiles. Each storey had a wooden floor, the first floor being 17½ feet above ground, the others at intervals of 7½ to 8 feet. In the main, this tower must have resembled the Roman light-house at Boulogne,

[1] No full publication of the Yorkshire coastal signal-stations yet exists. For Huntcliff, *J.R.S.*, ii, 213-232 ; for Scarborough, Collingwood, *The Roman Signal Station on Castle Hill, Scarborough* (pamphlet published by the Scarborough Corporation, 1925) ; for the whole subject, Haverfield in *J.R.S.*, ii, 201-214, and recently Macdonald, " Die Küstenverteidigung Britanniens gegen das Ende der röm. Herrschaft," in *Fünfundzwanzig Jahre röm.-germ. Kommission*, Leipzig, 1929, with plans of Goldsborough, Scarborough, and Huntcliff. The Exmoor example was dug and published by H. St. George Gray, *Trans. Devonshire Assoc.*, xliv, 703.

[2] For ancient light-houses in general, see art. *Pharos* in Daremberg and Saglio's *Dictionnaire*. An illustration of the Alexandria light-house is given in Rostovtseff's *Hist. of the Ancient World*, i, 369.

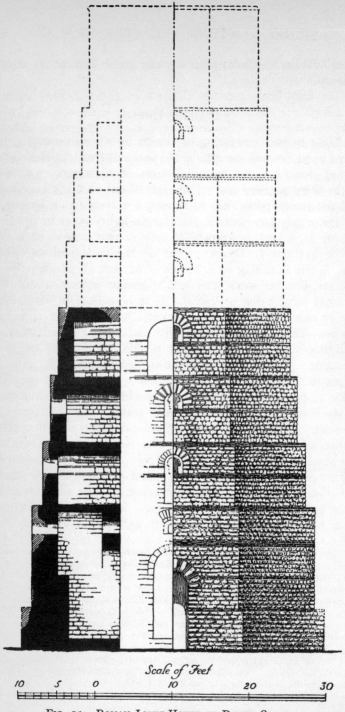

Scale of Feet

10   5   0   10   20   30

FIG. 15.—ROMAN LIGHT-HOUSE IN DOVER CASTLE.
Partial reconstruction in section and elevation from the south, by
R. E. M. Wheeler.

which like it was octagonal in plan and telescopic in profile, but was 200 feet high.[1]

The light-house on the Western Heights has now entirely vanished, but for a mass of masonry, traditionally known as the " Devil's Drop " on account of its lumpish shape and the hardness of its mortar, embedded in the " Drop Redoubt." Of the tower's original plan and dimensions nothing definite is known, but its foundations were seen when the redoubt was being built in 1861, and it appears to have been constructed, at least in part, of re-used materials, a fact which suggests that it was erected at a late date in the Roman period.[2]

[1] Early antiquaries did not in general recognise the Roman origin of this eastern tower : Stukeley (*It. Cur.*, ed. 1, p. 121) and Gough (Camden, i, 245) did so, and it was measured in 1872 (*A.*, xlv, 333-336) and is described in Mothersole, *Saxon Shore*, 122-126 ; but the only satisfactory account is by Wheeler " The Roman Light-houses at Dover," in *A.J.*, lxxxvi, forthcoming), who has very generously placed his MS. and plans at my disposal.

[2] Before it fell into ruin in the eighteenth century, the western tower was a more conspicuous object and better known to antiquaries than the eastern. *Cf.* Leland, ed. Toulmin Smith, iv, 50 ; Lambarde, *Perambulation of Kent*, ed. 2, 1596, p. 158 ; Camden, *Britannia*, tr. Philemon Holland, p. 345 (" a Watch towre to give night light and direction to ships ") ; Mothersole, *Saxon Shore*, p. 128 ; and now Wheeler, " Roman Light-houses," *cit.*

CHAPTER V

FRONTIER WORKS

§ 1. PRELIMINARIES

General Features of Roman Frontiers.[1]—A frontier, considered as something drawn on the ground and not merely drawn on the map, may mean three different things :—

(*a*) A continuous mark, designed to show people where a certain territory begins and ends. This may easily take the form of a ditch having no capacity to be used as an obstacle. It was with such a ditch that Scipio found the Carthaginian territory marked off from that of Carthage's native subjects, and this ditch became the boundary of the Roman province of Africa.

(*b*) A chain of fortified posts. This is a military frontier, the natural type for use where external enemies are feared. Such a chain of posts absolutely requires good communication from one post to the next; and therefore a road usually connects the various forts. Thus the frontier of Trajan's Arabian conquests consisted of a fortified road, intended to protect Roman Arabia against the desert tribes.

(*c*) A continuous barrier or obstacle, such as the Romans used in Britain and in Upper Germany and Raetia.

These three elements may be combined in various ways. The continuous mark may occur alone, but this is naturally rare ; a chain of posts connected by a road serves also as a continuous mark ; an obstacle is *ipso facto* a mark, and is not of much use unless patrolled by means of fortified posts.

---

[1] The fundamental work on the Roman frontier-system is Fabricius, art. *Limes* in *P.-W.* I refer to this hereinafter as *Fabricius*, and desire to acknowledge extensive debts to it.

But however they are combined, they are three distinct ideas, and must be kept separate in thought.

The Romans used the word *limes* to express any of these ideas or any combination of them. Literally, a *limes* is something that goes across; and its proper meaning is a path or track, such as the balk between the ploughed strips in a field, the path of the sun across the sky, or a ship across the sea, or a way through a wood. In a military sense, *limes* primarily means a line of march, especially a road by which one invades an enemy's territory. This is the regular sense of the word in the early years of the Empire.[1] But a further sense attaches the word to one particular strategic road—the transverse road forming the outward edge of the road-network thrown over a conquered country.[2] Hence the word comes to mean simply a frontier-line of whatever kind, with all its appurtenances; and ultimately the whole frontier district.[3]

Pre-Hadrianic Frontier-lines in Britain.—As the Roman armies advanced in their conquest of Britain, temporary frontiers must have formed and dissolved again constantly. The only one belonging to the earlier stages which we can identify with fair certainty is the Fosse, the frontier of Ostorius Scapula in A.D. 47. Tacitus (*Ann.*, xii, 31, 2) says that Ostorius took measures to prevent insurrections among the conquered tribes *cunctaque castris Antonam et Sabrinam fluvios cohibere parat*. No river Antona is known, and, even if it were, the sentence would not construe. Dr. Henry Bradley (*Collected Papers*, p. 243) proposed, by altering one letter, to read *cunctaque cis Trisantonam*, "and prepared to hold down everything this side of the Trent and Severn," showing reason to believe that Trisantona was the ancient name of the Trent. On this view, Tacitus's phrase would be a description of the course of the

---

[1] Tac., *Ann.*, i, 50 ; *silvam Caesiam limitemque a Tiberio coeptum scindit.* Velleius, ii, 120 : *penetrat interius, aperit limites.* Here *limites* are simply ways cleared in the forest. Fabricius, 572-574.

[2] Tac., *Agr.*, 41, 2, uses *limes imperii* in this sense ; also Tac., *Germ.*, 29, *limite acto*, seems to imply the same meaning.

[3] As a general sketch of the subject, Pelham, " The Roman Frontier System," in *Essays in Roman History*, though twenty years old, is still serviceable as an introduction. Fabricius's article contains a full bibliography ; but reference may here be made to the most important collections of detail : *Das obergermanisch-rätische Limes der Römerreich* (= *ORL*), and the parallel series *Das römische Limes in Oesterreich*.

Fosse, and the conclusion would emerge that the Fosse, with
its remarkably straight course and its obvious lack of utility
as an ordinary traffic-line, was intended as a *limes* in the sense
of a transverse fortified road acting as the frontier—a purely
temporary frontier—for a conquered district. The discovery
of a Claudian fort at Margidunum, on this road, confirms this
view (*J.R.S.*, xiv, 252-256; *cf.* also Ekwall, *English River
Names*, *s.v.* Trent).

Another temporary frontier is that of Agricola between the
Forth and Clyde. Here, according to Tacitus (*Agr.*, 23, 2)
Agricola established a chain of forts across the isthmus. We
have already examined the relics of one such, at Bar Hill
(p. 35). But the sites of others are known. At Mumrills
(*J.R.S.*, xviii, 193), Rough Castle (*R.W.S.*, 232 *seqq.*), Castlecary (*P.S.A.S.*, 1903, 271), Cadder (*P.S.A.S.*, 1917-18, p. 178),
and Old Kilpatrick (Miller, *Old Kilpatrick*, 10-14) various indications—partly structural, partly consisting of pottery and
other datable finds—make it clear that Agricola's temporary
frontier anticipated the line of the Antonine Wall, and that its
forts were planted on sites which were used again by the
engineers of the second century. But the case of Bar Hill
shows how short a time Agricola held this line. When he
advanced into central Scotland, many of his forts along this
temporary frontier were abandoned.[1]

Agricola intended to conquer the whole of Scotland, and
when this project was frustrated by his recall it does not
appear that he had time to organise a definite frontier-line.
Nor do we know of any attempt to do so during the thirty-odd
years that elapsed between his recall (A.D. 84-85) and the
accession of Hadrian (A.D. 117), although during this period it
is certain that many forts were built or rebuilt in various parts
of Britain. The details of this period are still obscure (*cf.*
Macdonald, "The Agricolan Occupation of North Britain," in
J.R.S., ix), but what evidence we have suggests that the work
of planning and constructing a permanent frontier was not
taken in hand until the British revolt at the beginning of
Hadrian's reign.

[1] Anderson, *Cornelii Taciti de vita Agricolae*, pp. lx-lxvii; *cf.* Haverfield,
"Agricola and the Antonine Wall," in *P.S.A. Scot.*, lii, 174-181.

§ 2. HADRIAN'S FRONTIER [1]

First Phase of the Hadrianic Frontier.—The line chosen for the new frontier was already occupied by a road dating back to the time of Agricola ; indeed, it may well have been one of Agricola's temporary frontiers. This road, now locally called the Stanegate, runs perhaps from Corbridge (a Flavian site, probably a *castellum* of Agricola ; *Northumberland County History*, vol. x, p. 478) westward, its course being at first doubtful, to Chesterholm, Carvoran, Nether Denton, Watchcross, and—again doubtfully in detail—to Carlisle (certainly a Flavian site ; claimed as possibly pre-Agricolan by Bushe-Fox in *Archaeologia*, lxiv, 295-314, as Agricolan by Haverfield and Atkinson in *C.W.*[2], xvii, 235-250). Of the intermediate sites, Nether Denton was probably founded not later than A.D. 100 or thereabouts (Bushe-Fox, *op. cit.*) ; Carvoran and Chesterholm were presumably rebuilt in connection with the Hadrianic frontier, and their earlier strata (supposing these to exist) have not been explored.

The original plan for a frontier, so far as we can at present reconstruct it, seems to have been as follows. Take the Stanegate as a line of forts : north of it, dig a continuous ditch by way of frontier-mark, and build new forts along this ditch where necessary. This plan was carried out. Along the Stanegate, certain new forts were built ; we know of two, one at Haltwhistle Burn and one at Throp near Gilsland (*C.W.*[2], xiii, 363-381). The Haltwhistle Burn fort is a rectangular stone-and-earth structure, two-thirds of an acre in extent, with two gateways, and various characteristics suggest that its purpose was less to accommodate a garrison than to serve as a dump for stores, looked after by a mere handful of men. The fort at Throp is nearly the same size (0·627 acre, *C.W.*[2], xiii, 365) but almost square, and its rampart is of turf, 16 feet wide, on a stone foundation, with an 8-foot berm separating it from a single ditch 16 feet 6 inches wide and 6 feet deep. There were two single gateways, and floors inside the fort showed where buildings had stood. In both these forts the objects found were sufficient to prove that they had been occupied for

---

[1] Mr. F. G. Simpson has very kindly read this section and suggested several improvements.

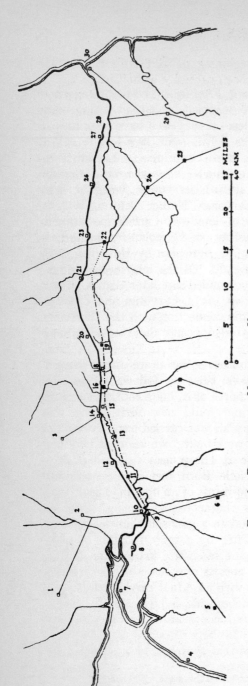

FIG. 16.—DIAGRAMMATIC MAP OF THE VALLUM AND STANEGATE.

■ Sites certainly or probably dating from the first century.
□ Sites certainly or probably connected in origin with the Vallum-Stanegate frontier.
—— Vallum. — · — · — · Stanegate.

1. Birrens (Blatobulgium).
2. Netherby (Castra Exploratorum).
3. Bewcastle.
4. Beckfoot.
5. Old Carlisle (Petrianae).
6. Old Penrith (Voreda).
7. Bowness-on-Solway.
8. Burgh-by-Sands.
9. Carlisle.
10. Stanwix.

11. Watchcross.
12. Castlesteads.
13. Nether Denton.
14. Birdoswald ((?C)amboglanna).
15. Throp.
16. Carvoran (Magnae).
17. Whitley Castle.
18. Haltwhistle Burn.
19. Chesterholm (Vindolanda).
20. Housesteads (Borcovicium).

21. Chesters (Cilurnum).
22. Corbridge (Corstopitum).
23. Halton Chesters (Hunnum).
24. Ebchester (Vindomora).
25. Lanchester (Longovicium).
26. Rudchester (Vindobala).
27. Benwell (Condercum).
28. Newcastle (Pons Aelius).
29. Chester-le-Street.
30. South Shields.

N.B.—Newbrough is on the Stanegate, S.W. of 21.

a short time about the beginning of Hadrian's reign. The Haltwhistle Burn fort had been carefully demolished.

These facts suggest that the Stanegate was adopted about the beginning of Hadrian's reign as a frontier-line and additionally fortified for that purpose ; also that it was in part deprived of this function when, shortly afterwards, the Wall was built. Until recently, those best acquainted with the complicated problems of the Hadrianic frontier have supposed that there were three main phases in its development : (i) the Stanegate frontier ; (ii) the Vallum [1] with its forts ; (iii) the Wall linking up the forts. This view was put forward in several places, about the year 1920, by Mr. F. G. Simpson and the present writer working in conjunction (*e.g.* Simpson and Shaw, " The Purpose and Date of the Vallum and its Crossings," *C.W.*[2], xxii (1922) ; Collingwood, " Hadrian's Wall : a History of the Problem," *J.R.S.*, xi (written 1922) ; Collingwood, *Roman Britain* (written 1922) ; and elsewhere). The threefold division of phases was made necessary by the fact that the Wall fort of Great Chesters lies less than a mile from Haltwhistle Burn, and they cannot therefore have been simultaneously occupied ; but it seemed clear that Great Chesters was built before the Wall, because its ditches underlay the Wall, which had actually

[1] The Vallum is the name used to denote the Hadrianic frontier ditch. Technically, the name is incorrect. The proper Latin word for a frontier ditch is *fossa*. *Vallum* is a word with a definite range of meanings. It is derived from *vallus*, a stake, and means, properly, a palisade. In military language it is the palisade round a camp, consisting of stakes (*valli*) driven into the *agger* or mound of upcast earth from the ditch. Hence it is naturally enough used of any barrier or defence, especially a bristly or spiky barrier : the Alps, the " beard " of an ear of wheat, regarded as a defence against predatory birds, and so forth (see Lewis and Short, *s.v. vallum*). From its general sense of " barrier," it comes to be used of Hadrian's Wall, which the Romans themselves called *murus*, when emphasising its architectural character, *vallum* when emphasising its function as an obstacle. As a rule, they called it simply *vallum*. Thus it is called *murus* by Spartian (*Vita Hadriani*, § 11, and *Vita Severi*, § 18) in describing its erection or repair, but *vallum* by the Antonine Itineraries, the *Notitia Dignitatum*, and the inscription *C.I.L.*, vii, 940, *ob res trans vallum prospere gestas*. Early antiquaries (in fact, no less a person than the Venerable Bede) finding two words, *murus* and *vallum*, in their authorities, and two works, the Wall and the frontier ditch, on the ground, wrongly argued that *murus* meant the Wall and *vallum* the frontier ditch, whose character as a frontier ditch was not recognised until the late nineteenth century, when Haverfield so explained the work in 1896 (*C.W.*[1], xiv, 419).

collapsed owing to their presence. In 1925, however, it was found that, though these ditches certainly underlay the *narrow* Wall, they stopped short of the *broad* Wall, in such a way as to prove that the fort was contemporary with it (*A.A.*⁴, ii, 197). Great Chesters, therefore, is not a " Vallum fort " but a " Wall fort," *i.e.* a fort added to the scheme when the Wall was built ; and therefore we are free to simplify the hypothesis by uniting the first and second phases. In 1928 additional evidence for this simplification was found at Birdoswald. Here the Vallum had been found in 1896-97 curving round the south end of the fort (*C.W.*¹, xiv, 415) which seemed to make Vallum and fort part of the same scheme ; but in 1928 it was found that the Vallum had curved to avoid, not Birdoswald fort as we know it, but something else, and probably something much smaller. This makes it possible to hold that the neighbouring fort at Throp might be contemporary with the Vallum ; it certainly could not be contemporary with Birdoswald fort, but we can now assume that it was superseded by this fort exactly as Haltwhistle Burn was superseded by Great Chesters.

Though the Vallum thus appears not to avoid Birdoswald fort, there are others which it does avoid in such a way as to suggest contemporary origin. These are Rudchester (*C.W.*¹, xv, 178), Halton Chesters (*Northumb. Co. Hist.*, vol. x, 468), Castlesteads (*C.W.*², ii, 384), Benwell (*North. C.H.*, xiii), and probably others. The case of Carrawburgh (*C.W.*¹, xiv, 416) is dubious. Thus we arrive at a very rough provisional scheme of the Vallum-Stanegate frontier, which we may describe (in the present state of our knowledge) as follows :—

Sketch of the Frontier in its First Stage.—On the east, the frontier begins at Newcastle, Hadrian's bridge (Pons Aelius) over the Tyne. Here, or quite near by, the Vallum begins. A fort stands on the hill-top of Benwell, a commanding situation 2 miles to the west. The next is nearly 7 miles farther on at Rudchester. Thence it is just over 7 miles to Halton Chesters, and thence 5½ miles to Chesters, where the frontier crosses the North Tyne. Hitherto the whole system has been new and, so far as we know, unprepared by any previous structures on the same line ; but, after Chesters, contact is established with the Stanegate. The Vallum, for 16 miles westward from Chesters, is gradually converging with the

Stanegate; and in the whole of these 16 miles it never [1]
bends to avoid a fort. There are three forts in these 16 miles :
Carrawburgh, Housesteads, and Great Chesters; but Great
Chesters is certainly later than the Vallum, Carrawburgh is
probably the same, and Housesteads alone of the three seems
earlier than the Wall, but, lying on a hill-top away from the
Vallum, is not near enough to it to cause a deflection. In the
Chesters-Carvoran area, therefore, the Vallum-Stanegate frontier may be conceived as involving four forts : three,[2] Chesterholm, Haltwhistle Burn, and Carvoran, being on the Stanegate ;
and one, Housesteads, on a commanding site north of the
Vallum.

At Carvoran, the Vallum and the Stanegate almost meet,
and run close together for 2½ miles to Throp. Beyond this
they diverge again. The Vallum crosses the Irthing and runs
along its north bank; the Stanegate remains south of it,
and 2½ miles farther reaches the fort (an old fort perhaps
incorporated in the new frontier-scheme) of Nether Denton.
But on the Vallum there are fortlets of some kind at Birdoswald
and Pike Hill (*C.W.*[2], xxviii, 381-382), keeping in touch with
the Stanegate through signal-stations of which one, at Mains
Rigg, has been identified (see above, p. 59). The next fort, 5¼
miles from Nether Denton, is on the Vallum : it is Castlesteads,
whose contemporaneity with the Vallum seems established by
the deflection of the Vallum (*C.W.*[2], ii, 384). And hence, once
more, the Vallum and Stanegate converge to meet at Stanwix
—possibly a Vallum fort—where the Stanegate runs into
Carlisle and comes to an end, while the Vallum continues on
the south bank of the Eden. The fort of Burgh-by-Sands
(*C.W.*[2], xxiii, 3-12) may be contemporary with the Vallum,
which ends in the marshes close by, at Dykesfield, 66 miles
from Newcastle.

East of Newcastle and west of Dykesfield this phase may very
well have involved the construction of isolated forts—South
Shields and Bowness-on-Solway—but of this we have no proof.

Description of the Vallum.—The Vallum consists of a ditch,
generally about 30 feet wide and 7 deep, with steep sides and

[1] Except in the doubtful case of Carrawburgh.
[2] A fourth, at Newbrough, has been found while this book was in the press :
but at present only fourth-century relics have turned up there.

a flat bottom, the upcast from which has been arranged in two continuous mounds set well back from its two edges. Each mound is on average 25 feet wide and sometimes still as much as 5 feet high, and is separated from the ditch by a berm about 20 feet wide. The whole work is thus on average about 100 feet across from centre to centre of the mounds. These are normal measurements, but the work is not uniform in scale.

Details show that the ditch was the essential thing. It is never interrupted, even where it has had to be cut through hard rock or carried across a deep ravine or a peat-moss. In these cases it has been modified in various ways with the plain intention of preserving its continuity at all costs ($C.W.^2$, xxii,

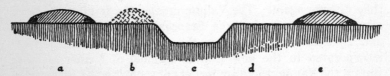

a　　　　b　　　　c　　　　d　　　　e

FIG. 17.—DIAGRAMMATIC SECTION OF THE VALLUM.

30 feet = 1 inch.

(a) South mound, made of clean upcast ; turf kerbs at either side, remains of original vegetation beneath.
(b) Marginal mound, varying greatly in size and not always present, on south berm ; made of mixed soil.
(c) Ditch.
(d) North berm, sometimes with a marginal mound.
(e) North mound, resembling (a).

361 *seqq.*). But its flat-bottomed section, its relation to the mounds on either side, and, above all, its relation to the topography of the country through which it runs, prove conclusively that it had no military significance (*op. cit.*, 355-367). It is a ditch but not a military ditch : the only alternative consistent with the facts is that it should be a frontier-mark.

But there remain two curious points. First, the wide berms ; secondly, the placing of forts on the northern side of the ditch. With regard to the first, Fabricius (628-629) suggests that they provided unmetalled roads along which patrols could walk or ride, sheltered by the mounds and enabled by the rectilinear lay-out of the work to see along it for considerable distances. It may be remarked that the mounds are generally provided

with kerbs of turf or stone to prevent them from spreading
unduly, but that no traces of palisades have ever been found
in them. On the other hand, the relation of the Vallum both
to the forts and to the lie of the land strongly suggests that
the patrol-track was to the north of it, on or near the line
later followed by the Wall.

As to the placing of the forts, the strangeness of their being
placed outside the frontier-line which they were to defend is
mitigated by supposing that the defence was conceived as an
active, offensive defence, conducted by troops operating in the
open, not hiding behind their fortifications. If the garrison of
a fort was to be used in this way, it could only be hampered by

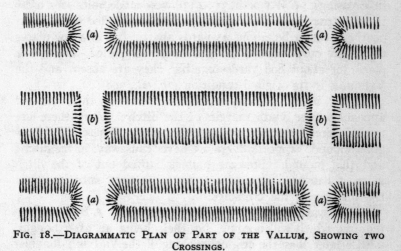

Fig. 18.—Diagrammatic Plan of Part of the Vallum, Showing two
Crossings.

50 feet = 1 inch.

(a), (a), Gaps in mounds ; (b), (b) causeways across ditch.

having the ditch and mounds of the Vallum between it and
the enemy.

Alterations in the Vallum.—The continuous and symmetrical
plan of the Vallum as described above is subject to two kinds
of variation. First, the details and dimensions vary slightly from
place to place ; but this variation, though significant as reveal-
ing the purpose of the work, is not otherwise important.
Secondly, there are irregularities due to alterations in the
Vallum after its completion. These are of three types :—

(*a*) Close to forts, the Vallum is generally invisible on the surface. This has long been known (*e.g. C.W.*[1], xiv, 415 : " both its mounds and its ditch vanish in [the] vicinity " of Birdoswald and Carrawburgh), but it was only in 1928 that proof was discovered that the filling-up of the Vallum ditch, near Birdoswald at any rate, had been done, deliberately and completely, very soon after it was first dug (*C.W.*[2], xxix, 309).

(*b*) Almost all along its length, the Vallum has been systematically broken through at regular intervals by digging a breach in either mound and throwing earth into the ditch to make a causeway. These " crossings," as they are called (Simpson and Shaw, " The Purpose and Date of the Vallum and its Crossings," *C.W.*[2], xxii, 353-433), were made quite soon after the construction of the Vallum, and were intended to occur, as nearly as might be, about 45 yards apart ; but in a few places they were only marked out and never completed, and in one place, for about 800 yards together, they are absent and the Vallum is in its original condition (*op. cit.*, 398).

(*c*) In many places—indeed, in most—a third mound appears on the south margin of the ditch ; rarely there are two additional mounds, one on either side. Where the " marginal mound " appears, there are never causeways in the ditch ; and this mound represents material lifted out of the ditch when it has been cleaned out at some time subsequent to the making of the crossings.

What was the purpose of these crossings ? A hypothesis is required which will account for their being an afterthought, a little later than the original making of the Vallum ; for their regular occurrence at so short an interval ; and for their cancellation by the cleaning-out of the ditch. The most probable view is that they were made when the Wall was built, in order to facilitate transport of building-stone from quarries south of the Vallum to the line of the Wall north of the Vallum. Certain it is that the vast majority of the quarries used *were* south of the Vallum, that some such device was absolutely required, and that no other roads for carrying stone across the Vallum are visible (*op. cit.*, 420 *seqq.*).

Hadrian's Wall.—The Vallum-Stanegate frontier presumably belongs to the early years of Hadrian's reign. It is in all probability later than A.D. 118, the probable date of the revolt which created the necessity for it. We possess no conclusive archaeological evidence that it may not be earlier than this ; but any attempt to push its date back into the reign of Trajan encounters the difficulty that, according to the results of expert botanical analysis, the Vallum ditch at Birdoswald " could only have been open a year or two before the re-filling with the peat " (*C.W.*[2], xxix, 309), *i.e.* before the construction of the Wall. On the other hand, the Vallum-Stanegate frontier must be earlier than *c.* 122-127, the date of Aulus Platorius Nepos, the governor whose name appears on the milecastles of the stone Wall (*C.I.L.*, vii, 660, 661, 662 ; *J.R.S.*, xii, 65). Hadrian visited Britain in 121 or 122, and, says his biographer Spartian, *multa correxit murumque per LXXX M.P. primus duxit qui barbaros Romanosque divideret* (*Historia Augusta, vita Hadriani*, § 11. For other ancient writers, see Collingwood, " Hadrian's Wall : a History of the Problem," in *J.R.S.*, xi). It is tempting to conjecture that the Vallum-Stanegate frontier had been constructed before his visit, and that the addition of the Wall was the result of that visit.

The Wall is about 73 miles long. It begins at Wallsend, where the lower reaches of the Tyne were in view (*A.A.*[4], vi, 174). Here a fort lies on a hill north of the river, and the Wall returns in a southerly direction to run into the river below low-water mark. From Wallsend the Wall runs to Newcastle, after which it picks up the Vallum. It runs close beside the Vallum, always to the north of it, successively to Benwell, Rudchester, Halton Chesters, and the North Tyne at Chesters. West of the North Tyne, the new phase of the frontier involved the building of new forts, perhaps at Carrawburgh, certainly at Great Chesters and Birdoswald. This entailed the abandonment of the Stanegate forts at Haltwhistle Burn, Throp, and probably Nether Denton ; [1] but the Stanegate forts at Chesterholm and Carvoran were retained in use. West of Dykesfield the Wall is prolonged to Bowness-on-Solway, running out into the water, as at Wallsend, where the estuary ceases to be fordable.

At every Roman mile was built a milecastle, a fortlet varying in size from about 50 by 60 feet to about 65 by 75 (internally),

---

[1] And, we must now add, Newbrough.

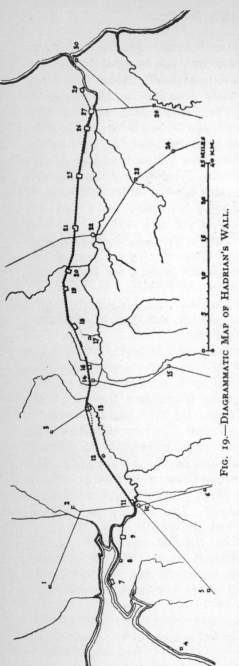

FIG. 19.—DIAGRAMMATIC MAP OF HADRIAN'S WALL.

———— Narrow stone wall.   ———— Narrow stone wall with broad foundation.
········· Turf wall.   ===== Broad stone wall.

The exact distribution of the above four types of wall is not yet established in all its details. Forts in contact with the Wall are exaggerated in size so as to show their relation to it in plan. Names in italics are given in the *Notitia Dignitatum* as those of forts *per lineam valli*.

1. Birrens (Blatobulgium).
2. Netherby.
3. Bewcastle.
4. Beckfoot.
5. Old Carlisle (*Petrianae*).
6. Old Penrith (Voreda).
7. Bowness-on-Solway.
8. Drumburgh.
9. Burgh-by-Sands.
10. Carlisle (Luguvallium).
11. Stanwix.
12. Castlesteads.
13. Birdoswald ((?C)*amboglanna*).
14. Carvoran (*Magnae*).
15. Whitley Castle.
16. Great Chesters (*Aesica*).
17. Chesterholm (*Vindolanda*).
18. Housesteads (*Borcovicium*).
19. Carrawburgh (*Procolitia*).
20. Chesters (*Cilurnum*).
21. Halton Chesters (*Hunnum*).
22. Corbridge (Corstopitum).
23. Ebchester (Vindomora).
24. Lanchester (Longovicium).
25. Rudchester (*Vindobala*).
26. Benwell (*Condercum*).
27. Newcastle (*Pons Aelius*).
28. Chester-le-Street.
29. Wallsend (*Segedunum*).
30. South Shields.

provided with a gate to north and south and barrack-buildings inside. Each mile was divided into three equal lengths by two turrets, about 13 feet square internally, which have been already described (p. 60) as signal-stations incorporated with the Wall.

The purpose of this new frontier-work is obviously in part a new purpose; but its novelty must not be exaggerated.

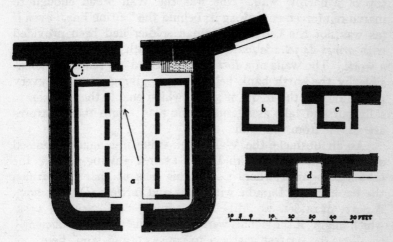

FIG. 20.—MILECASTLE AND TURRETS.

45 feet to an inch.

(a) Poltross Burn Milecastle.   The milecastle (No. 48) is of one build with the Wall; it has gateways north and south, two barrack buildings, an oven, and steps leading up to the rampart walk.   It is built to the gauge of the Broad Wall, but at a little distance to east and west the Wall is reduced to narrow gauge on Broad Foundation.
(b) An isolated turret (Risehow, on the Cumberland Coast).
(c) A turret incorporated in Narrow Wall (Appletree; 50 b).
(d) A turret incorporated in a short length of Broad Wall, reduced on either side to Narrow (Willowford West; 48 b).

First and foremost, the Wall is an elevated sentry-walk, running from fort to fort and studded with signal-stations. The sentries are now much more comfortably off, for they have regular quarters in the milecastles and the Wall protects them, the Vallum which never did, from snipers. But further, the Wall is, what the Vallum was not, an obstacle. An obstacle to what ? It has too often been assumed that it was meant as an obstacle to hostile armies; and certainly it has in many ways the aspect of a fortification. But it lacks the essential characteristic of a fortification. It cannot be defended. In order to defend a wall you must be able to bring reinforcements to a threatened point ; but the top of the Wall was reached only by stairways at forts and milecastles, and by ladders (it would appear) at the turrets ; and ladders 500 yards apart are a very poor means of bringing reinforcements to the top of a narrow wall. Nor was the Wall broad enough to march reinforcements along it, behind the " firing line," even if (as was not the case) the Roman soldier had been provided with *armes de jet* adequate for dealing with an attack on such a work. The walls of a fort of this period are rendered defensible by the earth bank behind them, giving access to every point, and by the frequent gates, which enable the garrison to sally out and take assailants in the rear ; both these features are absent from the Wall.

As an obstacle, the Wall is of value not against massed attacks of a military kind, but against raiding-parties, the *latrunculi* against whom Commodus tells us that he fortified the bank of the Danube with forts and fortlets (Dessau, 395). A party of raiders would be seriously impeded by such a work, which might, if the signals were working, delay them sufficiently to allow the nearest garrison to come up and stop them ; or else, if they got through, the garrisons could get under arms and catch them on their way back, laden with booty and faced with the problem of lifting it over the Wall after the fatigues and possible casualties of the raid. " Escaping raiders are always handicapped by the fact that they are tired, having to do a double journey, whereas the defenders are fresh. The looter has to carry his loot ; the defender carries only his arms. On the top of this, put a wall in front of the raider and his position becomes extremely difficult " (T. H. Clarke, in *C.W.*[2], xxvii, 237 ; *cf.* Collingwood, " The Purpose of the Roman Wall," in *The Vasculum*, Oct., 1921, and *Antiquity*, vol. i, p. 25).

Broad Wall, Narrow Wall, Turf Wall.—We know the Wall best as a structure 7 feet 6 inches thick, with stone faces and a concrete core. The faces are normally (not always ; *A.A.*[4], iv, 114) made of small dressed stones, each able to be carried by a man ; the core, of rough stones lying in mortar, sometimes forming a single solid mass and sometimes roughly coursed in

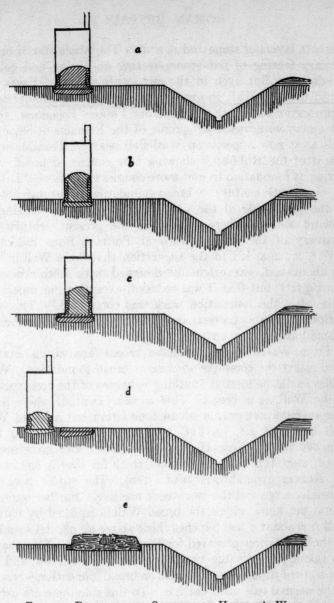

FIG. 21.—DIAGRAMMATIC SECTIONS OF HADRIAN'S WALL.

25 feet to an inch.

(a) Broad wall.   (b) Narrow wall.   (c) Narrow wall on broad foundation.
(d) Narrow wall behind broad foundation.   (e) Turf wall.

alternate layers of stone and mortar.   The whole stands on an
ordinary footing of flat stones resting on a clay and cobble
foundation.   But even in the eighteenth century it was observed that the Wall, in some places, stands on a foundation of
disproportionate width (Warburton, *Vallum Romanum*, 1753,
has a map with, inset, a " profile of the Remains of Severus's
Wall as it now appears on Wall Fell near St. Oswalds when
clear'd of the Rubbish," showing four courses of broad Wall
serving as foundation to four more courses of narrow).   Late in
the nineteenth century, a broad foundation projecting always
on the south side of the Wall was discovered by digging at
Gilsland and elsewhere.   Early in the present century the
discovery of the same feature at Poltross Burn milecastle
(*C.W.*[2], xi, 404) led to the suggestion that " the Wall in this
neighbourhood was originally designed with a thickness of
about 9 feet, but that it was reduced, except in the milecastle
walls, after the foundation work was completed."   This suggestion is probably correct, and is borne out by the distribution
of broad and narrow structures.

From Wallsend to Newcastle recent excavation enables
us to assert the complete absence of broad foundation.   West
of Newcastle, as soon as anything is known of the construction
of the Wall, it is broad.   This is near Denton, where however we have not only a broad foundation but a broad Wall
built on it (*A.A.*[4], iv, 111) from 9 feet 1 inch to 9 feet
5 inches thick.   Near Heddon-on-the-Wall, the structure is
broad, and stands 9 feet 7 inches thick for over 4 feet above
the Roman ground-level (*ibid.*, 120).   The stones here are
unusually large and the work very massive.   Farther west, we
do not yet know where, the broad Wall is replaced by narrow
Wall (*i.e.* about 7 feet 6 inches thick above all offsets) standing
on the foundation prepared for the broad Wall.   This change
has taken place by the time we get to St. Oswald's, and the
new state of things—narrow Wall on broad foundation—persists
as the normal rule until Carlisle.   To this rule there are exceptions of three kinds :—

(i) On the tops of the precipitous crags in the Housesteads
region, the broad foundation is absent, and the Wall is purely
narrow.

(ii) At Great Chesters the broad foundation lies not under,

but immediately in front of, the narrow Wall. The two works converge at Cockmount Hill, and west of this the broad foundation underlies the narrow Wall.

(iii) At Harrow's Scar, where the Wall begins again after crossing the Irthing at Willowford, the broad foundation is absent and continues so for about 3½ miles ; but the situation is complicated by the Turf Wall, a structure forming a loopline to the narrow stone Wall for 1¾ miles (Harrow's Scar to Wall Bowers) and thereafter coinciding in line with the Stone Wall, it appears, to about Banksburn (*C.W.*², xxviii, 382-383).

The Turf Wall is a turf-work about 20 feet wide, with a 6-foot berm (*op. cit.*, 383), which appears to have been erected as a temporary structure on the line prepared for the stone Wall (*op. cit.*, 381). This line was in part utilised, in part abandoned, when the stone Wall was built. The reason why it was partly abandoned may have been that the original line was too near the precipitous banks of the Irthing and was damaged by landslips. That the Turf Wall stood only a short time before being demolished appears from the character of the material in its ditch, indicating that this ditch had been deliberately filled up when it was quite new (*op. cit.*, 380). The old theory that the Turf Wall was Hadrian's Wall and the Stone Wall that of Severus (*cf. C.W.*¹, xiv, 190-191 ; xv, 342-343 ; Mommsen, *Provinces of the Roman Empire*, Eng. trans., vol. ii, 351 ; *Encycl. Brit.*, ed. 11, art. *Roman Britain*) was exploded in 1911 (*C.W.*², xiii, 297-397), and every fresh discovery makes its resuscitation more obviously impossible.

West of Carlisle no broad foundation is known, and it seems probable that in this region the Wall is always narrow (MacLauchlan, *Memoir written during a Survey of the Roman Wall*, p. 75, and excavation by the writer at Beaumont in 1928 ; on the other hand, at Drumburgh Haverfield reports the Wall 9½ feet broad at foundation, intermediate between the two types ; *C.W.*¹, xvi, p. 85).

The present hypothesis is that the stone Wall was originally designed to stretch from Newcastle to Carlisle and to be 10 Roman feet thick. It was not to be built along the summits of the crags near Housesteads, these crags themselves being a sufficient defence to the patrols ; and in the Birdoswald region, where the deep Irthing valley lay close behind the chosen line, a weaker barrier of turf was allowed to do temporary duty. When this broad Wall was partly built, the decision was made to reduce it in width and extend it in length by making it continuous, and also (for this afterthought may have occurred at the same time) prolonging it to Wallsend and Bowness.[1]

§ 3. THE ANTONINE WALL [2]

Historical Outline.—In the years 142 and 143 the frontier was moved forward from the Tyne-Solway line to the Forth-Clyde line. Traces of the campaigns in which Q. Lollius Urbicus, the legate of Antoninus Pius, advanced from Hadrian's Wall and conquered the Lowland districts are to be found, on the one hand, in the great supply-base at Corbridge, built at this time (*Northumberland County History*, vol. x, p. 478), and in other archaeological relics of his advance, notably at Newstead (*cf.* p. 34) ; and, on the other hand, in the numerous bodies of British troops, doubtless raised from the newly-conquered tribes, which built the forts and towers of the Odenwald Limes in Germany in the years 145-146 (Fabricius, 593). The new or Antonine Wall, with its attendant works, was probably complete by the end of 143, and, with a few outposts to the north, seems to have been continuously held for a dozen years or more. To what extent Hadrian's Wall was denuded of troops in order to garrison the new line we do not know. It is, however, certain that the two Walls cannot have been fully garrisoned with auxiliaries at the same time. To hold the two Walls, with their outposts, would have required about 60 auxiliary regiments, or about 30,000 men. But the total number of auxiliaries in Britain was probably about 20,000 to 25,000. Nor is it reasonable to suppose that every

---

[1] The standard work on the Wall is still J. C. Bruce, *The Roman Wall*, ed. 3, 1867, but it is altogether out of date where technically archaeological or historical questions are concerned. Almost everything of importance before 1922 is mentioned in " Hadrian's Wall : a History of the Problem," in *J.R.S.*, xi. Since then, the chief additions have been published in the form of contributions to *C.W.* and *A.A.*, almost every volume of which contains something of importance on the subject. The annual reports in *J.R.S.* are useful, but slight, and views there expressed in any given year, on the strength of unfinished work, are open to correction.

[2] I am greatly indebted to Sir George Macdonald for reading this section in MS. and correcting and improving it at many points.

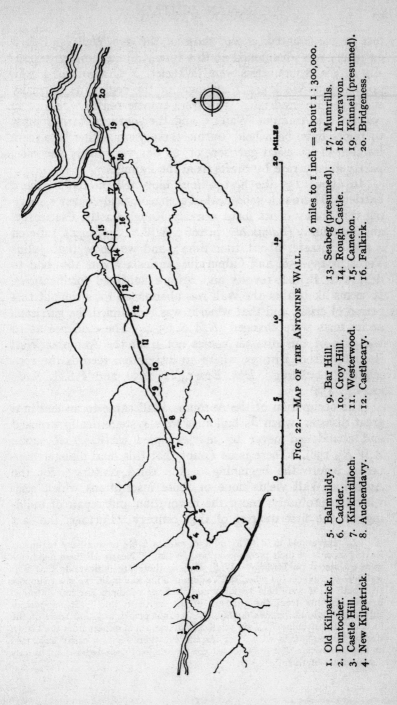

FIG. 22.—MAP OF THE ANTONINE WALL.

6 miles to 1 inch = about 1 : 300,000.

1. Old Kilpatrick.
2. Duntocher.
3. Castle Hill.
4. New Kilpatrick.
5. Balmuildy.
6. Cadder.
7. Kirkintilloch.
8. Auchendavy.
9. Bar Hill.
10. Croy Hill.
11. Westerwood.
12. Castlecary.
13. Seabeg (presumed).
14. Rough Castle.
15. Camelon.
16. Falkirk.
17. Mumrills.
18. Inveravon.
19. Kinneil (presumed).
20. Bridgeness.

fort in the country, except those of the two Walls and their outposts, was abandoned at this time ; though many, especially in Wales, doubtless were (Wheeler, *Y Cymmrodor*, xxxiii, pp. 45-46). We know that some of the regiments normally encamped on Hadrian's Wall were transferred in whole or in part to the Antonine Wall ; [1] and the southern barrier must therefore have been held, during these years, either by a mere fraction of its usual garrison, or, as was very likely the case, partly at any rate by drafts from the legions.

In about 155 the first serious blow fell on the northern barrier. There is a good deal of archaeological evidence showing that many of its forts, notably Rough Castle, Castlecary, and Balmuildy (*Balmuildy*, p. 106 ; *R.W.S.*, 395 seqq.), suffered a grave disaster about that time ; and we know that Julius Verus in 157-158, and Calpurnius Agricola about 162, had to deal with British revolts and restore damaged fortifications. It seems likely that the Wall was abandoned for a time at this period of crisis, and that when it was reoccupied the garrisons of its forts were changed (*R.W.S.*, 354. The evidence as to the date of this disaster comes not from the Antonine Wall itself but from Birrens, where an inscription records the consequent rebuilding ; *Eph. Epigr.*, ix, 1230, and *P.S.A. Scot.*, xxxviii, 454).

The occupation of the Antonine Wall came to an end in a great disaster, when its buildings were systematically wrecked and abandoned never to be reoccupied (*R.W.S.*, cit., 402 ; *A.W.R.*, 158). There is no doubt that this final disaster happened before the beginning of the third century ; for the Antonine Wall yields none of those inscriptions which elsewhere so profusely record the restoration and repair of buildings in the first quarter of that century. Further, the fact

---

[1] *Cf.* Haverfield in *A.W.R.*, p. 156, with a table of auxiliary regiments leaving records of their presence on both Walls. " Nearly all these regiments were quartered on Hadrian's Wall, and, as there are indications that that wall was not evacuated when the Vallum of Pius was built, we must suppose that both walls were held together and that the northern line was defended by detachments from the garrison of the southern line." In support of this suggestion, Miller (*Balmuildy*, cit., p. 109) points out that some of the forts on the Antonine Wall are smaller than one would expect from the known size of the regiments which left inscriptions there—a fact easily explained on the assumption that they housed not the whole of these regiments but only detachments of them.

that coins become rare on the Antonine Wall in the reign of Marcus Aurelius and cease altogether about 180 has been taken to prove the identity of this final disaster with the occasion about that time (Cassius Dio, lxxii, 8) when the Caledonians and Maeatae broke "the Wall" (only one Wall is mentioned) and destroyed a Roman army (*A.W.R.*, 158 ; *P.S.A. Scot.*, lii, 222).

But there was another barbarian inroad in 197 (Dio, lxxvi, 12), when Clodius Albinus took all the available forces from Britain to Gaul to contest his claim to the throne of the Empire. On this occasion there was no one to resist the barbarians, and it is therefore likely that they were more able to inflict damage on buildings than they had been *c.* 180. The fact that systematic destruction, of a kind that could not have been carried out under siege conditions, is found on Hadrian's Wall (*C.W.*², xiii, 321-322) and in the fortresses of York (*J.R.S.*, xv, 193) and Chester (*ibid.*), and in all these cases can be dated to the late second century, suggests that a vast campaign of leisurely and thorough demolition was undertaken at some time during that period ; and it is natural to connect the demolition of the Antonine Wall structures with this campaign. But it is easier to ascribe these events, as a whole, to 197 than *c.* 180 ; and although the question cannot be considered as settled, it is at any rate well to bear in mind the possibility that the Antonine Wall, temporarily lost a second time *c.* 180 (for evidence of a second temporary loss, *cf. R.W.S.*, 396), was not finally lost until the closing years of the century.

"Why," ask the authors of the *Antonine Wall Report*, " did Pius thus advance into Scotland ? . . . It was plainly an advance such as the English have often had to make in North-West India, to ensure the frontier from dangerous attack. The particular form which it assumed may be explained by a characteristic feature of Roman frontier policy, by which a broad belt of uninhabited land, a *glacis* on a great scale, was maintained outside the actual frontier, and the danger of night raiding and cattle lifting, as of more serious attack, was considerably diminished " (*A.W.R.*, p. 157). That is doubtless true. But the northern line was strategically weak. It was extremely easy to outflank it by crossing the narrow waters of the two great firths ; and in its rear lay a vast expanse of wild country, extending from Galloway to the Clyde and Annan valleys, ungarrisoned and unpatrolled by Roman forces and offering harbour and vantage-ground for hostile concentrations. So glaring are the strategical faults of the Antonine Wall, that no one can be surprised at its short life and violent end.

Description of the Antonine Wall.—However bad the Antonine Wall may be strategically, it is well designed tactically. For over 36 miles, from Old Kilpatrick on the Clyde to Bridgeness on the Forth, it runs for the most part along the southern edge of a level and often marshy depression, which it dominates in a striking manner from the brow of an almost continuous range of hills. It chooses its ground not on the summit of these hills, but in general some 30 or 40 yards away from the summit on the northern slope, so as to command the slope more completely ; and its forts are regularly placed on the hill-tops where such sites are available, so as to give the best possible view on all sides and to observe both the movements of enemies and the signals of friends (*A.W.R.*, 3 ; *R.W.S.*, 94-95).

The whole complex of works is far simpler than those of Hadrian's Wall. They have been planned and executed, not by a series of experiments and modifications, but at a single blow ; the design is practically homogeneous throughout, and the task of archaeological analysis is enormously simplified in consequence.

The Wall itself is everywhere built on a heavy stone foundation about 14 feet broad. On either side this is finished off with a massive kerb, and it is pierced from time to time by culverts. As a rule it follows the slope of the ground, but in at least one place it is stepped on a steep slope (*R.W.S.*, 116). Upon this stone base—the regular type of foundation for permanent earth or turf-work—was built a rampart of sods. It was thought at first that the sods lay face downward (*A.W.R.*, 125), but a study of the measurements involved later suggested that they had been laid grass to grass (*R.W.S.*, 192). The faces of this rampart were not vertical ; they battered with a slope of about $2\frac{1}{2}$ to 1, or roughly 70°. In places they still stand over 5 feet high, and if it is assumed that the rampart-walk along the top was 6 feet wide, the height of the rampart—exclusive of a wooden parapet, of which traces have not been found— would be 10 feet (*A.W.R.*, 130). But this turf structure only appears in the western three-quarters of the Wall's length. East of that, it is an earthwork sheathed with clay, a type of rampart found here and there in forts. This construction has been found in several trenches east of Falkirk (*P.S.A. Scot.*, xlix, 222) and further research has shown that all the eastern part is made of clay, in the manner described, and that the division between the two constructions is the road which passed through the Wall to Camelon (*P.S.A. Scot.*, lix, 285).

In front of the Wall is a ditch, normally about 40 feet wide and 12 feet deep, with sides cut to a slope of 26° to 30°, and the usual square drainage-channel in its bottom (*A.W.R.*, 133-134; *R.W.S.*, 101). Naturally, the ditch varies somewhat in size according to the nature of the ground, and when cut through rock shrinks to a width of 20 feet or even, when the rock is very hard, may suffer complete interruption (*R.W.S.*, 123, 126). The upcast from the ditch is thrown out on its northern margin, precisely as in the case of the ditch of Hadrian's Wall. The mound so formed, when measured, is found to account for all the material taken out of the ditch; it has been arranged in a rough kind of way to lie flat when the ground is flat, and to stand up in a ridge when the northern lip of the ditch is by nature lower than the southern (*A.W.R.*, 122, 138).

The ditch is separated from the Wall by a berm, generally 20 feet wide. It seldom falls below this width, and often exceeds it; thus measurements of 27, 35, 56, and 67 feet are given, and in one case, on Croy Hill, it is over 50 feet wide for a considerable distance and reaches a maximum of 116 (*R.W.S.*, 106-107; *A.W.R.*, 64). In view of the narrow berms usually associated with Roman earthwork and turf-work, this wide berm is remarkable. Attempts to explain it on tactical grounds (see *A.W.R.*, 134) ignore the fact that the berm of an earth or turf fort is as a rule far narrower, and the same is true of the Hadrianic turf wall near Birdoswald, which, as we have seen, has a 6-foot berm. For the same reason, no explanation based on engineering considerations (*cf. A.W.R.*, 135) is tenable. It is perhaps easier to suppose that the builders of the Antonine Wall were influenced by the precedent of Hadrian's Wall, where a wide berm had been adopted for sound constructional reasons.

The Expansions or Platforms.—At various places there are semicircular platforms projecting from the south side of the Wall. They are made of turf, like the Wall itself, and are solidly based either on a stone foundation or on living rock. Excavation has shown that, in one case at least, they were added to the Wall after its original construction, though possibly not long after (*A.W.R.*, 77). The stone foundation of that platform was 18 feet across from north to south ; and it has been estimated (*R.W.S.*, 262) that the standard size was about 15 to 20 feet from north to south by about 30 from east to west, but that some were smaller than this, and that there may have been two standard sizes. The number of these objects, definitely located, is not large. " There are at least two on the western slope of Croy Hill, two in Bonnyside grounds, and probably two in the Tentfield Plantation to the east of Rough Castle. There may be others " (*R.W.S.*, 258).

It has been pointed out (*A.W.R.*, 145 *seqq.*) that these expansions might serve as emplacements for artillery. The *onager*, a stone-throwing machine, was often placed upon a turf platform when in service (Ammianus Marcellinus, xxiii, 4), and many stone balls, doubtless ammunition for such weapons, have been found along the Wall. And they have some general resemblance with the gun-emplacements recently explored in the semi-permanent camp at Cawthorn in Yorkshire (*J.R.S.*, xvii, 191). On the other hand, it is contended that they are beacons, stands on which signalling-fires could be lit (*R.W.S.*, 265). It is certain that there must have been a properly-organised signalling-system on the Antonine Wall as on other Roman frontier-lines, and it is not unreasonable to see traces of such a system in these expansions, with their obvious resemblance to the turret-sites of Hadrian's Wall.[1]

Forts of the Antonine Wall.—It is clear, however, that the Antonine Wall has nothing corresponding to milecastles. The only ways through the barrier, so far as we know, are at the forts and the place near Falkirk where the road to Camelon

---

[1] Sir George Macdonald points out to me that for the most part the forts lie in sight of their next neighbours, so that, as a rule, intermediate signalling-posts are not needed ; but that the Croy Hill expansions occur precisely where such posts were necessary to maintain communication between the forts of Croy Hill and Bar Hill.

and Ardoch crosses the line : here was a gate with a guard-house (*R.W.S.*, 248). But the forts are at once rather smaller and much closer together than on Hadrian's Wall. There are nineteen forts to 36 miles, as against seventeen forts to 73 miles ; making an average interval of 1·8 mile as against 4·3. The forts on the northern line are two and a half times as close together as those on the southern, which would seem to render milecastles unnecessary. And the spacing of the forts is more uniform ; they are never more than 4600 yards apart and never less than 2450 (*R.W.S.*, 246). The largest fort, so far as we know, is Mumrills (over 6½ acres : *P.S.A. Scot.*, lix, 282) ; the smallest Rough Castle (1 acre). Castlecary is 3½ acres, Bar Hill 3 acres, Balmuildy 3¼ acres, Old Kilpatrick 4 acres.

In construction they are so far uniform that stone central buildings (headquarters and granary in particular) and wooden barracks are everywhere found. The ramparts may be of clay (Mumrills), turf, uniform with the Antonine Wall (Rough Castle, Bar Hill, Old Kilpatrick) or stone (Balmuildy, Castle-cary). Gun-emplacements are sometimes found, as at Bal-muildy. Double or more usually triple ditches are the rule, and a special feature is the annexes, almost as strongly defended as the forts themselves, which contained the dwellings of the civil population connected with the fort. These fortified annexes, so common in Scotland, are unknown at present in England.[1]

The structural relation of the forts to the Wall reflects the unity of the work ; for the normal state of things is that the fort-ramparts are of one build with the Wall, even when they differ from it in construction, and make T-shaped junctions with it, more like the milecastles of Hadrian's Wall than its forts. There are two known exceptions to this rule : Bar Hill, which for no very obvious reason is an isolated fort lying 20 or 30 yards away from the Wall (*R.W.S.*, 188), and Old Kilpatrick, which was built as a base-camp for sea communications at the commencement of the whole affair, so that the Antonine Wall abuts on it as on a pre-existing structure (*Old Kilpatrick*, 6-10).

[1] Since the above was written, what appears to be an annexe defended by a stone rampart-wall has been found at Brough-by-Bainbridge, as I learn from Professor J. P. Droop.

The ancient names of these forts are entirely unknown. In the Ravenna Cosmography (a compilation of the sixth century) there is a list of ten names of " cities connected with one another in a straight line where Britain is narrowest from Ocean to Ocean," and this clearly refers to the Antonine Wall ; but the relation between these ten names and the nineteen known forts cannot be determined.

The Building of the Antonine Wall.—At intervals along the course of the Wall, " distance-slabs " have been found ; that is to say, slabs recording the name of the Emperor Antoninus Pius, together with the fact that such and such a unit built a certain length of the Wall. Seventeen of these have been found, of which a certain number are duplicates.[1] A close study of these slabs, combined with a scrutiny of the records describing the places at which they were found, has led Sir George Macdonald to the conclusion that the entire length of the Wall —36 miles—was divided up into nine approximately equal lengths, each length consisting of two adjacent stretches from fort to fort ; there were nineteen forts, cutting up the Wall into eighteen stretches : of these the first and second made one length, the third and fourth another, and so on. These 4-mile lengths were assigned to working-parties, of which there were six : two drawn from the Second legion, two from the Sixth, and two from the Twentieth. These six parties, working simultaneously each at its allotted 4-mile length, would construct the eastern two-thirds of the Wall at one blow ; then they would be moved westward, and two parties would be turned on to each of the three remaining lengths. A working-party would set up two distance-slabs for each length constructed, one at each end.

All went well for the first four lengths ; but in the fifth length a serious obstacle was encountered in the shape of the basalt and dolerite mass of Croy Hill. Here the digging of the ditch became very laborious, and in places had to be given up as impossible. This dislocated the whole scheme. The working party in charge of the fifth length only succeeded in doing a fraction of its allotted task ; the party responsible for the sixth length had to begin work in the middle of what ought to

[1] What follows is drawn from Macdonald, " The Building of the Antonine Wall," in *J.R.S.*, xi.

'have been the fifth ; and the result was that when each party had done one length by itself and one in co-operation with a second party, there was a length of about 4 miles left over at the western end. The natural way of dealing with this was to divide it up among the six working parties, and this was done.

The method of dividing up a long line of works into large sections, allotted to a few strong working-parties, would seem a great improvement on the method, used on Hadrian's Wall, of dividing it into very short lengths allotted to the centuries of legions. The latter method had been long in use as applied to the ramparts of forts and other comparatively small structures, and for these it was suitable enough ; but its application to a Wall over 70 miles long was cumbrous and wasteful, and the abandonment of this method by the Antonine engineers is another proof of the care and skill with which the staff-work preparatory to the building of the Antonine Wall was done.[1]

[1] The fundamental works on the Antonine Wall are the Glasgow Archaeological Society's *Antonine Wall Report* (1899), and Sir George Macdonald's *Roman Wall in Scotland* (Maclehose, 1911). Since the latter's publication the chief works are Macdonald, " Discoveries on the Line of the Antonine Wall," in *P.S.A. Scot.*, xlix, and " Further Discoveries on the Line of the Antonine Wall," *ibid.*, lix ; Haverfield, " Agricola and the Antonine Wall," in *P.S.A. Scot.*, lii ; Macdonald, " The Building of the Antonine Wall," in *J.R.S.* xi ; Miller, *The Roman Fort at Balmuildy* (1922), and *The Roman Fort at Old Kilpatrick* (1928), both published for the Glasgow Archaeological Society. A second edition of Macdonald's *Wall* is promised.

CHAPTER VI

TOWNS

§ 1. Town-Planning, Size and Shape

ROMAN provincial towns fall into two classes : a larger pattern, laid out in a plan of streets crossing each other at right angles (*cf.* Haverfield, *Ancient Town-Planning*, Oxford, 1913) ; and a smaller pattern, which has no such formal plan, and consists of a group of houses clustered by the side of a road or at the place where two roads meet, or where a road crosses a river. These may be conventionally referred to as large towns and small towns respectively, but it must not be forgotten that all towns of the Roman period were small by our standards, and that many of the " large towns " of Britain were no larger than Henley or Abingdon.

The areas of some of the chief towns of Roman Britain are roughly as follows : London 330 acres, Cirencester 240, Verulam 200, Wroxeter 170, Colchester 108, Silchester 100, Caerwent 44, Lincoln 41, Caister-by-Norwich 35. Here are a few Continental Roman towns for comparison : Nimes 790, Autun 494, Milan 329, Lyons 314, Vienne 214, Turin 127. In a modern town the population runs from 50 to 100 per acre, but the latter figure is reached only in densely-packed industrial areas. An industrial town with a quarter of a million inhabitants will cover about 2500 acres ; a residential town of 50,000 will cover about 1200 acres. What we know of Romano-British towns (especially Silchester, the only one whose plan we know pretty completely) suggests that they were not more densely inhabited than a modern residential town. At that rate, Roman London can hardly have had 25,000 inhabitants ; it is more likely to have had 15,000.

A large town has a forum in the middle (see below, on Public Buildings), and round this as a centre the town is laid

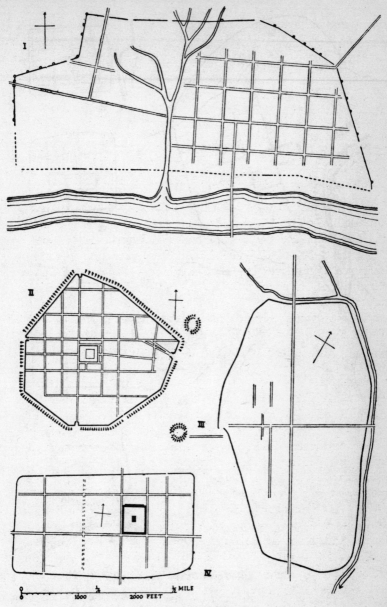

FIG. 23.—TOWN-PLANS.

1600 feet to 1 inch = 1 : 19,200.

I, London.   II, Silchester.   III, Cirencester.   IV, Colchester.

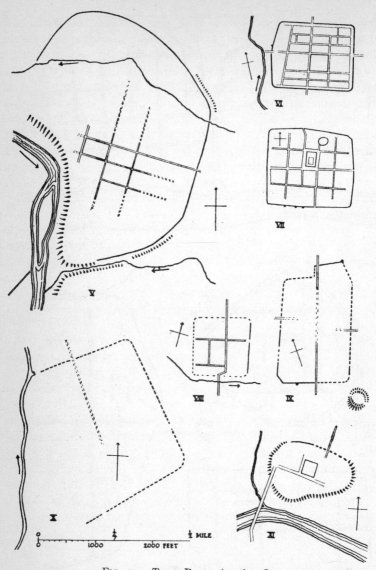

FIG. 24.—TOWN-PLANS (*continued*).

1600 feet to 1 inch = 1 : 19,200.

V, Wroxeter.   VI, Caister-by-Norwich.   VII, Caerwent.   VIII, Alchester.
IX, Aldborough.   X, Leicester.   XI, Corbridge.

out in rectangular *insulae*. The size of these varies a good deal from town to town. In London the normal insula seems to have been 480, or perhaps 240, feet square [1] (*Roman London*, 48, and Fig. 8). At Colchester, they seem to have been 330 feet square (*J.R.S.*, ix, 153-154). At Silchester they vary in size from a large type about 410 feet square to a small type about 290 by 260. At Caerwent they seem meant to be normally 280 feet square. At Wroxeter *insulae* about 310 by 380 feet have been found. The central *insula* containing the forum is generally larger than the rest ; in London perhaps about 550 by 480, at Silchester 525 by 410, at Colchester about 660 by 450. At Caerwent, on the other hand, it is rather smaller than the others.

Town-plans of this kind probably in many cases date back to the Flavian period. Tacitus says that Agricola (77-85) urged the Britons to build *templa fora domos* (*Agr.*, 21 ; ed. Anderson, pp. 100-106, with plans of towns, etc.). Before that time, the towns must have already made a considerable growth, but probably in an irregular fashion (*Roman London*, 47 ; *cf. J.R.S.*, ix, 144, on Colchester).

It is popularly fancied that all Roman towns were rectangular in outline. This is an error due to a confusion between towns and military camps. Roman towns, if we may take the line of their walls as fixing their shape, are not very often rectangular in outline [2] unless they began life as military fortresses ; and even then the original shape did not influence the final shape unless the original size was comparable with the final size. Thus, Cirencester has the irregular oval shape which is so common in Roman towns ; and at one time there may have been a fort there (*A.*, lxx, 195) ; but a fort of earth, perhaps 5 or 6 acres in extent, cannot have influenced the lay-out of a town extending over 240 acres.

§ 2. DEFENCES

All large Romano-British towns, and some small ones, are provided with defences, but these vary a good deal in character

---

[1] All these measurements are taken to the middle of the street.

[2] Of the numerous town-plans given in Blanchet's *Les enceintes romaines de la Gaule*, apart from purely military sites, not more than one-tenth are even vaguely rectangular.

and perhaps in date. At present no explorations have been made with the express purpose of discovering the date of any town walls in this country, except at Colchester; and consequently almost everything that is said on this subject is tentative.

The walls of Colchester (*North-East Essex, R. Comm. on Hist. Mon.*, 20-22), to begin with these because they were the first ones to be dated by excavation, are about 8 feet thick, built of concrete with cut stone faces and brick bonding-courses. Behind the wall is an earth bank 20 feet wide. Two rectangular and six semicircular bastions can be, or have been, recognised: the former are internal and contemporary with the wall, the latter are external and are post-Roman. The only gate of which we possess the plan, the so-called Balkerne Gate, is a vast structure 107 feet long and projecting 30 feet in front of the line of the wall. It has four openings, two 17 feet wide, for wheeled traffic, and two 6 feet wide for foot passengers. It is flanked by towers with a curious quadrant-shaped ground-plan. In its great width and the number of its openings it falls into line with gates of the Augustan period at Nimes, Autun, and Turin; and the excavations of 1913 and 1917 made it clear that the gate could not have been built later than about A.D. 85. It seems a fair inference that the walls and gates of Colchester were built soon after the destruction of the town by Boudicca in A.D. 61 (*E.A.S.T.*, N.S., xv, 182; *J.R.S.*, ix, 141-142).

London is provided with walls whose date has long been a matter of discussion. The view put forward by the Royal Commission on Historical Monuments (*Roman London*, 79) is that they were built during the half-century after A.D. 60. Hitherto it has been generally supposed that they are much later; but the late dating is unsupported by anything more definite than a rather vague presumption that so large a town must have taken a long time to grow, and that it would hardly need walls before the troublous times of the third century.[1]

---

[1] This summarises the very cautious argument of Haverfield in *J.R.S.*, i, 158. The view taken in the *V.C.H.* (p. 49) is that the wall was built about the end of the second century. These views are not here discussed in detail because they are superseded by the Royal Commission's, from which all future discussion must start.

The wall is built in the usual way, of concrete with a facing of cut stone and bonding-courses of brick. It has a plinth in front, above which its thickness varies from 7 to 9 feet (*Roman London*, 72). Portions standing as much as 14½ feet high are recorded, but it may be remembered that the walls of Roman towns are still standing to 25 feet (Cologne, Turin) and even more. Whether there was an earth bank behind the wall is not known.

The above description applies only to the landward wall of London. The wall along the river front is apparently later in date, and may be contemporary with the bastions, which were added to the wall at a date not exactly determined but probably not earlier than the third century. These bastions fall into two groups, one hollow, the other solid. The hollow bastions, like the river-wall, are built of new material; the solid bastions contain large quantities of re-used fragments such as are often found built into fortifications of the late Roman period (*ibid.*, 79-82). Of the gates, very little is known. Newgate, the only one of which we have a probable plan, seems to have had a double entrance with openings about 12 feet wide, flanked by large square towers, the whole about 100 feet in width (*ibid.*, 98).

The walls of Silchester resemble those of Colchester and London in having wide, massive gates and no bastions. Indeed, at Silchester bastions were never added, perhaps because at the time when such additions were being made the chief if not the only danger was from sea-raiders. The walls of Silchester are 9½ feet thick at the bottom, narrowing by offsets at the back to 7½ feet, and must have been at least 20 feet high. They are built of concrete faced with flints and bonded with courses of flat stones (*V.C.H. Hants*, i, 354). The east and west gates have double entrances, each opening about 13 feet wide, and are flanked by what look like round towers, but are really the wall itself curving inwards so as to allow the gates to be set well back from the line of the wall. The north and south gates are similarly planned but have single openings. There is an earth mound about 20 feet wide behind the wall, and a ditch immediately in front of it. At the back of the wall are what may be called internal bastions, about 200 feet apart, made by carrying the wall up to its full height without reducing its width, so that the top is $9\frac{1}{2}$ feet wide instead of $7\frac{1}{2}$ on a front of about 12 feet. Internal bastions exist elsewhere, *e.g.* at Colchester and Caerwent, and in the walls of Aventicum, which were built probably late in the first century (Stähelin, *Die Schweiz in röm. Zeit*, plan iii ; the polygonal shape of Aventicum is another point of resemblance with Silchester). The date of the Silchester walls is not known ; but it may be worth while to make two observations bearing on the question. (i) Plainly the earth bank existed before the walls, and conditioned their design. The wall has been crowded unnaturally in between the front of the earth bank and the back of the ditch. Had all three features been made at the same time, room would have been left for the wall to stand on a platform or berm between the bank and the ditch. Moreover, the plan of the gates is only explicable if the bank already existed before they were built ; that was the fact which compelled their builders to set them back from the line of the wall, in order to flank them with towers, instead of making the towers project. (ii) The wide double gates flanked by towers, and the absence of external bastions, bring to mind the walls of Colchester and London. It is therefore natural to conjecture that the walls of Silchester date from the late first or second century. If they are part of the town-plan, which is generally supposed to be Flavian, it follows that pre-Flavian Silchester was defended by an earthen rampart. But these are conjectures merely.

Caerwent, like Silchester, was defended at first by an earthen rampart and later by a stone wall, to which bastions were added still later (Ward, "The Fortifications of Roman Cærwent," *A.C.*[6], xvi, 1-36). The earthen rampart presumably dates from the origin of the town as such in the first century. The stone wall, 10 feet thick at the base and about $6\frac{1}{2}$ at the top, with internal projections not unlike those of Silchester, was added in the late second or early third century (Wheeler, *Prehistoric and Roman Wales*, 245), and six polygonal bastions were added to the south wall at some time after A.D. 330. The gates are incompletely known, since only the less important, at the north and south, now exist ; but these are single openings, 8 feet 9 inches (*A.*, lix, lx, 111) wide, without flanking towers, and were walled up before the end of the Roman age.

These are the only towns about whose defences enough is known to demand detailed notice. The walls of Wroxeter were apparently 9 feet thick (*V.C.H. Salop*, i, 224) with an 11-foot berm; those of Aldborough 8 feet thick (Eckroyd Smith, *Isurium*, Plate V; *J.R.S.*, xiv, 221); those of the small town of Alchester, near Oxford, 9 feet thick at the foundation, and built in the second century, supplementing an earlier earthen bank (personal information from the excavators of 1929). The Newport Arch at Lincoln is a remarkably well-preserved Roman gateway, but it tells us little except that the gate had separate openings for wheeled traffic and foot passengers.

§ 3. Public Buildings: Forum and Basilica

Romano-British towns are poor in public buildings. Only one theatre has been discovered; no public libraries or circi or aqueducts built of stone appear to have existed; and the temples were small and few. The chief public buildings to be seen in Romano-British towns are fora, amphitheatres, and baths.

The forum is an invariable feature of a large Roman town. It is the centre not only of the town-plan but of the life, both economic and political, of the town to which it belongs. Most towns in the Roman Empire were originally places of trade, and therefore essentially fora pure and simple; and though, as time went on, trade tended to be banished from the forum itself to the "shopping quarters" of the towns (*cf.* Stuart Jones, *Companion to R. Hist.*, 96), the forum remained "a piazza thronged by the citizens for purposes of intercourse and discussion, and surrounded by the public buildings in which the most important civic functions took place" (*ibid.*). In proportion, however, as civic life was a backward growth in this remote province of the Empire, we must think of the fora of Romano-British towns as retaining much of their original character as market-places.

The Silchester forum is a rectangle surrounded by a portico and measuring 310 feet by 275. In the centre is a courtyard about 140 by 130 feet, surrounded on three sides by a colonnade, from which open a score of chambers, some of which may have been shops, others what we may call city and county offices. The fourth side was formed by the basilica, a great hall 240 feet long (internally, apart from the apses), by 58 feet wide, with a central nave, terminating in an apse at each end, and side aisles whose columns have been estimated at not less than 27 feet high (*V.C.H. Hants*, i, 362). The nave may have been 60 feet high.

Of the forum at Wroxeter, excavated in 1923-27, no full account has yet been published, but its general arrangement is similar. It is a block 394 by 265 feet, with a portico along its front or east side and another on its south. The courtyard and ranges of shops or offices are the same in plan, and it was found that the front colonnade had been used for shops, facing the main street of the town. At the back was the basilica, 250 feet long, and having a nave 35 feet wide and aisles of 18 feet. At the south end, the only one explored, it had no apse (*J.R.S.*, xiv, 226; xv, 228; xvi, 224; xvii, 197). Behind this again, as at Silchester, was a row of offices.

A similar forum and basilica existed at Cirencester, but little is known of them beyond the fact that the basilica was 320 feet long and about 70 feet wide, divided in the usual way into nave and aisles, and having an apse at the west end (*A.*, lxix, 168-169).

The forum at Caerwent (*A.*, lxi, Plate XCI) is smaller, in conformity with the small size of the town. It is only 251 feet long by 182 wide, and its arrangements in general resemble those of the Silchester example—courtyard surrounded on three sides by colonnades and rooms, basilica (182 by 52 feet) at the back, and behind that another row of rooms.

Traces of a basilica have been recognised in London, lying east and west of Gracechurch Street in and near Leadenhall Market. It appears to have been, in the words of the Royal Commission's report on Roman London (p. 42), " a great aisled hall with an eastern apse and a total length of at least 350 feet and probably 420 feet." The forum would on this view lie to the south of this building.

In some ways the most interesting forum in Britain seems to have been at Colchester (Wheeler and Laver, " Roman Colchester," in *J.R.S.*, ix, 144). Here the central feature was the temple of Claudius; this stood in a great open square about

435 by 345 feet, surrounded on three sides by colonnades, forming altogether a block about 500 feet by 420. This, if the conjectural plan offered by Wheeler and Laver is correct, is the only known British example of a type of forum well known in other parts of the Empire. The other British fora, with their basilicas and rows of shops, are based on a pattern resembling the headquarters of the legionary fortress. Fora of this type were coming into fashion in the late first and early second century (*cf.* Schultze, *Basilika*, Figs. 30, 33, 36; Lehmann-Hartleben in *P.W. s.v. Städtebau*, col. 2072, 2117).

§ 4. BATHS

The habit of bathing in what we call Turkish baths was inherited by the Romans from the later Greeks, and became an essential feature of Roman everyday life. Every community with any pretensions to civilisation possessed a public bath-house, which was the centre of its social life ; and, in addition to this, rich men had private baths in their own houses.

The Roman bath-house consists of a series of rooms heated to different degrees. Normally there are three : the *frigidarium*, heated very little or not at all, and containing a cold plunge-bath ; the *tepidarium*, moderately heated, and the *caldarium*, heated enough to make the bathers perspire freely, and provided with hot water for washing. In addition, there may be dressing-rooms (*apodyteria*) ; there is usually a latrine, entered as a rule from a courtyard in front of the building ; and there is often a *sudatorium* or *laconicum*, a specially hot room, often circular in plan, approached sometimes directly from the *frigidarium* and sometimes from the open air.

The simplest type of public bath-house has a single unheated room serving as *apodyterium* and *frigidarium*, and having a plunge bath for cold water ; then the *tepidarium*, then the *caldarium*, beyond which is the furnace. A single furnace supplies all the heat required, which passes first under a metal boiler for heating the water, then under the raised hypocaust-floor of the *caldarium*, and then under that of the *tepidarium*. This type is often found in connection with small forts. Ordinarily, however, a fort has a slightly more elaborate bath-house, supplied with a *sudatorium* heated from a separate

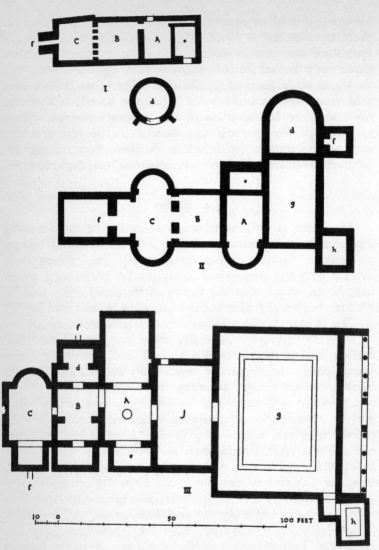

FIG. 25.—BATH-HOUSES.

40 feet to 1 inch = 1 : 480.

I Hardknot.   II Inchtuthil.   III Silchester.

(town baths as originally built)

(A) *frigidarium*.   (d) *sudatorium*.   (g) *courtyard*.
(B) *tepidarium*.   (e) cold plunge-bath.   (h) *latrine*.
(C) *caldarium*.   (f) furnaces.   (j) *apodyterium*.

furnace ; and often the plan is complicated by the addition
of an apse at one or both ends of the *caldarium*. In one
apse stood the laver (*labrum*) of hot water ; if there were two
apses, the other would contain a warm plunge-bath.

The same features are found in the public baths of towns.
It is generally easy, even in the largest bath-houses, to recognise the same fundamental scheme. Thus the great public
bath-house at Silchester has a portico facing the street ; then
a peristyle courtyard with a latrine opening off one corner ;
then an *apodyterium ;* and then, in the usual order, *frigidarium*,
tepidarium, and apsed *caldarium*. The recently discovered
first-century baths at Wroxeter have the same scheme, with
two circular *sudatoria* opening off the main hall.

In private houses the same plan is carried out on a small
scale, but with little or no essential alteration.[1]

§ 5. AMPHITHEATRES

The Romans had three kinds of building used for public
spectacles : theatres, circuses, and amphitheatres.

The theatre was a D-shaped building, whose straight side
was occupied by the stage. In front of the stage was the
semicircular " orchestra," and beyond this again were the
seats, in semicircular tiers rising higher and higher towards
the back of the auditorium. The Romans borrowed both the
theatre, as a type of building, and the drama, as a type of
literature, from the Greeks, and neither became a real national
institution. It is, therefore, the less surprising that only one
example of a Roman theatre has been found in this country.[2]

The circus was a kind of building established at Rome from
a very early date. It was essentially a race-course, a long
narrow plot of ground divided longitudinally by a wall (*spina*)

---

[1] Roman baths in general : Cagnat-Chapot, *Manuel d'arch. rom.*, ch. ix.
In Britain : Ward, *R.B.B.E.*, ch. viii. Individual examples are treated in
monographs on the sites concerned : among these may be mentioned
Silchester (*A.*, lix), Lydney (report forthcoming), *Newstead*, Inchtuthil (*P.S.A.
Scot.*, xxxvi), *Balmuildy*, Great Chesters (*A.A.*[2], xxvi), Hardknot (*C.W.*[2],
xxviii). Fair, " Circular Bath Buildings in connection with Cohort Forts,"
in *J.R.S.*, xvii, contains much useful information. Sir George Macdonald's
publication of the baths at Mumrills, and Professor Atkinson's of those at
Wroxeter, will be of great importance when they appear.

[2] At Verulam: *cf. V.C.H. Herts.*

at each end of which was a column or group of columns (*meta*) to serve as a turning point for the racers. Tiers of seats along either side, and carried in semicircles round the ends, might be made of wood or of stone. In Britain there is no certain example of a circus.

The amphitheatre was a new type of building invented towards the close of the Republican period but especially characteristic of the Empire. It consisted essentially of an elliptical open space (*arena*) surrounded by rising tiers of seats. Of the great stone amphitheatres seen in Italy and the south of France, Britain has no examples; but it has many earthen amphitheatres, still visible as elliptical earthworks and found on excavation to have had revetments of stone or wood. The only one that has been properly explored is outside the legionary fortress at Caerleon-on-Usk. It measured 267 by 222 feet, and accommodated about 6000 spectators. It consisted of an earth bank enclosing an arena—the arena being excavated to obtain material for the bank—and revetted with massive stone walls. The top of the inner wall must have been about 10 or 11 feet above the arena, the top of the outer wall about 30; the slope between these two wall-tops was covered with tiers of wooden seats. There were eight entrances, the chief being at the two ends, where roadways about 16 feet broad led into the arena. In the middle of each side was an entrance of rather complicated pattern comprising a pen to hold wild beasts; over the pen must have been a box for distinguished spectators. The four remaining entrances were smaller, and consisted merely of passages with a flight of steps leading up to the seats and down again to the arena. All the entrances were covered by barrel vaults in their outer half, where they passed beneath the higher part of the seating-banks. This building was erected about A.D. 80, and subsequently modified in details at various times; it remained in use for at least 200 years.[1]

This was a military amphitheatre, and unusually elaborate. More typical of Britain, perhaps, is the structure now known as Maumbury Rings, the ampitheatre belonging to the town of Dorchester. It is about 345 by 333 feet, and the top of its

---

[1] Full description in *A*., lxxviii, 111-218. Summary in *A.C.*, June, 1928 (lxxxiii), 1-32.

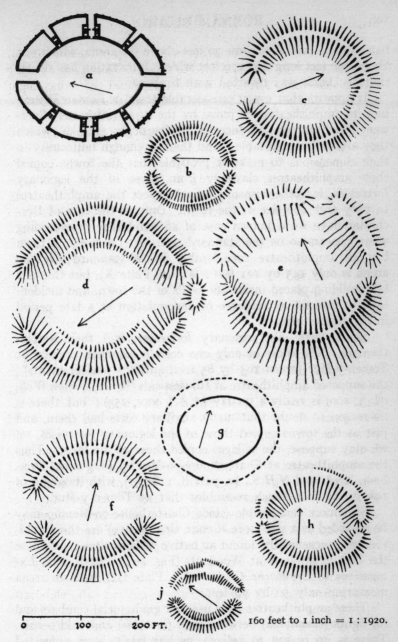

0   100   200 FT.   160 feet to 1 inch = 1 : 1920.

FIG. 26.—AMPHITHEATRES.

(*a*) Legionary fortress : Caerleon-on-Usk.   (*b*) Auxiliary fort : Tomen-y-Mur.
(*c*) Town : Silchester.   (*d*) Town : Dorchester.   (*e*) Town : Aldborough.
(*f*) Town : Cirencester.   (*g*) Town (late addition to) : Caerwent.   (*h*) Mining
village : Charterhouse-on-Mendip.   (*j*) Native village : Woodcuts.

bank stands even now some 30 feet above the arena, which was about 196 feet long and 176 feet wide. Excavation has shown that the bank was revetted with timber.[1]

It appears that every considerable town in Roman Britain had its amphitheatre, to judge by the cases (Silchester, Caerwent, Richborough, Cirencester, Aldborough, etc.), in which they are still recognisable ; and there is enough uniformity in their dimensions to make it probable that the towns copied their amphitheatres slavishly from those of the legionary fortresses, for otherwise one would expect the amphitheatres to vary with the size of the town. Only in the case of Dorchester have we a known case of an amphitheatre exceeding what appears to be the standard size. At Caerwent, a town has an amphitheatre considerably below standard size (its arena is only 145 by 121 feet : *A.*, lix, Plate X), but this is a late building placed inside the walls of the town, and incidentally of interest as evidence of depopulation at a late period in the town's history.

Small forts, like legionary fortresses, had their amphitheatres. We know of only one certain example, namely at Tomen-y-Mur (arena 105 by 85 feet, author's measurements) ; the supposed amphitheatre at Housesteads (Bruce, *Roman Wall*, ed. 3, 190) is really a quarry (*A.A.*[2], xxv, 253) ; but there is no reason to doubt that many auxiliary forts had them, and just as the towns copied those of the legionary fortresses, so, we may suppose, the villages copied those of the forts. Thus the amphitheatre at Charterhouse-on-Mendip (dug 1909, *Proc. Som. Arch. and N.H.S.*, lv, part ii, 118-137), with its arena of 105 by 80 feet, much resembles that at Tomen-y-Mur.

Still more remarkable (since Charterhouse-on-Mendip may be regarded as a site more Roman than native) are the amphitheatres occasionally found at native village sites. Of these the best example is at Woodcuts (Fig. 26 *j*; Pitt-Rivers, *Excavations in Cranborne Chase*, vol. i, Plate III), with an arena measuring only 50 by 70 feet.

These amphitheatres were used for gladiatorial combats and for fights (*venationes*) between men (*bestiarii*) and wild beasts. There is no reason to believe, as has lately been suggested

---

[1] Ward, *R.B.B.E.*, 230.

(Allcroft, *The Circle and the Cross*) either that the small village amphitheatres are pre-Roman or that they are "folk-moots" for the discussion of public business.

§ 6. THE TOWN HOUSE

The country houses of Roman Britain are described in a later chapter. Here it is only necessary to anticipate a few of the points there made, in order to explain how far the town house is a distinct thing calling for separate treatment.

The country house, probably originating in a rectangular cottage entered by a door in the middle of one side, develops under Roman influence into a building whose dominant feature is its façade. In the commonest type of villa, this façade consists of a veranda terminating at each end in a projecting wing and having the front door in its centre. This symmetrical façade, with the central door, remains the keynote of the villa-plan even when that plan develops from the so-called corridor house to the so-called courtyard house; for even in the latter type the main block of the house lies at the back of the courtyard, and the visitor approaching the front door crosses the courtyard and sees the façade with its central door in front of him.

In the town house this façade is absent. Corridors and courtyards are common enough, but their design is governed by principles quite other than those which control the architecture of the villa. It is therefore misleading to use terms like corridor house and courtyard house indifferently of town houses and country houses, as if the things denoted were the same; and it is positively false to say, as many writers have said, that the town and country houses of Roman Britain are indistinguishable in plan.

The commonest type of town house is a long narrow building, generally from 50 to 100 feet long, whose door is in one end. This end gives directly on the street, and the building is separated by a narrow lane, or even by a mere eavesdrip, from its neighbours on either hand. There is no room for an entrance in the middle of the side, and no question of anything even remotely like the wide-spreading façade of the average villa. A street composed of these houses appears simply as a row of gable-ends, each with its own door.

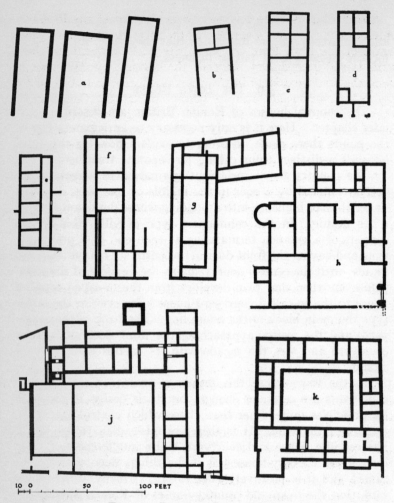

FIG. 27.—PLANS OF TOWN HOUSES.

80 feet to 1 inch = 1 : 960.

(a) Plain wooden strip houses (Wroxeter).
(b) Strip house with open front, rooms at back (Silchester xi, 4).
(c) The same with closed front (Silchester ix, 3).
(d) As (c) with shop-front added (Caerwent, site xvi, 5).
(e) Strip house with one corridor (Silchester xxviii, 2).
(f) Strip house with two corridors (Silchester ix, 1).
(g) Two-sided or L-shaped house (Silchester xxxiii, 5).
(h) Three-sided house, E-shaped (Silchester viii, 1).
(j) Three-sided house (Silchester xix, 2).
(k) Quadrangle house (Caerwent).

Streets of houses like this may be seen in almost any Roman provincial town. At Silchester, in the street leading into the centre of the town from the west gate ; at Caerwent, in the main street immediately west of the forum ; at Wroxeter, along the street explored in the years 1912-24 ; and at almost any other provincial town in Britain or on the Continent[1] where the dwellings, and not merely the public buildings, have been studied, houses of this type will be found to be the rule. But these long narrow houses opening at the end are practically never found except in towns.

In its simplest form, this town house—we may perhaps call it the strip house, because of its long narrow rectangular shape —is a barn-like one-roomed building containing no partitions. At an early date in the Roman period we actually find it existing in this form, *e.g.* at Wroxeter, where, underneath later and more complex buildings, houses of this type were found without any internal divisions, and open to the street on their whole width (*Wroxeter*, 1914, Plate XXX, showing three open-fronted houses, 73 by 30, 73 by 40, and 86 by 26 feet respectively ; built in the reign of Vespasian and pulled down after a short life, *ibid.*, p. 4. *Cf.* Jack, *Excavations . . . Kenchester*, 1912-13, Plate LVI).

The strip house develops by cutting off portions by means of partitions, in order to provide separate chambers. These are most often found at the back of the house, away from the street (*cf.* numerous examples at Silchester, *e.g. insulae* ix, x, xi) ; but it is also usual to cut off portions in front, facing the street, for use as shops. These are sometimes completely open to the street. Thus we reach a type of strip house especially common at Caerwent (*A.*, lxii, 429).

Little can be said, in the present state of our knowledge, about the origin of this house. The type has been well described and its wide distribution commented on by Oelmann (*Bonner Jahrbücher*, 128, pp. 77-97), who thinks that it may originally have been a Hellenistic plan, but that it already existed in the Celtic lands before the coming of the Romans (*op. cit.*, 93, with examples from the pre-Roman town at Mont Beuvray). Oelmann also points out that the natural function

---

[1] See, *e.g.*, the house plans from Zugmantel, Bregenz, Belgica, and Kempten in *Germania Romana*[2], part ii, Plates IX (5), XI (1, 2, 3), XII (1).

of these houses, whether or no they originate, as he is inclined
to think, in the temporary booths of a market, is to serve as
shops ; and that therefore they are always a sign of trade ;
and the fact that they occur especially at the centre and along
the main streets of towns like Silchester and Caerwent suggests
to him that these towns began life as markets, and only afterwards attracted the rich men who built themselves large houses
in their outskirts.

Convenience of access to the back rooms obviously requires
a passage along the side of the house ; and this addition is
often found. It is very common at Silchester, much rarer at
Caerwent ; and in many cases at Silchester there are two such
passages, one along each side of the house. The plan now
resembles what in a later chapter is called a tripartite corridor
villa, lacking wings ; but the resemblance is only superficial,
because the town house, even in this developed form, still
retains its original entrance at the end. Its roof was presumably constructed by raising the central span above the
penthouse at either side, and lighting the central rooms by
means of clerestory windows, as in the models mentioned on
page 130.

Where space permitted, it was easy to make such a house
more commodious by adding a room or two at one side, giving
the plan the shape of the letter L. Additions of this sort are
common at Silchester, and it is significant that the added room
is often either a new shop on the street-front or a room heated
with a hypocaust, a luxury rare in the original plan.

Among the larger Romano-British town houses, this L-
shaped plan is very common. Such houses often—at Silchester,
in fact, generally—have two wings, one rather longer than the
other, each consisting of a range of rooms with a corridor
along the front and perhaps another along the back. Not
infrequently the chief wing has corridors on both sides, the
lesser wing on one side only. The back corridor seems generally
to have been converted into a range of small rooms.

The L-shaped town house easily develops a courtyard. It
has only to build two walls at right angles from the ends of its
wings, and the thing is done. If a corridor is added along one
or both these walls, the result is a peristyle court with the rooms
of the house opening off two sides of it. And if more rooms are

wanted, they can be built along the other two sides of the quadrangle.

The larger town houses thus fall into three main types. First, the L-shaped is the commonest. Then comes a three-sided plan, with rooms or corridors running along three sides and the fourth side being open or closed by a wall. This type is rather like a winged corridor villa, and no doubt the two types influenced each other to some extent; but the resemblance is seldom close. The three-sided house is not so common in towns as it ought to be on any theory of mutual influence, for in fact it is the rarest of all the chief patterns of town-house; and when it does occur it sometimes shows a feature hardly ever present in the front of a villa, namely a projecting room opening off the centre of the corridor, giving an E-shaped plan. This same projection appears in other types than the three-sided, e.g. in several L-shaped houses, which thus become F-shaped.

Last comes the house with rooms, or at least corridors, all round the four sides of its courtyard. In order to avoid all confusion with villa types, we shall call this the quadrangle house. Of all the types of Romano-British house this is the most classical, and corresponds closely to the larger houses at Ostia (Rostovtseff, *Social and Econ. Hist. of the R. Empire*, 136. For examples of this plan in the case of villas, cf. Swoboda, *Röm. und roman. Paläste*, pp. 24, 25; in Britain villas are never so planned). So far as we yet know, such houses are not common in Romano-British towns. There is only one at Silchester; there are four at Caerwent, where the L-shaped plan so common at Silchester is almost absent; elsewhere they occur, e.g. at Colchester (*E.A.S.T.*, N.S., x, 323, house iii, Flavian date), and at Wall in Staffordshire (*A.J.*, lxxi, 360).

Whether these large houses had an upper floor is not known. The excavators of Silchester thought they had; but no actual traces of stairs have been found, and bearing in mind the fact that land inside a Romano-British town cannot have been so valuable as it was at Rome or Ostia, one would naturally assume that they were built only one storey high.

This classification of town houses has little, if any, chronological significance. It is possible that strip houses were sometimes altered into L-shaped houses after their original erection;

it is most improbable that any strip house ever developed by
successive additions into a quadrangle house.   The quadrangle
house existed fully developed in the Roman world before the
conquest of Britain, and was among the alternatives open to
the Romanised Britons as soon as they began to build towns
at all.

CHAPTER VII

VILLAS

§ 1. General Features and Types

" Villa," in Latin, means farm. It is an economic term ; it refers to the fact that the place so designated is an agricultural establishment. This is the sense in which we shall here use the word. There is a popular tendency to restrict its application to the country houses of the rich, with luxurious accessories and an ambitious plan ; but there is no good reason for any such restriction. Any house of the Roman period may be called a villa, provided that it was the dwelling of people, somewhat Romanised in manners, who farmed a plot of land ; as opposed to a town house on the one hand and a cottage on the other. Most of these Romano-British farms were self-supporting economic units ; they therefore carried on other industries beside farming ; and sometimes (as in the fulling establishment at Chedworth) these were on such a scale that we must suppose their produce to have travelled in the way of trade beyond the confines of the estate ; but no one, on that account, would say that Chedworth was a factory and not a farm.

Architecturally as well as economically, the Romano-British villa is a fairly definite entity, with a general character of its own, which it is the business of this chapter to describe. Of its construction and materials we shall say little ; they varied according to districts and to the wealth and taste of the owner ; but normally the villa seems to have been a one-storey timber-framed building standing on foundations of stone, for these foundations, as we find them, are too slight, as a rule, to carry anything either high or heavy. Tiled or slated roofs, painted plaster walls, and tessellated floors, were quite common ; in every villa except the poorest there were rooms heated by hypocausts, and generally a suite of baths.

Most of these villas lie south-east of a straight line joining Exeter to the mouth of the Trent. Beyond that, they occur only sparsely, *e.g.* in the Vale of York and the Welsh marches (*O.S. Map of Roman Britain*, ed. 2).

The Romano-British villa shows a considerable variety of ground-plans ; but comparative study reveals the existence of three main types, the corridor house, the courtyard house, and the basilican house. Of these the courtyard house appears to be an offshoot of the corridor house ; and we are left with two original types. But these again may possibly have a common origin. If it is assumed that they are descended from a common ancestor in the shape of a rectangular one-roomed building with a door in the middle of one side, it will follow that the basilican house develops by the insertion of longitudinal rows of posts to support the roof, while the corridor house develops by adding a veranda along the front to protect the door. It is also possible for both these developments to take place at once, if the front aisle of a basilican house turns into a veranda or corridor. This gives us three house-types, all very closely akin both in origin and in appearance :—

(1) The original rectangle divided into two longitudinal strips of unequal width, corridor in front and house proper behind. We shall call this the *bipartite* corridor house (Fig. 28 *a-d* ; Fig. 29).

(2) The same, divided into three longitudinal strips, corridor in front, then the main body of the house, then a second corridor which may be turned into a row of rooms. This we shall call the *tripartite* corridor house (Fig. 28 *e-k* ; Fig. 30).

(3) The same, divided as no. (2), but by rows of posts instead of solid partitions. This is the *basilican* house (Fig. 34 *a-h*).

The natural way of roofing these houses would be with a central ridged roof to which (1) adds a penthouse in front, and (2) and (3) both in front and behind.

This tentative pedigree of the Romano-British villa is based on evidence, mostly Continental, which will be quoted below as occasion arises. It must remain a guess until it has been tested by scientific excavation in this country. But by making the suggestion, the writer does not mean to take sides in the controversy as to whether the corridor house is classical or Celtic in origin. Very few elements in the Romano-Celtic civilisation of the north-western provinces were exclusively Roman or exclusively Celtic ; the Romans and the Celts had a good deal in common in civilisation, as well as in race and language, before the one conquered the other. After that event, the Romans taught the Celts much ; but—as invariably happens—they could teach no lessons that their pupils were not already prepared to learn.

§ 2. The Winged Corridor House

Most Roman villas in Britain are of the winged corridor type. In this type the corridor running along the front of the house stops short of its two ends, which project in wings either beyond the corridor or at least as far as its front line. This arrangement looks better than a wingless plan ; it gives more shelter to persons using the corridor ; and it saves space by throwing superfluous passage-room into the end rooms of the house.

This is the standard type of Romano-British country house ; a type not confined to Britain, but very common in France, Belgium, and Germany, and in all essentials recognisable even farther afield, linking itself up with the portico-houses of Pompeian wall-paintings (Rostovtseff, *Social and Econ. Hist. of the R. Empire*, Plate III, Figs. 1, 2), and other Mediterranean house-types (Swoboda, *Röm. und romanische Paläste*, 29 *seqq.*). In Britain and Gaul the main body of the house tends to be long and narrow, and is divided up by transverse partitions ; whereas in Germany it tends to be short and more or less square, and rooms are cut out of it round its edges, leaving an open space in the centre (characteristic German examples in *Germania Romana* [2], part ii, Plates XXIII, XXVII). There has been discussion in the past as to whether this open space was a courtyard or a covered hall ; some scholars (*e.g.* Schumacher, *Westdeutsche Zeitchrift*, xv, and others), holding that the corridor was the living room of the house and the squarish enclosure behind it an open courtyard, additional rooms being provided when required by roofing over parts of this yard.

This view has been disproved recently by the excavation of
a villa at Mayen, 18 miles west of Coblenz (*Bonner Jahrbücher*,
133, pp. 51-152), where the corridor was found to be a relatively
late addition to what was originally a one-roomed house. The
results of this excavation facilitate the understanding of the
Romano-British corridor house, where the attempt to find an
open courtyard behind the corridor has never been successful.

The earliest corridor houses in the Roman Empire were
simple rectangular buildings with no wings. The Pompeian
wall-paintings, all earlier than the eruption of A.D. 79, do not
show these features, which seem to have come into general
favour in the early second century (Swoboda, *op. cit.*, ch. iv,
esp. p. 87). On the Continent, wingless corridor houses of
a simple villa type are found, both bipartite (*e.g.* at Dortelweil
in Westphalia, Swoboda, p. 39) and tripartite (*e.g.* at Mau-
levrier near Caudebec in Normandy, *ibid.*, p. 54) ; but in Britain
the wingless pattern is almost entirely absent. So far as the
writer is aware, there is only one villa which is probably an
example of it, *viz.* Finkley (Hants ; see below, p. 135).[1] The
vast majority belong to the winged pattern. But whether
this means that the winged pattern had been firmly established
elsewhere before the Romanisation of the British country districts began, or whether it means that the British villas, like
the Mayen villa, were once wingless, and were brought into
line with the new fashion by adding wings, will not be known
until excavation is set on foot in this country with the express
purpose of determining the architectural history of our villas.

In the following paragraphs we shall review some examples
of British corridor villas, all belonging to the winged pattern,
but classified into two groups, bipartite and tripartite.

§ 3. The Bipartite Corridor House

A typical example is the villa at Mansfield Woodhouse
(Notts. ; Fig. 28 *a* ; *A.*, viii, 363 ; *V.C.H. Notts.*, ii, 28 ; *R.O.B.*,

---

[1] It is most regrettable that the complete plan of the villa at Yeovil
(Somerset ; *Proc. Som. A. and N.H. Soc.*, lxxiv, 122-143) could not be discovered ; what is known of it suggests that it may have been a wingless
tripartite house. In any case, the plan so far as we know it suggests town-
house, rather than country-house, analogies ; and perhaps Roman Yeovil
ought to be regarded not as a villa but as a small town.

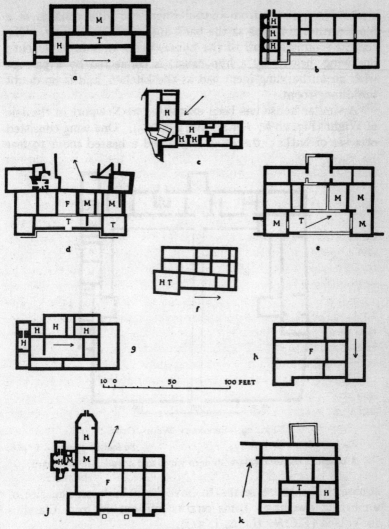

FIG. 28.—CORRIDOR VILLAS, BIPARTITE AND TRIPARTITE PLANS.

80 feet to 1 inch = 1 : 960.

(a) Mansfield Woodhouse, Notts.   (f) Frilford, Berks.
(b) Newport, I.O.W.   (g) Rodmarton, Glos.
(c) Hadstock, Essex.   (h) Cherington, Glos.
(d) Brislington, Som.   (j) Colerne, Wilts.
(e) Brading, I.O.W.   (k) Ely, Glam.

F = Flag paving. H = Hypocaust. M = Mosaic floor. T = Tessellated floor.

231). Here, apart from outbuildings, the villa consists of a block with five rooms at the back and one in each wing. The central room, the hall of the house, has a mosaic pavement ; one wing, heated by a hypocaust, is connected by a passage with an outbuilding identified as the kitchen, and is no doubt the dining-room.

A similar house has been excavated at Newport in the Isle of Wight (Fig. 28 *b* ; *J.R.S.*, xvi, 233-235). One wing consisted of a set of baths ; the other contained a heated room 19 feet

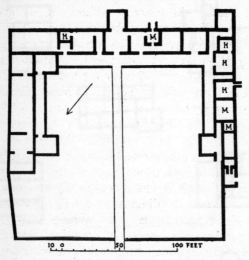

FIG. 29.—SPOONLEY WOOD, GLOS.

80 feet to 1 inch = 1 : 960.

A bipartite corridor villa with deep wings and a walled-in courtyard.

square. The house seems to have been built on the site of an earlier dwelling ; coins on the site extend from Claudius to Valens (*V.C.H. Hants*, i, 317).

These may be regarded as standard examples of the bipartite plan ; it may be modified by the addition of inessential features.

At Hadstock in Essex, for instance (Fig. 28 *c* ; *A.J.*, viii, 27), a very simple house of this type has been enlarged and improved by adding a wing at the back, containing heated rooms. As we have it, the plan is further complicated by later alterations; hypocausts have been inserted in the corridor and the centre of the main block, and one wing has been altered into a new set of baths. Pottery and coins show that the site had a long history.

Alterations of the same kind have taken place at Brislington (Somerset; Fig. 28 *d*; *V.C.H. Somerset*, i, 304; Haverfield, *Romanisation*, ed. 4, 38; *R.O.B.*, 224). Here two back wings appear to have been patched on at some time subsequent to the original building, giving the house a rough resemblance to what below is called the H-shaped type. One of these wings is a set of baths; the other resembles the so-called granary of the Mayen villa (*Bonner Jahrbücher*, 133, Plate VII). The central hall is flagged, as often in corridor houses, but it cannot be understood as an open courtyard, for neither in this case nor in any other is provision made for draining it of rain-water.

The well-known villa at Spoonley Wood (Glos.; Fig. 29; *A.*, lii, 551) may be taken as an example of the highest development of the bipartite plan. With its deep wings, it resembles Box (Fig. 30 *e*) except in the absence of a back corridor; and it is interesting because the bipartite plan very seldom develops to such proportions as this. It is not a courtyard house, although it has a completely-enclosed courtyard, outside which farm buildings were found; for the courtyard is not completely surrounded by buildings (*cf.* § 5, below).

Another large and luxurious bipartite house at Ridgwell (Essex; *A.*, xiv, 62) has deep wings terminating in apses; unfortunately the plan is not completely known.

§ 4. THE TRIPARTITE CORRIDOR HOUSE

We will begin, once more, by taking a typical example. At Brading (Isle of Wight; Fig. 28 *e*; Price, *Remains of Roman Buildings at Morton near Brading; V.C.H. Hants*, i, 313), is a villa 92 feet long by 56 wide apart from a projection at the back. It has a central range of five rooms; in front is a corridor with a wing at either end; behind is a narrower range of five rooms, the middle one projecting behind the house like the *sacellum* of many military headquarters-buildings. There are outbuildings which need not be here considered. Here, and in other examples of the type, the central rooms can only have been effectively lighted by clerestory windows above pent-house roofs in front and behind (*cf. Bonner Jahrbücher*, 133, p. 126).

The next examples show how this pattern was adapted to the purposes of the simpler, and poorer farm houses.

Typical of these humbler establishments is the villa at Frilford (Berks. ; Fig. 28 *f* ; *Oxford Arch. and Hist. Soc. Proc.*, N.S. iv, 233 ; *A.J.*, liv, 340 ; *R.O.B.*, 223). Here, as often in Germany, there is only one wing, which was plainly the chief living-room, for it has a hypocaust and a tessellated pavement. The whole house measures 73 by 40 feet.

A house at Rodmarton (Gloucestershire ; Fig. 28 *g* ; *A.*, xviii, 113-116), measuring 86 by 40 feet, in many ways resembles the foregoing, but though it has wings they do not project beyond the front of the corridor. The central hall is roughly pitched with stones (compare Cherington and Brislington), as if it were an open yard ; but the excavators saw no arrangements for draining it, and it was therefore probably roofed. Behind the hall is a range of three rooms heated with hypocausts and having mosaic floors ; at the south end is a suite of baths.

The villa at Cherington (Gloucestershire ; Fig. 28 *h* ; *A.*, xviii, 114, 117) ought clearly to be explained as a tripartite corridor house. The projecting wings show which is its front ; on this side is a deep corridor ; on the left, in the middle of the house, is the hall, paved with large rough stones ; on the right is perhaps a barn or stable. The whole house is only 82 by 54 feet, and no hypocausts or tessellated floors were found in it. We may imagine a high roof over the central part, with lean-to roofs over the front and back, as at Frilford and Rodmarton ; the roof plan in these cases being identical with that in a basilican house or in a simple town house with two corridors.

If the Cherington house had been enlarged and improved by adding a couple of heated rooms and a suite of baths projecting from one corner, the result would have been like the villa at Colerne (Wilts. ; Fig. 28 *j* ; *A.J.*, xiii, 328), where these refinements have the appearance of an afterthought, though the question was not raised by the excavators.

The little villa at Ely, just outside Cardiff (Glam. ; Fig. 28 *k* ; *J.R.S.*, xi) seems to date from the early second century. Its

wings are unusually large in proportion to the house as a
whole ; and a central wing at the back is a later addition, as
is a bath-building at the south-west corner.

We turn to rather more elaborate plans. One of these may
be called the H-shaped house. It has not only two corridors,
but two pairs of wings, one at the front and one at the back.
(The reader will observe that whereas all ordinary corridor
houses are symmetrical laterally, this type is symmetrical
longitudinally also.) Several examples of this are known ;
e.g. Chesterford (Essex ; Fig. 30 *a* ; *A.J.*, vi, 14), Gayton
Thorpe (Norfolk ; Fig. 30 *b* ; *Norf. and Norw. Arch. Soc.*,
xxiii) ; Ickleton (Cambs. ; Fig. 30 *d* ; *A.J.*, vi, 14) ; Hambledon (Bucks. ; Fig. 30 *c* ; *A.*, lxxi, 141). At Chesterford
the plan is extremely simple. A central range of rooms is
flanked by a corridor on each side, and at each end is a wing
projecting front and back. At Gayton Thorpe a rather larger
building of this pattern was found to have been occupied at
least from A.D. 150-170 to 300-320. In the other two cases
quoted there is an additional complication in the shape of a
room projecting from the middle of one of the corridors. At
Hambledon this is certainly the back corridor. At Ickleton
the plan is most easily understood if it is assumed that the foundations of the front corridor escaped the notice of the excavators, in which case the plan is substantially identical with
Hambledon.

A room projecting in this way from the middle of a corridor
is found, as we have seen, in what has been called the E-shaped
town house. The fact that it occurs at the back of the Hambledon villa shows that, unlike the corresponding feature in the
English Elizabethan house, it is not an entrance hall ; nor
does it appear to have that purpose when it occurs in town
houses.

Lastly, the tripartite villa may develop into a large and
luxurious country house, not much inferior to the courtyard
villas. An example of this occurs at Box near Bath (Wilts. ;
Fig. 30 *e* ; *A.J.*, lxi, 1). Here a tripartite villa has deep wings
on either side, projecting so far as almost to suggest a courtyard house ; and in fact the exploration of this villa was so
hampered by modern buildings that we cannot be absolutely
certain that the wings did not continue and form a courtyard.

But if the plan as we have it is correct, this villa is interesting as being the only considerable Romano-British country house

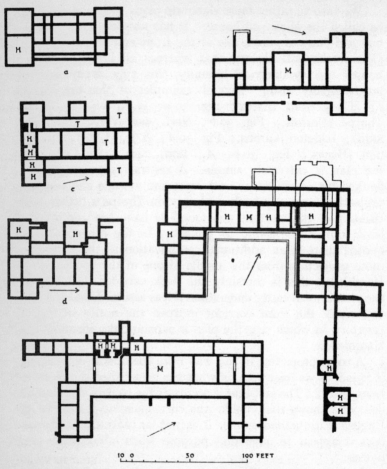

FIG. 30.—CORRIDOR VILLAS, TRIPARTITE PLANS.

(a) Chesterford, Essex.
(b) Gayton Thorpe, Norfolk.
(c) Hambledon, Bucks.

(d) Ickleton, Cambs.
(e) Box, Wilts.
(f) Folkestone, Kent.

F = Flag paving.   H = Hypocaust.   M = Mosaic floor.   T = Tessellated floor.

which might possibly have existed in a town. Had we found it at Silchester, we should have called it an example of the rare

three-sided town house ; but even so, it has a symmetry, when
seen from the front, which is hardly ever found in any town
house.

Another house of the same pattern, but without the
suggestion of town influence, exists at Folkestone (Kent ;
Fig. 30 *f* ; Winbolt, *Roman Folkestone*, is a popular account of
the excavation). The villa, which measures about 180 feet
by 81, shows two periods of construction, of which only the
later plan is known. A central range of eleven rooms is
bounded in front and behind by corridors, the back corridor
having been, perhaps as an afterthought, converted into a
series of rooms and baths. The central hall, 21 feet by 20,
has a mosaic pavement, the only one found.

How far inferior these finest British corridor houses are to
the best Continental examples may be seen by comparing
Folkestone, Ridgwell, or Box with Hosté (Belgium ; Cumont,
Comment la Belgique fut romanisée, 41 ; 450 by 100 feet, with
over forty rooms), or Nennig (Germany ; Fig. 31 *n* ; *Germania
Romana*[2], part ii, Plate XXII, 3 ; 350 by 150 feet, with between thirty and forty rooms).

§ 5. THE COURTYARD HOUSE

The largest and most wealthy Romano-British villas are
courtyard houses ; that is to say, they are built round a more
or less rectangular courtyard which is entered by a gate facing
the main part of the house.

Some kind of courtyard is normal in a villa of any type ;
you cannot very well have a farm without a farm-yard ; and
the buildings of the villa are ordinarily grouped round this
yard. Thus at Brading, Hambledon, and Stroud (Fig. 31 *a*,
b, *c*), there is a more or less symmetrical arrangement in which
the house stands across the far end of the yard with one or
more detached blocks of outbuildings on either side. At Clanville (Fig. 31 *f*) there are only two buildings altogether, standing
at right angles to one another ; this plan reappears at Ely,
Mansfield Woodhouse, and Folkestone (Fig. 31 *e*, *h*, *j*), and
in a modified way at Gayton Thorpe (Fig. 31 *g*). This way of
grouping the farm-buildings round a courtyard, of which other
examples could be given which could certainly be multiplied

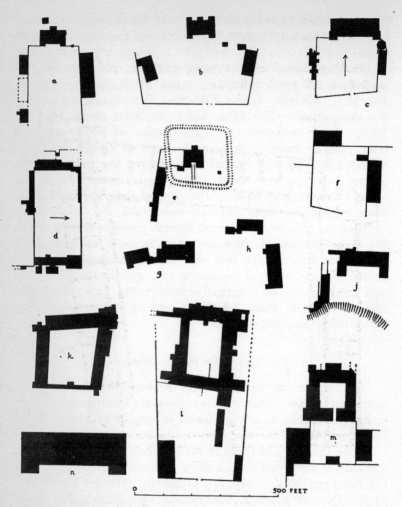

FIG. 31.—BLOCK-PLANS OF VILLAS.

320 feet to 1 inch = 1 : 3840.

(a) Brading, I.O.W.
(b) Hambledon, Bucks.
(c) Stroud, Hants.
(d) Pitney, Som.
(e) Ely, Glam.
(f) Clanville, Hants.
(g) Gayton Thorpe, Norfolk.

(h) Mansfield Woodhouse, Notts.
(j) Folkestone, Kent.
(k) North Leigh, Oxon.
(l) Bignor, Sussex.
(m) Woodchester, Glos.
(n) Nennig (main block only of a
    large continental villa for
    comparison of scale).

if the surroundings of known villas had been properly explored, does not constitute a courtyard villa. The true courtyard villa is one in which the courtyard is completely surrounded by buildings, not merely by an enclosure wall connecting a number of separate buildings.

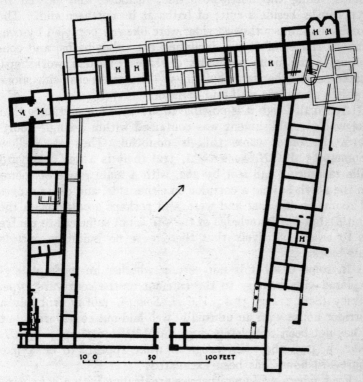

FIG. 32.—NORTH LEIGH, OXON.

80 feet to 1 inch = 1 : 960.

A typical courtyard villa. At an earlier stage it was a deep-winged corridor villa.

The essential features of the type may be seen from the plan of North Leigh (Oxfordshire ; Fig. 32 ; *R.O.B.*, p. 221 ; M. V. Taylor, *The Roman Villa at North Leigh*, pamphlet). The remains are complicated by the existence of three periods of building, which have never been distinguished satisfactorily for the entire site ; in the plan here shown an attempt has been made to represent the third period. The whole house measures nearly 300 feet each way, and lies round a courtyard about 190 feet long by 160 broad. A corridor or veranda runs all round this courtyard, only interrupted by the gate, with its porter's lodge, in the south-east side. The main range of rooms, along the north-west side, included four heated by hypocausts, beside a suite of baths at its northern end. The north-east and south-west sides were likewise occupied by continuous ranges of rooms, including two other baths, and consisting in the main, no doubt, of slaves' quarters, workshops, stables, and other farm-buildings. The south-east side alone consists of a mere wall and corridor.

At North Leigh it is possible to say with fair certainty that the whole establishment was contained within a single courtyard. In other cases this is doubtful. Thus at Wellow (Somerset ; *V.C.H. Somerset*, i, 312) there is a fine courtyard villa measuring 248 feet by 262, with a main range of rooms on the north having a corridor on either side, and other ranges of rooms on the east and west, and perhaps a corridor on the south ; but our knowledge of the site is not sufficient to enable us to assert positively that there were no buildings outside this block.

In some cases it is not certain whether an incompletely-explored villa belongs to the corridor or the courtyard type. Pitney (Som. ; Fig. 31 *d* ; *V.C.H. Som.*, i, 326) is probably a corridor house with an unusually well-laid-out courtyard ; but it has not been completely dug. At Littleton (Som. ; *V.C.H. Som.*, i, 324), the main range of what appears to be a fine courtyard house has been excavated.

Even where we know that we are dealing with a courtyard house, we cannot always be certain that there were not other buildings outside the main block. Sometimes there certainly were ; the entire courtyard house might stand, exactly like an ordinary corridor house, at the far end of an outer courtyard having the farm buildings to right and left. The best example is the magnificent villa at Woodchester in the Cotswolds (Glos. ; Lysons, *The Roman Villa at Woodchester*). If we compare the block-plan of this villa (Fig. 31 *m*) with that of, *e.g.* Brading (*ibid.*, *a*), we see at once that two things have happened to convert Brading into Woodchester : first, the Brading courtyard has consolidated itself into a single architectural unit, as at North Leigh (*ibid., k*) ; then, a second courtyard arranged like the first has been added in front. This means that the family lives shut off from the farmyard in a self-contained dwelling-house ; a conception whose luxurious character is reflected in the character of the building itself, whose rooms are more splendid than is usual in Romano-British villas. The most remarkable of these is the great central hall, whose roof was supported on four columns. This was not an atrium ; had the space between the columns been open to the sky, it would not have been paved with an elaborate mosaic, but would have contained a properly-drained *compluvium* for receiving rain-water. Similar halls are found in villas in Germany (*e.g.* Bilsdorf ; *Bonner Jahrbücher*, 133, p. 127).

A larger, but less symmetrical, example of the house with two courtyards exists at Bignor (Sussex ; Fig. 31 *l* ; Lysons, *Reliquiae Romano-Britannicae*, vol. iii). Here a corridor runs all round the inner courtyard, in a way reminiscent of North Leigh ; the outer courtyard is surrounded by a wall and entered by a gate, and contains farm buildings irregularly disposed.

The villa at Chedworth (Gloucestershire ; Fig. 33 ; *A.*, lix, 210 ; *A.J.*, xliv, 322 ; Buckman and Hall, *Notes on the R. Villa at Chedworth*) seems to represent a further development of the same type. The inner courtyard had a corridor all round it and rooms on three sides, thus resembling North Leigh ; but outside this is a second courtyard, whose sides are formed not by separate buildings as at Woodchester or Bignor, but by prolongations of the wings, so that the whole appears to be a corridor villa with exceedingly deep wings, having a small courtyard in front of the main living-rooms. Unfortunately, however, the plan is not completely known. The north side of the inner courtyard is mostly occupied by a large fulling establishment, too large to be easily explained as merely designed to satisfy the needs of the villa, and therefore evidence that cloth was prepared here on a commercial scale (Fox, " Notes on some probable traces of Roman fulling in Britain," *A.*, lix, 207 ; Rostovtseff, *Social and Economic Hist. of the R. Empire*, Plate XXXI, pp. 538-539 ; but *contra* Haverfield, *Trans. Bristol and Glos. Arch. Soc.*, xli, 161).

Courtyards of some kind are among the commonest features of classical architecture, but the Romano-British courtyard villa is not a copy of any classical house. Its essence lies in

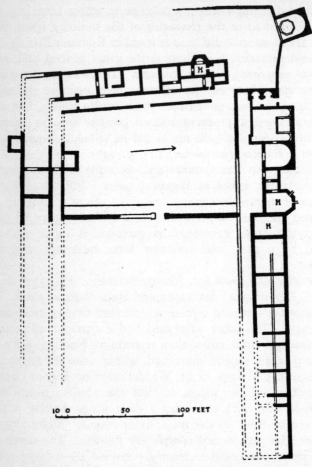

FIG. 33.—PLAN OF VILLA AT CHEDWORTH, GLOS.

80 feet to 1 inch = 1 : 960.

A courtyard villa with wings projecting to form the sides of a second courtyard.

the fact that its courtyard is a thoroughfare leading to the house, whereas the classical courtyard is a secluded space within or behind the house. Thus, in the ordinary Pompeian house (plans in Ward, *R.B.B.E.*, p. 140 ; Stuart Jones, *Companion to R. Hist.*, 163 ; *R.O.B.*, 225) the front door leads first to the *atrium*, the central hall of the house, and then, behind this, one finds the cool and quiet of the peristyle garden. This classical type of secluded courtyard is common in Continental villas (*e.g.* Chiragan in S.W. France : Joulin, *Les établissements gallo-romains de . . . Martres Tolosanes ;* Saint-Ulrich in Lorraine : Grenier, *Habitations gauloises*, 145 *seqq. ;* Westenhofen in Bavaria : *Germania Romana²*, part ii, Plate XXVIII, Fig. 2) ; but it never occurs in a British villa, though it does occur in British town houses.

The origin of the British courtyard villa is probably to be sought in the corridor house, with deep lateral wings as at Folkestone or Anthée (Belgium ; *Annales de la soc. arch. de Namur*, xiv, 165). Spoonley Wood is simply a corridor house of this kind which has been walled up into a courtyard ; and at North Leigh the extension of the wings right down the two sides of the courtyard seems to date only from the last period of building, the house having previously been a corridor house with deep wings.

This development produces a new type of courtyard house, turned, as it were, inside out : the courtyard is now in front of the hall and chief living-rooms, instead of behind them. It is a development especially characteristic of Britain, but it is not confined to Britain (*cf.* a good example at Mienne, Dept. Eure-et-Loire, Caumont, *Abécédaire*, 379), and it was certainly stimulated by classical models—partly by the classical peristyle courtyard, partly perhaps by such things as the forum of a town and the headquarters building of a fortress.

§ 6. The Basilican House

This name may serve to designate a special type of house which is fairly common in Britain, and is not unknown, though rare, on the Continent. (Swoboda, *Röm. und roman. Paläste*, gives a perfectly normal plan, Fig. 59, at Königshofen in Hungary, and a remarkable compound of basilican and corridor plans, Fig. 58, in the Sinsheimer Wald, and quotes an example from Normandy, p. 115. A basilican house at Kastell Larga, between Bâle and Belfort, is published in *Westd.*

Zeitschr., xxvi, 273, and parallels are quoted from Bachenau, Aulfingen, and Siblingen.)

This type, which has been described by Ward (*R.B.B.E.*, 174-182, and *cf. R.O.B.*, 227-230), is essentially a rectangular building with two rows of posts running along its length and dividing it into a nave and two aisles.   The entrance is sometimes, though apparently not always, in the middle of one side ; and internal partitions may be added to taste, forming rooms cut off from the general body of the interior.

The question has often been asked whether the central portion of a basilican house was a roofed nave or an open courtyard.   The right answer is that it was a roofed nave.   This is clear from a study of the British examples, in which the central space generally has a dirt floor and never has any means of draining off rain-water.   If it is asked how light was found for rooms cut out of this central space, *e.g.* at Clanville and Carisbrooke, the answer is that the Romano-Celtic house was roofed, in some cases at least, so as to permit of clerestory windows. This is shown by two small models of houses found at Kreuznach, one (*Bonner Jahrbücher*, 123, p. 233) representing a small house with a kind of lean-to running along each of its longer sides, while the other (*Germania*, vii, 74) has a lean-to on one side only, and thus resembles a corridor house with no wings (both models are republished in *Bonner Jahrbücher*, 133, pp. 124-126).

The corridor house at Mayen in its original form was a rectangular one-roomed house with an aisle running along one side at least, perhaps along both sides, and an entrance in the middle of one side (*Bonner Jahrbücher*, 133, pp. 58-59, 144 ; Plate V ; Plate IX, upper photograph) ; that is to say, it was a basilican house before it was converted into a corridor house ; and its internal arrangements led the excavators to infer with confidence that at this stage it was wholly roofed over, the aisle or aisles being merely a device to facilitate the spanning of a space 30 feet wide.

This throws some light on the question of the origin of the basilican house.   Ward (*R.B.B.E.*, 180-181) pointed out a general resemblance between the basilican house and an early type of Frisian and Saxon farm-house ; Swoboda (*op. cit.*, 115) finds parallels further afield, and concludes that it is " an old

Hellenistic form of peasant-house, which spread all over the Hellenistic-Roman cultural area." But the history of the Mayen house enables us to go a little further and to say that it was an early type in the Celtic world, perhaps established there before the Romans came (this phase of the Mayen building is dated at the beginning of the Roman period), and in any case superseded, as the Romanisation of the Celtic provinces advanced, by the corridor type. Its frequency in Roman Britain, therefore, is one of the many facts which show that Britain was a relatively backward area in civilisation.

One of the best examples of the basilican house is the villa at Clanville, near Andover (Hampshire ; Fig. 34 *a* ; *A.*, lvi, 2 ; *V.C.H. Hants*, i, 296 ; Haverfield and Macdonald, *Roman Occupation*, 227). A rectangular building 96 feet by 52, lying north and south, here forms the chief building of a farm ; its door, in the middle of its eastern side, gives on a courtyard, on the north side of which are outbuildings. Two rows of stone bases divide it into a nave and aisles, and beyond the western aisle lies a narrow corridor. The south end is cut off by a thick partition and divided into three rooms : the central room has a mosaic pavement, and one of the others appears to be a bath. Six other rooms have been made by inserting partitions ; two are heated with hypocausts, and the others have tessellated pavements. The central space has a dirt floor. Abundant window-glass and painted wall-plaster showed that the house had pretensions to comfort and elegance.

A simpler example in the same county has been found at Castlefield (Fig. 34 *b* ; *V.C.H. Hants*, i, 302). The rectangle is 66 feet by 41 ; at one end is a projecting chamber 22 feet by 14 externally, and apart from this the whole building is a single room. Coins were found dating from 238 to 378.

A still simpler house of this pattern exists at Holbury (Fig. 34 *c* ; *V.C.H. Hants*, i, 312). It measures 59 by 49 feet internally ; the two corners at one end are walled off into small chambers, and the rest of the house is divided into a nave and aisles by four massive bases. The fact that there is a hearth in the middle of each end shows that the entrance is at the side, as usual in basilican houses.

At Carisbrooke (Isle of Wight ; Fig. 34 *d* ; *V.C.H. Hants*, i, 316) there is a large basilican house, 118 feet by 50, much

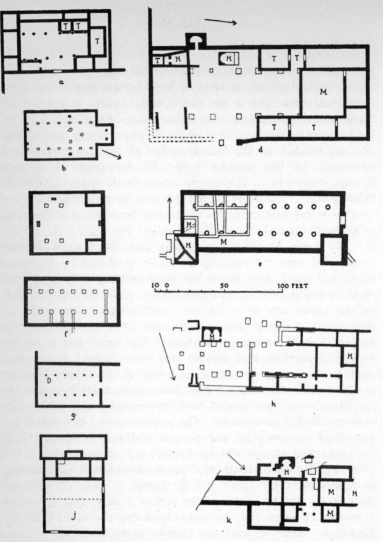

FIG. 34.—BASILICAN VILLAS, ETC.   80 feet to 1 inch = 1 : 960.

(a) Clanville, Hants (basilican villa).
(b) Castlefield, Hants (basilican villa).
(c) Holbury, Hants (basilican villa).
(d) Carisbrooke, I.O.W. (basilican villa).
(e) Stroud, Hants (basilican villa with wings).
(f) Ickleton, Cambs. (basilican outbuilding of a corridor villa).
(g) Spoonley Wood, Glos. (basilican outbuilding).
(h) Brading, I.O.W. (basilican outbuilding adapted as a dwelling-house).
(j) Finkley, Hants (villa of unclassified type, perhaps a wingless corridor villa).
(k) Yatton, Som. (villa of unclassified type, with entrance of classical pattern).

H = Hypocaust.   M = Mosaic floor.   T = Tessellated floor.

resembling that at Clanville. It lies north and south, and its entrance is on the east. At the north end are eight rooms, some at least of which seem to have been made by inserting partitions after the house was already built. Two of these, including the largest, 22 feet square, are floored with mosaics. At the other end is a suite of baths. Coins from 250 to 350 were found ; but the presence of an early Gaulish coin is suggestive when taken in connection with the primitive plan of the house.

Another house of the same pattern has been found at Thruxton (*V.C.H. Hants*, i, 298), but no plan of it exists ; and the villa at Lippen Wood, West Meon (Hants ; *A.J.*, lxiv, 1), may be yet another.

The most interesting of all the basilican houses is at Stroud, near Petersfield (Hants ; Fig. 34 *e* ; *A.J.*, lxvi, 33). It consists of a rectangle 140 feet by 52, from two corners of which project wings exactly like those of a normal corridor house. The excavator was careful to point out that these wings were contemporary in build with the main structure (p. 38), and were not later additions. The main block had been divided at first merely by two rows of wooden columns ; but at a later date a number of rooms had been cut off at its western end, in such a way as to leave the front aisle doing duty as a corridor. The easternmost of the rooms in the nave contained a hearth. The interest of this house lies in the fact that here, as in the Sinsheimer Wald (Swoboda, *op. cit.*, p. 113), but far more definitely and unambiguously, we have an example of the basilican principle and the corridor principle combined in the same house. If a few more partitions had been put in and the now unnecessary columns removed, the Stroud villa could never have been distinguished from a normal tripartite corridor house. It should be observed that the excavator regarded the door at the east end as a late addition, the original entrance being between the wings.

Buildings of the basilican type are found serving as outbuildings in farms where the house proper belonged to a more advanced type. Thus at Spoonley Wood (Fig. 34 *g*) a basilican barn or byre 60 feet by 40 was found (*A.*, lii, Plate XVII). At Ickleton (Fig. 34 *f*), one measuring 78 by 36 feet internally was found, with some partitions inserted as if for stalls (*A.J.*, vi, 14). Elsewhere (*e.g.* Brading, Fig. 34 *h* ; *V.C.H.*

Hants, i, 313 ; West Dean, *ibid.*, 311 ; Mansfield Woodhouse,
A., viii, 363 ; apparently Apethorpe, *V.C.H. Northants*, i, 191 ;
and Woodchester) large buildings of basilican plan have been
used partly perhaps as barns or stables or the like, but partly
also as quarters for the *personnel* of the farm, as is shown by
the rooms, hypocausts, suites of baths, and so forth, which
have been inserted in them by the building of partitions. The
fact that in these cases a socially lower class lives in a building
whose architecture connects it with an early phase of Romano-
Celtic culture, is not without bearing on the Romanisation of
the Celtic provinces.

§ 7. Outbuildings

All villas except the very humblest possessed buildings other
than the dwelling-house proper. These generally consist of
cottages, barns, stables, and so forth. It is noteworthy that
such buildings, even when they were undoubtedly dwellings,
very rarely conform to the architectural type of the villa. At
Gayton Thorpe, indeed, a winged corridor house has another
winged corridor house as an outbuilding ; but this is an exception. A basilican villa like Clanville has barn-like outbuildings ; a corridor villa like Mansfield Woodhouse has a
basilican outbuilding ; the outbuilding tends to show a more
primitive plan than the house proper (see above).

Sometimes the outbuildings of villas show a certain resemblance to the simpler kinds of town house. This is not un-
natural, since these town houses appear to have developed out
of a shed not wholly unlike the barn of a farm ; but in spite
of these occasional resemblances it is remarkable how closely,
as a general rule, the town house and the country house follow
independent lines of development.

When the outbuildings are incorporated with the dwelling-
house in a single block, as in the case of the courtyard villa,
it is sometimes still possible to detect their affinity to types
other than that which dictates the form of the dwelling-house.

§ 8. Other Types of Villa

Nearly all the villas in Britain fall into one of the above
three classes. Of the apparent exceptions, there are few

which must certainly be assigned to any other class ; most of them are incompletely known and would probably, with fuller knowledge, conform to the usual types. For example, at Holcombe in Devonshire (*A.*, xlv, 462), a very curious building appears to exist, in which rooms of various shapes radiate from an octagonal hall or court ; but this is evidently a suite of baths or other apartments attached to a large villa whose plan is otherwise unknown ; compare the hexagonal room, with variously-shaped apartments opening off it, in the corner of a courtyard villa at Keynsham (Somerset ; *J.R.S.*, xii, 264, with plan).

At Somerdale, again (Somerset ; *J.R.S.*, xiv, 232), is a villa which seems to consist of a suite of baths and three or four other rooms grouped round a flagged courtyard with a tank in it ; but here again the plan is probably incomplete. The baths are too large for a house 60 feet square and containing only three or four rooms.

There is, however, one large villa in Britain which demands separate treatment. This is at Yatton (Somerset ; Fig. 34 *k* ; *V.C.H. Somerset*, i, 306). It is not completely excavated, but the known portion, 60 feet by 150, presents unusual features. In the middle is a hall, on one side of which is something that may be the remains of a stair. This is the only case in which a Romano-British villa has yielded traces of an upper storey. In front of the hall is a porch, whose roof was supported by two columns ; and in front of that again there may have been a corridor running veranda-wise across the front of the house. On either side of the hall are living-rooms, and behind it a suite of baths. There are Continental analogies ; a central porch with columns, approached through a veranda or portico, is a feature of the great villa at Wittlich (*Germania Romana* [2], part ii, Plate XXII, Fig. 2).

A few small houses, hardly small enough to justify refusing them the rank of villa, are recalcitrant to classification. At Finkley in Hampshire (Fig. 34 *j* ; *V.C.H. Hants*, i, 303), is a house 83 feet by 59, made up of three parts. In front is a courtyard, paved with flints. Across the back of this there seems to have been a veranda. Then comes a square hall, paved with brick tesserae and containing a hearth ; on either side of it is a long narrow chamber. Finally, at the back, there is a range of two or three rooms—the partitions are not certain—whose walls were decorated with coloured plaster. The hint of a corridor in front, the central hall, and the living rooms at the back, connect this with corridor houses such as Cherington, Rodmarton, and Frilford. The coins in it go back to Trajan, which is unusual in a villa, and it is perhaps legitimate to guess that Finkley may be an example of the bipartite corridor house as it was before the projecting wings were added to its plan, with yards at back and front.

Finally, there are a few houses, but very few, which have the air of town houses strayed into the country. One such is at North Ash (Kent ; Haverfield, *R.B. in* 1914), and seems to be a strip house at one end of a rectangular yard, but this, too, may be a corridor house without wings. Another, which has the same general plan, has been found at Ashdon (Essex ; *A.J.*, x, 14). In the present state of our knowledge, we cannot say whether these are corridor houses before the development of the winged plan ; or whether they are houses belonging to villages of which the rest has not yet been discovered ; or whether they are merely the outbuildings of villas, or, finally, whether there is some other explanation of their plan. We have already called attention to a case in which a so-called villa with outbuildings appears to be in some respects better classified as a village ; and we have also noted that the outbuildings of villas occasionally approximate to the strip-plan of an ordinary town house.

CHAPTER VIII

TEMPLES

§ 1. CLASSICAL TEMPLES.

THE regular classical temple with its pediment supported on a range of columns, and its *podium* or raised table-like foundation, is not commonly found in this part of the Roman Empire. Only two British examples have been identified. At Bath, the temple of the goddess Sul (or Sul Minerva) was found in 1790, and although no plan was made it is clear from the relics still in existence that the building was of the classical type. The pediment, decorated with reliefs showing the panoply of Minerva with her gorgon shield in the centre, is now at Bath ; and it is fairly certain that it was supported on four columns, and formed a classical façade about 26 feet wide. The temple, in fact, seems to have been a small pseudo-peripteral building (*i.e.* with free-standing columns in front, supporting the pediment, and attached columns round the other sides), like the well-known temples at Nimes and Vienne.[1]

At Colchester, Tacitus tells us (*Ann.*, xiv, 31, 6), there was a temple of the deified Claudius, which was regarded by the Britons of Nero's reign with especial hatred as " a stronghold of eternal tyranny " (*quasi arx aeternae dominationis*). This must have been a building in the regular classical style, standing on a *podium*. Such a *podium* has recently been identified in the foundations of the early Norman castle (Fig. 35 *c*). There are two vaults, each 92 feet 9 inches long and 19 feet 10 inches wide, separated by a partition 5 feet 9 inches thick. These vaults, which are built in a recognisably Roman fashion, form

---

[1] Drawings in Lysons, *Reliquiae Romano-Britannicae*. See also *V.C.H. Somerset*, i.

FIG. 35.—TEMPLES.

80 feet to 1 inch = 1 : 960.

(a) Silchester (Hants) : insula vii.
(b) Weycock (Berks.).
(c) Colchester (Essex), substructures.
(d) Corbridge (Northumberland).
(e) Silchester, church ; insula iv.
(f) Lydney (Glos.).
(g) Silchester ; insula xxx.
(h) Harlow (Essex).
(j) Silchester : insula xxxi.

(k) Wroxeter (Salop).
(l) Worth (Kent.)
(m) Chesterford (Essex).
(n) Carrawburgh (Northumberland).
(o) Caerwent (Mon.).
(p) Silchester, temple of Mars ; insula xxxv.
(q) Housesteads (Northumberland), Mithraeum.

the hollow interior of a building now embedded in the castle. Originally this building must have been about 105 feet long by 80 feet wide (the Maison Carrée at Nimes is 87 by 45 ; Esperandieu, *La Maison Carrée*, Nimes, 1923, p. 5 ; the temple at Vienne is 78 by 47 feet according to a local guide-book). A cross-wall inside one of the vaults suggests that about two-fifths of the way from the south end of the building to the north end there was need to support a heavy load lying transversely on it ; this would be the front wall of the temple *cella*, which at the Maison Carrée occupies just this position. It has therefore been suggested that the Colchester building is the hollow *podium* of the temple of Claudius, which, to judge from the existing remains, had rows of free columns in front and on either side ; and, further, that round it vestiges of a *forum*, in whose centre such a temple may well have stood, are still discernible. Bearing in mind the fact that the vaults are certainly of Roman construction (*cf.* Ashby in *J.R.S.*, x, p. 89), and that it is difficult to offer any other explanation for them, the suggestion is extremely plausible.[1]

The nearest approach to the classical temple, beside these two, is one excavated at Wroxeter (Fig. 35 *k*). A rectangular enclosure, 98 feet by 56, facing a little south of east, contained, in its front portion, a courtyard with a cloister round three sides, and, at its back, a very massive foundation on which stood a *cella* about 30 feet by 25 externally. There was no *podium*—the foundation was not raised above the floor level of the courtyard—but the plan of placing a temple inside a cloistered enclosure recalls examples at Pompeii and elsewhere. This building was dated by the excavators not earlier than Hadrian's reign and perhaps later ; it is significant that the nearest parallel is in the Trajanic colony of Timgad.[2]

At Corbridge (Fig. 35 *d*) a building was found which in some ways resembles a temple of the classical type. It is a rectangle 24 feet long by 15 feet 8 inches wide, facing a little south of east. In front of its door, at the east end, seems to have been a colonnade of four columns recalling the ordinary classical temple façade. At the opposite end was an apse. The

---

[1] Wheeler and Laver, " Roman Colchester," in *J.R.S.*, ix, 146 *seqq.* Royal Commission on Hist. Monuments, *North-East Essex*, pp. 24-26.

[2] *Wroxeter*, 1913, pp. 2-9.

excavators, judging by the style of the masonry, assigned the
building to the middle of the second century ; and it is worth
noting that this would make it a little later than Hadrian's
temple of Venus and Roma at Rome, which consists of two
apsed *cellae* placed back to back, a portico in front of each.[1]

Circular temples of Roman date are not uncommon. They
consisted as a rule of a cylindrical *cella* surrounded by a circular portico, the whole surmounted by a flattish conical roof.
The temples at Tivoli and in the Forum Boarium at Rome are
famous examples. In Britain there is an example at Silchester
(Fig. 35 *a*). The *cella* is circular internally and about 37 feet
in diameter ; externally it is sixteen-sided, and the portico
wall is likewise sixteen-sided, and about 65 feet in diameter
over all.[2]

Another example is at Weycock in Berkshire (Fig. 35 *b*).
Here an octagonal building, 28 feet in diameter internally, is
surrounded by an outer octagonal wall, the whole about 63
feet in diameter. The identification of this building as a
temple is not certain, but is supported by the existence of
octagonal temples elsewhere. At Trier, for instance, a circular
cella is surrounded by an octagonal portico (no. 42 in the
" Tempelbezirk " ; Loeschcke, *Die Erforschung des Tempel-
bezirkes in Altbachtale zu Trier*, 1928, p. 34).[3]

It may be mentioned here that there are other types of
Roman circular buildings beside temples ; namely tombs and
certain portions of bath-houses. In the past these have often
been mistaken for temples ; but they do not show the distinction between *cella* and portico, forming two concentric rings,
which is characteristic of the ordinary round temple.[4] There
are also octagonal buildings which cannot be temples ; *e.g.*
just outside the villa at Stroud near Petersfield (*A.J.*, lxvi, 33) ;
here again, the wall is single and there is no distinction of *cella*
and portico.

[1] *Corbridge Report* for 1913, pp. 15 *seqq.* (site 40). The measurements
quoted are given in the excavation report, but do not tally with the plan.

[2] *A.*, liv, 206.

[3] *A.J.*, vi, 114. A possible, but insufficiently explored, example of an
octagonal temple in a circular enclosure is at Caerwent, *A.*, lxiv, 447.

[4] It is true that, *e.g.*, in the case of no. 3 at Trier (*cf.* Loeschcke, *op. cit.*,
pp. 7, 22), a round temple may have foundations consisting of one ring only ;
in that case it has no *cella*, but is simply a canopy or pavilion supported on
a ring of columns.

At Lydney (Fig. 35 *f*) there is a remarkable temple based
on the plan of a basilica. It was built late in the fourth century, and was the centre of the cult of the god Nodens. It is
a rectangular building, facing south-east, about 60 by 80 feet
externally. At its northern end is a row of three small chambers
or chapels, separated from the north wall of the temple by an
ambulatory. In line with the side walls of the outermost
chapels are two ranges of piers running along the temple and
dividing a central nave from two aisles. In each of the aisles
are two more chapels, projecting outwards at the sides of the
building. After a collapse due to insecure foundations, the
intervals between the piers of the nave were filled up with walls
to give additional strength. The basilica type of temple
reappears, but much less elaborately planned and entirely
without chapels, at Pesch in the Eifel (Germany ; *Bonner
Jahrbücher*, cxxv).[1]

§ 2. ROMANO-CELTIC TEMPLES

Far commoner, in this part of the Roman Empire, than
any of the classical temple-types, or all put together, is the so-
called Romano-Celtic temple. This is a square or rectangular
cella surrounded on all sides by a portico or veranda. It has
obvious affinities with classical types ; it is not unlike a small
peristyle temple, and was probably developed in Gaul, Germany,
and Britain under the influence of Greco-Roman architecture.
Temples of this kind are especially common in the lower Seine
valley, below Paris, and in the district between Trier and
Cologne ; but they are not uncommon in Central France and
Switzerland, and about fifteen are known in Britain (examples,
Fig. 35 *g, h, j, l, m*).[2]

Normal examples of the type have been found at Silchester
(three ; *A.*, lii, 745, and lxi, 206), Richborough (two ; *Ant. J.*,
viii, 318), Caister-by-Norwich (two, identified by an air photograph ; *Antiquity*, iii, 183 ; a third building which may be a

[1] Bathurst and King, *Roman Antiquities in Lydney Park*, 1879. Excavations now (1928-29) in progress, conducted by the Society of Antiquaries,
will be reported upon in the near future. I am indebted to Dr. R. E. M. Wheeler
for permission to reproduce his plan in advance of publication.

[2] Wheeler, " A Romano-Celtic Temple near Harlow, Essex, and a note
on the type," in *Ant. J.*, viii, 300-326, with a map, plans, etc.

temple of a different pattern is visible in the same photograph), and one each at Harlow, Essex (*Ant. J.*, viii, 300), Lancing (*ibid.*, 318), Chanctonbury Ring (*ibid.*, 318), Great Chesterford (*ibid.*, 319), and Worth (*Ant. J.*, viii, 76). In these cases the *cella* is ordinarily from about 12 to about 20 feet square internally, and the whole external measurement of the building varies between about 35 and 75 feet square. The only considerable deviation from the square shape is at Chanctonbury Ring, where the *cella* measures 24 by 17 feet internally. Concerning their internal arrangements little is known ; one Silchester example (Fig. 35 *p*, p. 138) had a platform across the back of the *cella*, and at Great Chesterford some kind of cylindrical object seems to have stood just inside the door. Nor do we know much about their architecture. Whether the *cella* had a ridged or a pyramidal roof is quite uncertain, but there is evidence that in some cases at least the veranda had a separate penthouse roof.[1]

Abnormal examples of the Romano-Celtic temple occur at various places. At Caerwent, for example, is one (Fig. 35 *o*) with a *cella* 19 feet square internally and having an apse at the back (*A.*, lxii, 4 ; Haverfield, *Romanisation*, ed. 4, p. 37). At Benwell a temple was dug in 1862 and found to be 16 feet square, with an apse to the south and an entrance to the north, and to east and west were found walls which appear to have been relics of the veranda. At each side of the apse was an altar, dedicated respectively to Anociticus and Antenociticus ; sculptured fragments included parts of shafts and capitals (*Arch. Aeliana*, ser. 2, vi, 169). When this is compared with the Caerwent temple and, more especially, with No. 1 in the Trier " Tempelbezirk," where a Romano-Celtic temple was found to terminate in an apse having a base for an altar or statue in exactly the position of one of the Benwell altars (Loeschcke, *op. cit.*, p. 21, and Plate II), its Romano-Celtic character cannot be doubted.

Finally, what must probably be regarded as a Romano-Celtic temple was excavated at Carrawburgh in 1876 (Fig. 35 *n*).

---

[1] Dr. Wheeler calls my attention to two other examples: (i) on Jordan's Hill, Weymouth (excavated but not planned in 1843 ; *Trans. Dorset N.H. & Ant. Field Club*, 1923, p. 18 of reprint) ; (ii) on Farley Heath, Albury (*Surrey Arch. Coll.*, xxxvii, 1927, p. 183).

It measured 46 by 44 feet over all—a normal size for a temple of this pattern—and had an outer wall 3 feet thick, inside which, as often happens, the ground was artificially raised. In the middle was a cistern measuring 8 feet 6 inches by 7 feet 9 inches, and 7 feet deep ; this was filled by a spring, the sacred spring of the goddess Coventina, whose home the temple was. Numerous altars and other votive objects had stood round about the cistern, and had at some time been swept into it ; it also contained many thousands of coins and other things that had been thrown in by way of offering them to the goddess. The coins would seem to indicate that the worship of Coventina was carried on from the time of Hadrian to that of Gratian. No *cella* was found in this temple, and it is not certain whether the cistern took its place, or whether it was overlooked by the excavators, or, finally, whether the temple belonged to a somewhat different type of building (*A.A.*², viii, 20).

§ 3. MITHRAISM

A special type of temple is the Mithraeum. The worship of Mithras (for an account of which see Cumont, *Les mystères de Mithra*, Eng. tr. *The Mysteries of Mithra*) dates from a very remote period in the Near East, having been traced back to the fourteenth century B.C. (Cumont, *op. cit.*, p. 2) ; in the sacred books of Zoroastrianism, the religion of the Persian Empire, Mithras is the god of light—not of the sun, but of the light which uses sun, moon, and stars indifferently as its vehicles. He is by a further development of ideas, the god of fertility and victory, the god of armies (*ibid.*, 4-5). Influenced by Babylonian, Greek, and other currents of thought, Mithraism had long been a flourishing religion in the East before it began to penetrate the Roman Empire, which it did largely in consequence of the Eastern campaigns conducted by Trajan, Verus, and Septimius Severus (*ibid.*, 35). No doubt it actually appeared in Rome earlier than this, indeed it is said to have been introduced during the Republican period (Plutarch, *Pompey*, 24) ; but of the vast number of Mithraic documents which we possess, none is dated earlier than the Flavian period and few are earlier than the Antonine age. Yet there are no Mithraic

monuments on the Antonine Wall ; and in fact it is not until
the third century that we reach the great period of Mithraism,
at any rate in the extreme north-west of the Empire.   The
triumph of Mithraism in this period is characteristically sym-
bolised by an altar from Housesteads, on which a second-
century dedication to Iuppiter Optimus Maximus has been
replaced, in A.D. 252, by one to the Invincible Sun-god Mithras.

Mithras was worshipped in an underground or partly underground building, having a central aisle and on either side a
long, narrow raised platform of earth or stone, to accommodate
the worshippers.   It was entered at one end, and at the other
end was the sanctuary where, dominating the whole congrega-
tion, stood what we may call the altar-piece—a sculptured slab
representing Mithras killing the bull.   Mithras, in tunic and
trousers, flowing cloak and Phrygian cap, throws himself on
the falling bull and averts his eyes in pity as he plunges his
dagger into its throat.   Below the bull are a dog that jumps
up to lick its blood, a snake and a scorpion.   On either side is
a torch-bearer in Phrygian dress, one holding his torch upwards,
the other downwards.   Round about may be other accessories
—a circular frame with the signs of the zodiac ; the four winds,
one in each corner ; the four seasons ; the chariots of the sun
and the moon ; scenes from the legend of Mithras ; and so
forth.   Other sculptures were often present ; especially a
representation of the birth of Mithras from the rock.

The only Mithraeum in Britain that has been identified
with certainty and explored more or less completely [1] is at
Housesteads (Fig. 35 q).   It measured 54 feet long by 16 feet
wide, and had a flagged central aisle 6 feet 6 inches wide between raised platforms at least 2 feet high.   Running water—
an essential, as it would seem, of the Mithraic liturgy—was
provided by a spring.   At the far end was a sanctuary with a
relief of the Birth of Mithras still standing in its place between
two altars ; fragments of a " Bull-killing " littered the floor.
Here, as often on the Continent, it appeared that the temple
had been deliberately wrecked (A.A.[2], i, 263 ; A.A.[2], xxv, 255,

---

[1] A subterranean building at Burham, Kent, may be a Mithraeum, but
the identification is not certain (P.S.A.[2], xvi, 1896, 248-249).   There were
certainly many Mithraea in the north, but no others have been properly
excavated.

for the wrecking of a Mithraeum, *cf. e.g.* Drexel, *Das Kastell Stockstadt*, O.R.L. Lief. xxxiii, 26 ; Behn, *Das Mithrasheiligtum zu Dieburg*, 1928, p. 7 : " of the hundreds of Mithraea, very few are undamaged . . . all others have been more or less completely destroyed "). Behn ascribes the destruction at Dieburg to the invading Germans of the late third century, *ibid.*, p. 45 ; but that does not account for the case of House-steads, where it seems natural to suppose that the ruin of the Mithraeum was brought about either by the Picts and Scots in 367, or by the Christians.[1]

§ 4. CHRISTIANITY

Relics of Christianity in Roman Britain are very rare. Setting aside everything that belongs to the period following the Roman evacuation, we are left with a few examples of the chi-rho monogram or chrismon and a few—not too certain—tombstones (see below, ch. xi, § 9), and one undoubted Romano-British church. This was found at Silchester in 1892 (Fig. 35 *e*). It was 42 feet long by 33 feet wide across the transepts. Across the entrance end was a narthex or porch ; at the other end the nave terminated in an apse, and outside the narthex was a square base, probably to hold a laver (*A.*, liii, 563 ; *V.C.H. Hants*, i, 364).

A less certain Christian church was found in 1923 at Caerwent, and will shortly be published in *Archaeologia*. It is a small oblong building with an apse at the east and a narthex at the west, and dates from the latter part of the Roman period or perhaps later.

---

[1] The building at Colchester described as a Mithraeum in the *Illustrated London News*, May 24, 1930, is in the present writer's opinion a water-tank.

CHAPTER IX

TOMBS

§ 1. The Burial

Hominem mortuom in urbe ne sepelito neve urito is a regulation of the Twelve Tables (x, 1) ; and, in obedience to this ancient law, Roman tombs are regularly placed outside the settlement to which they belong. Most often they are grouped along the roads leading out of it ; and although cases exist where, in defiance of the law, a few burials have been made within the limits of a town, the general rule holds good that where tombs are found in any considerable number, the limits of the settlement have already been left behind.[1]

As the quotation from the Twelve Tables shows, the Romans of the Republic practised both cremation and inhumation. But in the early Imperial age cremation had become almost universal, and there is no certain example of a Roman inhumation-burial in Britain before the late second century. After A.D. 150 inhumation seems gradually to have been reintroduced, at first as an exception, then with increasing frequency until, during the third century, it becomes the rule, and supplants cremation almost entirely by the end of that century. The earliest known inhumation-cemetery in Britain is at Chester ; it was in use during the second half of the second century and closed about A.D. 200 (Haverfield, *R.B. in* 1913, p. 14 ; *R.B. in* 1914, pp. 41-42).

---

[1] Examples of burial within a town : Caerwent, *Archaeologia*, lviii, 151 ; lix, 292 ; lx, 126 ; lxii, 414, 417, 421. Colchester, *Phil. Trans.*, 1761, 285-286 ; Morant, *Colchester*, i, 184 ; *Jour. Brit. Arch. Assoc.*, v, 86. London, *Roman London* (Royal Comm. Hist. Mon.), 30, with the sound observation that " isolated burials are of comparatively small importance to the historian " trying to fix the limits of a given town at a given time, but " cemeteries . . . are a different matter " and " lay outside the main areas of habitation."

A cremation-burial consists essentially of a receptacle called an urn, containing the burnt remains, which is deposited in a grave.[1] The urn is as a rule either an earthen jar, of ordinary domestic type, or a glass vessel, in which case it is generally a square bottle with a fluted handle. Sometimes, however, cinerary urns of stone or metal (*e.g.* leaden cylinders) are found. Coins are sometimes found among the ashes ; failing these, an earthenware urn can be dated by its shape and fabric, and it is almost always accompanied by vessels of various kinds constituting a " grave-group," which is often susceptible of accurate dating, as well as by other grave-goods. The grave may be a mere hole in the ground, or it may be a cist—an underground structure of stone slabs or tiles. Such a grave was probably almost always marked by a monument of some kind above ground, a standing tombstone or something more elaborate. But tombstones easily fall a prey to the vandalism of people in search of building materials, and the vast majority of Roman cremation-graves known to us have been found without anything above ground to mark their position. Sometimes the urn is lodged in a funeral monument standing above the ground ; in that case it occupies a chamber inside the monument.

An inhumation-burial consists of a grave containing the body, which is laid out at full length, on its back. The position tends to differentiate Roman inhumations from those of pre-historic date, in which the skeleton often lies on its side with its knees drawn up towards its chin ; on the other hand, the orientation may serve to differentiate them from those of the Christian period, which have their feet to the east, while in Roman inhumations, though the eastward position is quite common, there is no definite rule. Generally speaking, grave-goods of recognisably Roman date are found in Roman inhumation-burials : a coin in the skeleton's mouth—the passage money for the ferry across the Styx—earthen or other vessels, toilet articles, ornaments, and so forth. It is, however, so rare to find weapons in Roman graves, that when weapons of that date are found in a grave it may legitimately be called a barbarian grave (*e.g.* Fremersdorf, " Gräber der einheimischen

---

[1] The *columbarium*, a building full of pigeon-holes in which urns are placed, has not been found in this country.

Bevölkerung römischer Zeit in Köln," in *Prähist. Zeitschrift*, xviii, 283). The coffin is an optional feature. Wooden coffins, made of boards, were common, but perishable, and few have survived. Leaden coffins were often used ; they were frequently ornamented with scallop-shells, cable mouldings, and other patterns. Stone coffins are more often found than any other kind ; sometimes they are roughly finished, and evidently intended to be buried ; sometimes they take the form of ornamented sarcophagi, which were placed in a recess or chamber in the tomb, where they could be seen.[1]

Some graves are supplied with a pipe, affording communication between the deceased and his surviving friends. In graves of a certain type, the so-called " altar-tombs," this is a regular feature (Cagnat-Chapot, *Manuel d'archéologie romaine*, i, 340) ; libations to the dead being poured into the focus of the altar and descending by the pipe in the grave ; but in Britain, where two examples of " pipe-burial " are known (at Caerleon and Colchester ; Wheeler, *Ant. J.*, ix, 1-7), the altar above ground was absent, as it is in certain other cases of the sort, or else has been removed.

§ 2. THE MONUMENT

We now turn to the monument, *i.e.* the structure standing above ground-level to mark the place of the burial.

The simplest type of monument is the tombstone. This may vary from a shapeless slab, rudely cut with the name of the deceased, to an elaborately carved and inscribed stone. So far as the inscription is concerned, the reader is referred to the chapter on *Inscriptions*. With regard to the sculpture, it need only be said that it consists sometimes of a portrait of the deceased, sometimes of symbols of his occupation or of mortality ; for instance, a legionary soldier who had been in the fleet may have two dolphins and a trident on his tombstone (*C.I.L.*, vii, 185, in the British Museum, from Lincoln), or a

---

[1] The best representative collection of burials in Britain is that contained in *Roman London*, 153-169, where specimens of every type are described and illustrated. Much useful detail is given in Ward, *R.E.B.*, 136-149. Coffins of various kinds are figured in *B.M. Guide to Antiq. of R.B.*, 14-16, 101-102. Good examples of grave-groups are published in Westell, *Roman and pre-Roman Antiquities in Letchworth Museum*.

smith the implements of his trade (*Eph. Epigr.*, ix, 1077, at Chester), while elsewhere we find lions, sphinxes, etc., or merely decorative patterns. A special motive is the "sepulchral banquet," in which the deceased is shown reclining on a couch with a table beside him, on which are meat and drink ; often a slave stands to serve him.[1]

The next type of monument in order of simplicity is the earthen mound or barrow. Here we may quote Mr. O. G. S. Crawford (*Wessex from the Air*, 16), who says : " The peculiar features of Roman barrows would appear to be these :—

1. The sides are steep and the mound conical in shape.
2. The mound is sometimes surrounded at the base by a small bank placed *inside* the ditch.
3. They are often placed in a row by the side of Roman roads or tracks.
4. Single examples are often found near Roman villas."

He goes on to enumerate various examples ; *e.g.* the Six Hills near Stevenage, Herts., a group of steep-sided conical barrows beside what is probably a Roman road, each encircled by a bank ; the Bartlow Hills, with high conical profile and Roman remains ; a group of four beside the Roman road along the top of the Mendips ; a group of three close to Badbury camp, beside the Old Sarum-Dorchester Roman road ; and a large isolated example, 15 feet high, near Kingston Lisle in Berkshire. He concludes : " It is now possible for the first time to recognise some barrows at sight as being Roman. When they appear conical in profile . . . their Roman age and character may now be regarded as proven. When barrows occur in a row by the side of a Roman road, the same conclusion will probably be found correct, even if characteristic structural features are absent " (*op. cit.*, 17). A large Roman barrow on Mersea Island, 110 feet in diameter and 22 feet high, has been excavated, and found to contain a nucleus built of tiles and mortar, in which was a chamber 18 inches square and $21\frac{1}{2}$

---

[1] For examples of tombstones, see any collection of inscriptions ; *e.g.* *Roman London*, 170-174 ; *V.C.H. Somerset*, i (Bath) ; *A.*, lxxi (Cirencester) ; Ward, *R.E.B.*, 149-152 ; *Germania Romana*[2], part iii (a fine collection of examples from Germany). The best collection of illustrations for Britain is Bruce, *Lapidarium Septentrionale* (Newcastle, 1875), with admirable woodcuts, but the text is unsatisfactory by modern standards. Haverfield, "The Sepulchral Banquet on Roman Tombstones," *A.J.*, lvi, 326-331.

inches high, containing a globular glass urn in a cubical leaden casket (Haverfield, *R.B. in* 1913, 42-43 ; *R.B. in* 1914, 43 ; Crawford, *Antiquity*, i, 431).

The most elaborate kind of monument is the masonry tomb. This may be either rectangular or circular in plan. The rectangular tomb may have had various kinds of superstructure : it may have resembled a large altar like the tomb of Fabius Alpinus in the British Museum (*B.M. Guide to Antiq. of R.B.*, 16), or it may have been a little building resembling a house or temple, or it may have been a mausoleum like the famous examples at Saint-Rémy in Provence, or Igel near Trier, or one of the smaller tombs of which there are many in France and Germany and Italy (Cagnat-Chapot, *Manuel d'archéologie romaine*, i, 342-353 ; *Germania Romana*², part iii). In Britain the foundations of such tombs are not uncommon (*cf.* for example, *A.*, xxii, 336 ; xxxvi, 120 ; Bruce, *Roman Wall* ³, 330), but in no case have we enough left to reconstruct the original monument.

The circular tomb (Cagnat-Chapot, *op. cit.*, 353-356) is a development of the barrow. The conical earthen mound is rendered more substantial and impressive by surrounding it with a retaining wall at its base, so that the cone stands on a masonry drum ; and this drum may rise to any required height, so as to form in itself the whole tomb (the classical example is the tomb of Caecilia Metella on the Appian Way), and may be enriched with architectural ornament. Plain circular foundations for the drum of a tomb of this type exist, *e.g.* at Pulborough (*Sussex Arch. Coll.*, xi, 141 ; 60 feet external diameter, wall 11½ feet thick), and High Rochester (now destroyed ; Bruce, *Wall, loc. cit.*). A more elaborate type, with buttresses round the outside, perhaps merely to resist the thrust of the earth, but perhaps forming a base for columns, is exemplified at Keston (Fig. 36 *b* ; *A.*, xxii, 336 ; 30 feet external diameter, wall 3 feet thick, with a doorway possibly indicating that the interior was not filled with earth). The most elaborate type has a skeleton of masonry inside it, designed partly to consolidate the drum and partly to support some heavy object —a statue or the like—on the top of the cone. The only British example is at West Mersea (Fig. 36 *a*), where the masonry ring, 65 feet in diameter, has twelve buttresses externally and six walls, radiating like the spokes of a wheel from a central hollow hexagonal structure, inside. Mr. A. W. Clapham has shown (*A.J.*, 1922, 93-100) that it falls into line with a group of circular buildings with "cart-wheel" plans, all derived from the Mausoleum of Augustus, and all certainly tombs; the closest

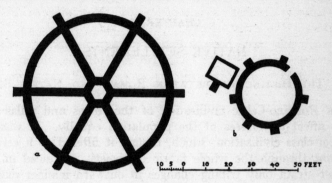

FIG. 36.—TOMBS.

(*a*) West Mersea, Essex. 40 feet to 1 inch = 1 : 480. (*b*) Keston, Kent.

parallel to the West Mersea building is a tomb on the Via Appia, outside Rome.

Reference may here be made to the walled cemeteries of which several examples have been found in Kent (Springhead, Lockham, Sittingbourne, etc.; see forthcoming account in *V.C.H. Kent*).

CHAPTER X

NATIVE SETTLEMENTS

§ 1. The Distinction between Roman and Native Sites

THE Romano-Celtic civilisation of the towns and villas did not affect all classes of the population equally. It was an upper-class civilisation, which, though it filtered to a certain extent through the whole fabric of society, produced in the lower strata only trifling changes in outward manner of life. How far these were accompanied by changes in thought, religion, education, legal status, and so forth, this is not the place to inquire. In the main, the position laid down by Haverfield in his *Romanisation of Roman Britain* (ed. 1, 1906 ; ed. 4, edited by Sir George Macdonald, 1922) still holds good ; but a certain change of emphasis is now needed on the subject of " the dwellings of the peasant poor " (*op. cit.*, ed. 4, 45). Haverfield was concerned to point out that even here the traces of Romanisation were definite and unmistakable. He was right, and his contention is now accepted by every one who is competent to judge. But there is another side to the question, which later research has tended to emphasise ; namely, that these traces are very slender, and that, although " there is no discernible breach in the scale " (*ibid.*, 46), yet the scale runs down to vanishing point.

For practical purposes a division can be made on an architectural basis between Roman and native settlements. From this point of view a Roman settlement means either a military site or a town, large or small, where the houses are built in the manner described in Chapter VI, or a villa, as defined in Chapter VII. There are hundreds of settlements of Roman date in Britain which conform to none of these types. They include farms which, although they possess rude hypocausts and use a few Samian vessels, belong architecturally not to the type of the villa but to the type of the hut. They include villages which, however many features of Roman origin they may present, are still architecturally Celtic villages, clusters of huts and not groups of houses. When we approach the lower end of the scale we reach settlements only distinguishable by a single sherd or two of certainly Roman pottery from prehistoric sites ; and vanishing point is reached when we find sites resembling these but lacking even the shred of evidence that demonstrates their Roman date. On the Ordnance Survey Map of Roman Britain (second edition) an attempt has been made to enter all known villages of this kind ; but it has been necessary to exclude from the map a large number of sites concerning which there is a moral certainty that they are of Roman date, on the ground that no Roman objects have been found in them, either because they possessed none, or because insufficient search has been made.

§ 2. VILLAGES

The number of native sites hitherto excavated is very small in proportion to the number of Roman. This is not because they are fewer ; it is because they have been in the past less interesting to antiquaries in search of " finds." Sites of this humble quality are attractive only to the excavator who approaches his work from a rigidly scientific point of view, in search, not of collector's specimens or *objets d'art*, but of knowledge. And this attitude is rare. Had it not been for the genius of a single man, the late General Pitt-Rivers, whose work of fifty years ago was animated by a spirit, and directed by methods, far in advance of his time and still appreciably in advance of ours, our accurate knowledge of Romano-British villages would to-day be non-existent ; for all other work on the subject owes its existence to his example or its instructive-ness to his results.

One of the best examples of a Romano-British village is Woodcuts in Dorset (Pitt-Rivers, *Excavations in Cranborne Chase*, i ; 1887). It contained as many as 95 pits, relics of wattle huts with floors sunk below the level of the ground, and was surrounded by a rampart and ditch. So far, the settlement is purely native in character. But these huts were in many cases walled with painted plaster like a Roman house, and some of them were even fitted with rude T-shaped hypocausts (*op. cit.*, 15, 29). There was, moreover, a tiny amphitheatre, 110 by 140 feet, with an arena 50 feet by 70 (*ibid.*, 23 ; *cf. supra*, ch. vi, § 5, and Fig. 26 *j*). The pottery and other relics make it clear that this village had existed before the Roman period, though perhaps not very long before ; and that it did

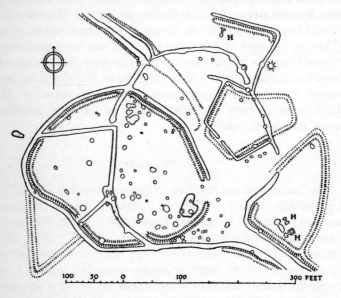

FIG. 37.—ROMANO-BRITISH VILLAGE, WOODCUTS COMMON, DORSET.

160 feet to 1 inch = 1 : 1920.

Banks are shaded : ditches are shown by double lines, pits are shown by rings.

H = Hypocaust.

not come into effective contact with Roman civilisation until some time after the conquest. It is noticeable that there are no brooches of the Continental first-century types which are so common at the strictly Roman sites in the south of England. Roman coins, too, become common at Woodcuts only in the early second century. In the third century the village was still flourishing, but in the fourth it seems to decay, and there is no evidence that it was inhabited in the later part of that century. The character of the occupation is profoundly peaceful. Great quantities of agricultural implements were found, but not a single weapon of any kind, not even hunting weapons. As for the extent of the Romanisation, it would hardly be true to say that Roman influences, once they had made their appearance, were predominant. General Pitt-Rivers found that the rampart surrounding the village was probably later than the time of Carausius (*ibid.*, 9), but it shows no trace of the influence of Roman fortification. Nor, in spite of the hypocausts and the painted plaster, do the huts show the influence of Roman house-planning. Even the humblest kind of strip house is wholly absent.

On the whole, Woodcuts is typical of the Wessex villages. Others are Rotherley (Pitt-Rivers, *op. cit.*, vol. ii), Casterley (*Wilts. Arch. Mag.*, xxxviii), Stockton Earthworks (*ibid.*, xliii), Cold Kitchen Hill (*ibid.*, xliv), and Upavon and Rushall Downs (*ibid.*, xlii ; I quote a few examples where recent excavation has taught us something of the history of the site). Rotherley is much like Woodcuts in its general character, but poorer and even less Romanised ; it has no hypocausts or painted plaster. Nor does there seem to be any evidence that it was inhabited after the end of the third century. Cold Kitchen Hill, also, seems to have been deserted before the end of the Roman period, in this case about the middle of the fourth century, and the same may be true of Casterley. The other sites named were inhabited down to the end of the century, and perhaps longer. The question how far, and why, these villages were abandoned in the latter part of the Roman period is one which has not yet been seriously discussed ; nor is it very much use discussing it until more facts have been collected by excavation.

A considerable group of Romano-British villages in Anglesey has been studied. The best known of these is Din Lligwy (*A.C.*, 1908). It seems to have been a foundation of the third century on the site of an earlier and larger village ; and although most of its houses are wholly un-Roman round huts, others are more or less rectangular, and the wall that surrounds the whole village is laid out in a polygonal shape whose straight sides are no doubt a testimony to Roman influence. The same combination of round hut and straight walls reappears on the mainland at Rhostryfan (*A.C.*, 1922, 1923 ; Wheeler, *Prehist. and Rom.*

Wales, 264). Other Anglesey villages (*e.g.* Rhyddgaer with coins of the second and third centuries ; *A.C.*, 1861, 37 ; 1857, 218 ; Caerleb, with a rectangular plan and a coin of Postumus, *ibid.*, 1866, 209 ; 1908, 71 ; and others, *cf.* Wheeler, " Roman and Native in Wales," in *Trans. Hon. Soc. of Cymmrodorion*, 1920-1921), bear out the general inference that in this region the native settlements were coming under Roman influence in the second and third centuries.

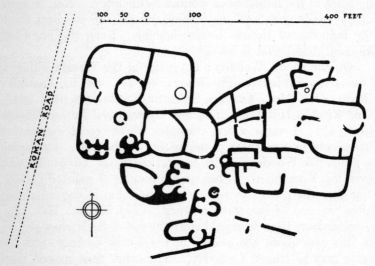

FIG. 38.—ROMANO-BRITISH VILLAGE, EWE CLOSE, WESTMORLAND.

200 feet to 1 inch = 1 : 2400.

The whole settlement is built in stone walling, shown in black. The houses are not sunk pit-dwellings, as on the dry chalk lands of the south, but stone beehive huts. The more or less quadrilateral enclosures were probably not roofed.

Even in the north of England and in Scotland we can trace the same process. In the north of England there are great numbers of so-called " British settlements " which, when excavated, betray their Roman date by one or two chance finds. Here we are very near the lower end of the scale of Romanisation. Apart from a potsherd or two, and perhaps a far-away reminiscence of Roman lay-out, these sites might easily be altogether pre-Roman, and in the almost complete absence of Roman influence they present a remarkable contrast with the Wessex villages. Examples are a lake-dwelling on the Costa beck near Pickering, where a single pot of Roman type was associated with a quantity of ware whose character was purely prehistoric (*J.R.S.*, xvi, 221) ; Ewe Close in Westmorland, where a few Roman potsherds appeared in a village of round stone huts (*C.W.*², viii, 355 ; ix, 295) ; Urswick Stone Walls in Lancashire, where a rectilinear enclosure seemed to form an addition of Roman date to a settlement that may have been earlier (*ibid.*, vii, 72), and *cf.* W. G. Collingwood (*Lake District History*, ch. ii, for a general discussion of these sites in one district). In Scotland the best example is Traprain Law in Haddingtonshire (*P.S.A. Scot.*, xlix, l, liv-lviii), where a site of strictly native type yielded considerable numbers of Roman objects.

§ 3. ISOLATED FARMS

The less Romanised population of Britain lived partly in villages and partly in isolated farms. On what principle these two types of settlement were distributed we do not know ; but it is certain that both existed. It is possible that many of the smaller so-called villages were really single farms in the sense that they consisted of one estate with a main dwelling-house and a number of cottages for labourers. In economic character though not in degree of Romanisation, these establishments resembled villas.

As an undoubted example of an isolated farm, the settlement on Rockbourne Down, Hants, may be mentioned (Heywood Sumner, *Excavations on Rockbourne Down*, 1914). An enclosure, pentagonal in shape and measuring 1100 by 700 yards, is surrounded by a wooden fence and a ditch whose rectilinear lay-out suggests Roman influence and whose construction is dated to the third century. The houses were mere wattle huts, as it seems, but they contained three rough hypocausts, one of them suitable for use in a bake-house and were surrounded by small ditches for draining away the surface-water. Coins showed that the site had been occupied from about the middle of the third century to after the middle of the fourth, and pottery told the same tale.

§ 4. FORTIFIED SITES

Almost all the settlements mentioned above were surrounded with walls or ditches and to that extent fortified. These fortifications have no military meaning. Their purpose is to keep out thieves and wild beasts. But there are other works of a defensive kind which are too strong and too elaborate to be altogether explained in this way. The great hill-forts of the pre-Roman period, of which we have numerous examples in Britain, were for the most part dismantled after the Roman conquest, if not before it ; Caesar's account of his own experience in Gaul shows how formidable they might be, and by the analogy of Mont Beuvray, whose inhabitants were removed to the newly-founded city of Autun in the neighbouring valley, we may be fairly certain that Dorchester was built to house the transplanted population of Maiden Castle, and that Wroxeter stood in the same relation to the hill-fort on the Wrekin, and Caerwent to that on the hill a mile to the north ; and something similar happened at other places. But in some instances the change from a hill-site to a valley-site was accomplished considerably before the Roman invasion, *e.g.* at Winchester and Chichester. On the other hand, these hill-forts were not entirely abandoned. The evidence of coins shows the people continued to live in Maiden Castle throughout the Roman occupation, and recent excavation has even suggested a possibility that the great earthworks of Cissbury may have been thrown up late in the Roman period (Toms, " The Cissbury Earthworks," in *Sussex Arch. Coll.*, lxvii).

Evidence of this kind becomes more definite in Wales. Here several strongly-walled hill-top towns have been partially excavated, with the result that they appear in many cases to have been either fortified or re-fortified in the Roman period. The hill-top town of Tre'r Ceiri, with its massive stone walls, is dated to the second century (Wheeler, *Roman and Native in Wales, cit.*, 55) ; in the similar site at Penmaenmawr no occupation has been detected earlier than A.D. 100 (*ibid.*, 61) ; Dinorben was rebuilt in the Roman period (*ibid.*, 64) ; and other examples are forthcoming. These are true fortifications, but not fortresses ; they would keep out not only thieves but armed bands of raiders, and yet their inhabitants, to judge from the

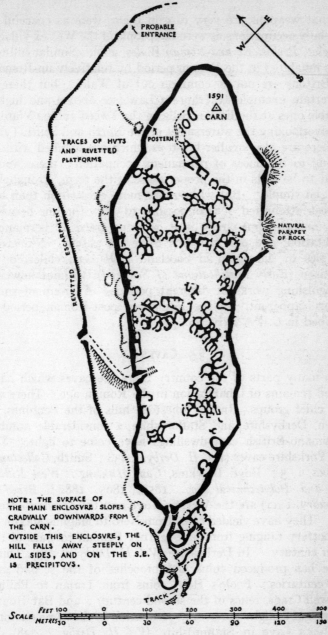

↑ PROBABLE
ENTRANCE

1591
△ CARN

TRACES OF HVTS
AND REVETTED
PLATFORMS

← POSTERN

REVETTED ESCARPMENT

NATVRAL
PARAPET
OF ROCK

NOTE: THE SVRFACE OF
THE MAIN ENCLOSVRE SLOPES
CRADVALLY DOWNWARDS FROM
THE CARN.
OVTSIDE THIS ENCLOSVRE, THE
HILL FALLS AWAY STEEPLY ON
ALL SIDES, AND ON THE S.E.
IS PRECIPITOVS.

TRACK ↗

Scale
Feet 100 · · · · 0 · · · · 100 · · · · 200 · · · · 300 · · · · 400 · · · · 500
Metres 30 · · · · 0 · · · · 30 · · · · 60 · · · · 90 · · · · 120 · · · · 150

Fig. 39.—Hill-top Town, Tre'r Ceiri, Carnarvonshire.

fact that weapons are very rare in them, were as peaceful in their daily occupations as were the people of the Wessex villages (Wheeler, *Prehistoric and Roman Wales*, 266). Similar hill-top towns inhabited in the Roman period by relatively un-Romanised Britons are not so common out of Wales ; but there is one certain example at Traprain Law (see above) and highly probable ones at the Eildon Hills on the Tweed and on Warden Hill, overlooking the watersmeet of the North and South Tyne.

There are also smaller hill-tops which are fortified without seeming to be places of permanent occupation ; these would appear to be forts in the proper sense of the term, strongholds pure and simple. But without far more excavation than has yet been attempted, it is impossible to draw the line between a hill-fort with hut circles in it, showing traces of permanent inhabitation, and one in which these are absent. Numerous examples in the south of Scotland have been collected by Christison (*Early Fortifications of Scotland*), without however distinguishing works of different periods. A group of small hill-forts apparently of the Roman or post-Roman period is described in *C.W.*², xxiv, 78.

§ 5. Caves

In many parts of the country there are caves which have yielded remains of inhabitation in the Roman age. There are three chief groups. In the limestone hills of the Pennines, in Craven, Derbyshire, and Staffordshire, a considerable number of Romano-British cave-dwellings have come to light. The chief Yorkshire caves (*V.C.H. Derby*, i, 238 ; Smith, *Collectanea Antiqua*, i, 5 ; Boyd Dawkins, *Cave Hunting ; West Riding Geol. and Polytechnical Soc.*, 1859, 1865, 1882 ; *Bradford Antiquary*, 1911) are the Victoria Cave and the Dowkerbottom Cave. They have yielded coins from Nero to Magnus Maximus, and pottery ranging from first-century Samian to ware of the fourth century. In Derbyshire (*V.C.H. Derby*, i, 233), Thirst House has produced coins and brooches of the second and third centuries ; Poole's Hole, coins from Trajan to Philip ; Cresswell Crags, relics of the second century ; and Bat House, evidence of a slight temporary occupation in the same century. At Thor's Cave in Staffordshire (*V.C.H. Derby*, i, 238) the occupation lasted a long time.

In the Mendips there are several caves—Wookey Hole, Gough's Cavern at Cheddar, Uphill, Burrington—which yield Roman remains mostly of a late date. Thus at Wookey Hole there is a certain amount of occupation throughout the period, but the coins suddenly become common in the reigns of Valentinian I and Gratian (*A.*, lxii, 565 ; *V.C.H. Som.*, i, 356).

A few caves on the Devonshire coast deserve mention, of which the chief is Kent's Hole, near Torquay ; here Samian and other Roman pottery has been found, and coins of Valentinian (*V.C.H. Derby*, i, 240).

CHAPTER XI

INSCRIPTIONS

§ 1. INTRODUCTORY

THE Latin alphabet was introduced into Britain before the Roman invasions, and used by the moneyers who struck coins for the British kings ; but we do not know of its being put to any other use in this country till the conquest ; nor has any example been found, on this side of the Channel, of the Celtic inscriptions in Latin letters that are known in Gaul. When the Romans came to Britain they brought with them the habit of setting up inscribed stones as religious dedications, as records of building work, as tombstones and as milestones, and also of inscribing weapons, domestic utensils, pigs and ingots of metal, and so forth, with the name of the owner. Many kinds of utensil, and also bricks and tiles, were often stamped in addition with the name of the maker or makers. This indicates a widespread knowledge of reading and writing ; but it is noteworthy that inscriptions, which are extremely common in the first and second centuries, become rarer in the third and almost cease in the fourth, with the exception of tombstones ; these go on, among the Romanised Britons, far beyond the date of the Anglo-Saxon settlements, in Wales and other western districts.

The value of inscriptions as historical material is so great that it can hardly be exaggerated. Apart from modern forgeries, which are rare and in general easily detected, they are contemporary and authoritative documents, whose text if legible cannot be corrupt, and whose cumulative value, in the hands of scholars accustomed to handling them in the mass, is astonishing. They are the most important single source for the history and organisation of the Roman Empire.

§ 2. TECHNIQUE

Roman inscriptions are always cut in capital letters, but these may be either " monumental " or " cursive." Monumental lettering, at the beginning of our period, is stiff and severe, but shows on the average a high degree of elegance and good taste ; as the period advances, a tendency towards the florid and picturesque shows itself, and ligatures or combined letters, rare in the first century, become very common and often very complicated in the third. Cursive lettering consists of the monumental alphabet modified by adaptation to the rapid use of the stylus or brush. It is seen in its purity in scribbles on tiles, etc., but it influences monumental lettering, because the mason cuts the letters as they have been chalked for him, perhaps carelessly, on the stone. It is common, especially in the fourth century, to see an inscription degenerate into cursive forms towards its end. For similar reasons, early inscriptions by unskilled masons are akin to late work in style, and have not the characteristics of the best contemporary monumental work. In good monumental work the strokes of the letters are always cut with a chisel to a V section ; this does not apply to rough work, which is done with a punch or a mason's pick.

Words are abbreviated at will by docking their ends to taste, and when so abbreviated they show the plural by doubling the last letter ; but the medieval system of abbreviation, by leaving out letters in the middle of a word, is coming into use during our period, and seems first to assert itself as a very rare provincialism in rude unskilled work perhaps as early as the second century. A word may be divided at the end of a line in almost any desired way. Between the words stops are usually, but not always, placed ; they are always central to the letters, not level with their foot like a modern full-stop, and in good work they generally consist of a small triangle or a leaf. In rougher work a dot is sufficient, or the stop is omitted altogether. Where the end of a word comes at the end of a line the stop is usually left out, unless it is required to fill up space. Occasionally stops are placed at the end of every syllable.

Britain is remarkable for the disproportionate quantity of rough and unskilled work in its inscriptions This is partly because it was the province remotest from the centres of civilisation ; partly because the inscriptions of the civilised south have mostly perished and those which survive mostly belong to the north, where they were cut by half-barbarian soldiers ; and partly because the grits and sandstones of England do not readily lend themselves to fine mason's work.

§ 3. RELIGIOUS DEDICATIONS

These are generally altars ; or they may be bases for statues, portions of temples, or inscribed votive offerings.

An altar may be a few inches high, or anything up to five feet or more. It was normally placed on a stand, foundation-offerings in the shape of coins being laid under its corners ; but, when found, altars have almost always been dismantled, and often deliberately defaced, hidden, or turned to some non-religious use. An altar consists of three members : a capital, on the top of which is a hollow " focus " in the centre, to hold a fire and receive offerings, and a " bolster " or roll on either side, conventionally representing bundles of firewood ; below this, a shaft called the " die," and a base at the bottom, generally matching the capital in size. The whole is almost invariably cut out of a single stone.

On the die, sometimes overlapping to the capital or the base, is the inscription. This was generally both cut and painted, sometimes painted only ; errors in cutting could be corrected in the painting, a consideration applying to all types of lapidary inscriptions. The essential parts of such an inscription are the name of the deity or deities, in the dative ; the name of the donor, in the nominative ; and a verb signifying " dedicates." The deity may be one of the classical gods or goddesses (Aesculapius, Apollo, Bellona, Ceres, Diana, Hercules, Juno, Jupiter—generally in the form I.O.M. for *Iovi Optimo Maximo* —Mars, Minerva, Neptune, Silvanus, Venus, Volcanus, or the like), with or without an epithet such as *sanctus*, *invictus*, *conservator ;* or one of those personified powers which were constantly tending to swell the bulk of the Roman pantheon, such as the Genius of a place or a person or an institution, Bonus Eventus, Fatum Bonum, Fortuna, Discipulina, Nemesis, Numen Augusti (the godhead of the divine Emperor), Salus,

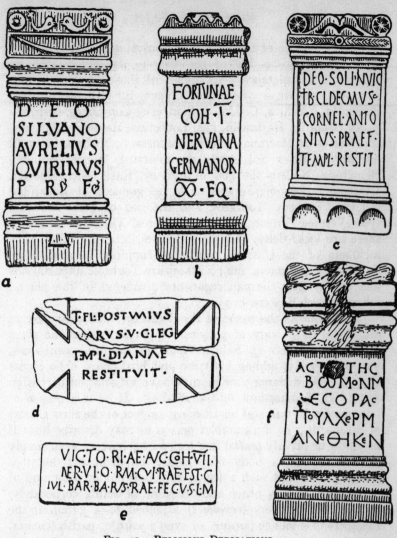

FIG. 40.—RELIGIOUS DEDICATIONS.

(a) (Near Stanhope in Weardale.) Altar. "To the god Silvanus, Aurelius Quirinus, prefect, made (this)."

(b) (Birrens.) Altar. "To Fortune; Nerva's First Cohort of Germans, 1,000 strong, with a cavalry contingent."

(c) (Rudchester.) Altar. "To the Invincible Sun-God, Tiberius Claudius Decimus Cornelianus Antonius, prefect, restored this temple" (*i.e.* the Mithraeum).

(d) (Caerleon.) Slab. "Titus Flavius Postumius Varus, senator and legate, restored this temple to Diana."

(e) (Great Chesters.) Base for a statue. "To Imperial Victory, the Seventh Cohort of Nervii, commanded by Gaius Julius Barbarus, prefect, made this and paid its vow."

(f) (Corbridge.) Altar. "Thou seest me, an altar of Astarte; Pulcher set me up."

Victoria ; or one of the very numerous non-Roman divinities whom the religious life of the Empire welcomed with its characteristic tolerance. Examples of these, in Britain, are Ancasta, Anociticus and Antenociticus, Barrex, Belatucader, Brigantia, Cocidius, Condates, Contrebis, Corotiacus, Garmangabis, Grannus, Harimella, Isis, Loucetius, Maponus, Matunus, the Matres or Matronae (Mother-goddesses), Mithras (with all his various titles, Sol, saecularis, invictus), Mogon, Mountis, Nemetona, Nodens the god of Lydney, Ratis, Ricagambeda, Rigisamus, Saegon, Serapis, Sul the goddess of Bath, the Sulevae, Tanarus, Toutates, and the god or gods variously spelt Veteres, Viteres, Vitires, Hueteres, Vhiteres. Many of these are local Celtic gods or goddesses, often identified with members of the classical pantheon (Iuppiter Tanarus, Mars Cocidius, Sul Minerva, etc.) ; others are Teutonic importations due to the Low German regiments quartered in the north ; others are of Eastern origin.

Then follows the name of the dedicator. This may be an individual or a body of persons. If an individual, he gives his name in brief—Q. Fabius Victor, or the like—sometimes, but very rarely, adding his tribe and birthplace, if he comes from a great distance ; or he may have a Latinised barbarian name like Nemnogenus or Gamidiahus. If he is a person of importance, he will add his title, *e.g.* prefect of the First Cohort of Spaniards ; or if a humbler person he may describe himself as officer or private (*miles*) in a legion or cohort, or even simply " sculptor." If a body of persons, the dedicator describes itself as such and such a legion or cohort under command of so-and-so ; or any other body capable of acting corporately, such as the hunters (*venatores*) attached to a garrison, the members of a village (*vicani*), or even a ward or parish (*vicinia*) in a town.

The dedication generally ends with an abbreviated formula like D. (*dat*), P. (*posuit*), F. (*fecit*), D.D. (*dono dedit*), REST. (*restituit*), or, most common of all, V.S.L.M. (*votum solvit libens merito*, " paid a vow willingly and deservedly ").

It is assumed that the object dedicated is obvious to the reader ; but it may be mentioned—*aram, templum, signum* (statue)—and a fuller description may be given of what exactly the dedicator did : he " had the temple rebuilt and repainted,"

PLATE I

FIG. 41
ALTAR TO COCIDIUS FROM BEWCASTLE

FIG. 42
ALTAR TO MARS AND NEMETONA
AT BATH

or " built it from the ground," or the like. It is also optional
to add more fully why he did it—as the result of an oracle or
dream or command of the gods, or to celebrate a victory or
safe journey or successful hunting expedition, or in gratitude
for recovery from disease. And the date, in terms of consulships, is sometimes added.

§ 4. HONORIFIC INSCRIPTIONS

These are usually cut on the bases of statues to eminent
persons ; they include the name and titles of the person
honoured, the name of the person or body responsible for the
statue, and the reasons for its erection. They are rare in this
country, but a remarkable example at Caerwent (Fig. 43 *d*)
records the dedication of a statue " by the Republic of the
Silures, by order of its Senate "—an important light upon local
self-government in Roman Britain. Some inscriptions naming
emperors, which may be milestones (§ 5, below), perhaps belong
to this class.

§ 5. MILESTONES

These almost always recorded, often elaborately, the name
and titles of the emperor, and sometimes added a numeral with
or without the name of the place from which the miles were
measured. They are generally columnar stones, squarish or
oval or round in section, 4 to 6 feet high ; the inscription
is often very roughly cut, and frequently gives the date in
terms of the tribunician power and other titles of the emperor
under whom the road was built or repaired.

§ 6. BUILDING RECORDS

These are inscriptions, varying in size from great slabs many
feet long to single stones a few inches each way, recording the
erection or repair of buildings. When a fort, a gateway, a
public building of any kind, was either constructed or exten-
sively restored, such an inscription, sometimes highly ornate,
was set up in a prominent place, such as over the main entrance.
The more ambitious specimens are often very elaborate ; the
simplest do no more than name the working-party responsible
for this part of the structure.

FIG. 43.—INSCRIPTIONS FROM THE TWO WALLS AND ELSEWHERE.

(a) (Old Kilpatrick.) Distance-slab from the Antonine Wall. "To the
    Emperor Caesar Titus Aelius Hadrianus ANTONINUS PIUS, august,
    pious, father of his country, a vexillation of the Twentieth Valerian
    Victorious Legion built 4,411 feet of the Wall."

(b) (Carvoran.) Centurial stone from Hadrian's Wall. "The century of
    Claudius built 30½ paces."

(c) (Milking Gap.) Milecastle-slab. "The Emperor Caesar Hadrian Augus-
    tus's Second Augustan Legion, under Aulus Platorius Nepos, proprae-
    torian legate."

(d) (Caerwent.) Base of statue "to (Claudius) Paulinus, legate of the Second
    Augustan Legion, proconsul of Gallia Narbonensis, imperial proprae-
    torian legate at Gallia Lugudunensis; set up by the commonwealth of
    the tribe of the Silures, by decree of their tribal senate."

(e) (Wroxeter.) Tombstone. "Marcus Petronius, son of Lucius, of the
    Menenian tribe, from Vicenza; aged 38; a soldier of the Fourteenth
    Legion 'Gemina'; served 18 years; he was a standard-bearer; he
    lies here."

A large building-record contains the following elements.
First come the name and titles of the emperor ; in the nominative, if he or rather his representatives are the actual builders,
or the dative, if the building is regarded as erected in his honour,
or the ablative, if the intention is merely to state that it is
erected in his reign. Or the text may begin with the name
of a god, if the building is a temple ; or with a formula like
" in honour of the Divine House " (*i.e.* Imperial family) which
however has not yet been seen in this country. The emperor's
titles are generally given very simply in the early period, and
get more and more elaborate ; early third-century emperors
were fond of recording their entire pedigree on such occasions
—their adoptive pedigree, of course, not their actual one. If
the emperor is not the builder, here comes the name of the
person or body erecting the structure, and this is followed by
a description of the building—*portam cum turribus, horreum,
balneum*, or the like. If it is a reconstruction, we are told that
it was previously ruinous, *vetustate corruptum* or *dilapsum*, or
burnt down, *vi ignis exustum*, or hitherto unfinished, *iam pridem
a solo coeptum ;* never that it was destroyed by the act of the
emperor's enemies. If it is a new building, there may be a
phrase like *a solo* qualifying the verb (*facere, perficere, aedificare,*
etc., or in the case of reconstruction *restituere, renovare*, etc.),
with which the whole generally ends. If the emperor is the
builder, we are told that he acted *per* so-and-so, his representative ; and the names of the people actually directing the
work are sometimes added.

Building-records are often far less elaborate than this. Sometimes the emperor is omitted altogether, and the text begins
with a statement of the building's purpose : thus we find
" Aqueduct for the second *Ala* of Asturians, under Ulpius
Marcellus, Imperial propraetorian governor," at Chesters. And
where work was done by legionary soldiers, working in separate gangs of a century, each gang signed its own section of
building by cutting " Century of so-and-so " on a walling-
stone, with or without a numeral showing, in paces or feet,
the length of the section. This practice, which grew up in
connection with building the ramparts of forts, was applied to
the Wall of Hadrian, and some hundreds of " centurial stones "
from that structure are still preserved (Fig. 43 *b*). The Antonine

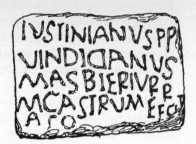

IMPP·VALERIANVS·ET·GALLIEN·S
AVGG·F·VAERINVS·N·BILISS·M·S
CÆS·COHORTI·VII·CNTVRIS·ASO
LO·RESTIT·VN·PR·D·EST·CVM·N·BM
V·C·LEGATVM·AVG·G·PR·PR·ET
VITVIASIVM·LÆT·N·N·VM·EG·EG
II·AVG·CVRATE·DOMIT·POTENTIN
PRAEE·LEG·EIVSDEM·C·

a

IVSTINIANVS·PP
VINDICIANVS
MAS·BIERIVR·R
M·CASTRVM·R·
A·SO EFCT

b

IMP·CÆSAR·M·ANTONIVS
GORDIANVS·P·F·AVG
PRINCIPIA·ET·ARMAMEN
TARIA·CON·LAPSA·RESTITV
IT·PER·MECILVM·F·SC·M·LEG
AVG·PR·PR·CVRANTEM·AVR
QVIRINO·PR·COH·I·L·GOR

c

d

....MAXI
CoS·III·M·E·M·NÆL·ANTNIN·PO
CoS·II·AVG
PORTAM·CVM·MVRIS·VETVSTATE·DI
LPSIS·IVSSV·ALEN·SENEC·INSV
CoS·CVRANTE·ODEAN·ADVENTR
NG·NN·CoH·I·VANG·N·Co·EO
CVM·ÆMSALVIAN·R·
SV·AN·GLO·REST·

FIG. 44.

Wall was built not by centuries but by vexillations working on longer sections, and the ends of these sections were marked by " distance-slabs," rather ornate in character, recording the name of Antoninus Pius, the vexillation that had done the work, and the length of the section (Fig. 43 a). For the methods of dividing up the work on the two Walls, see Chapter V, sections 2 and 3.

§ 7. TOMBSTONES

The Twelve Tables forbade burial within the city ; and in all Roman sites it is usual to find the tombs arranged along the roads outside the inhabited area. In a small place there was often one special quarter used as a cemetery (the Alyscamps at Arles is an example of this on a large scale) ; but in a large place the burials tend to radiate round the inhabited area. This gave rise to the practice of building large tombs and setting up large tombstones, which are sometimes fine works of art. In Britain, the tombstone is generally a large slab, often gable-topped, and often more or less elaborately decorated ; sometimes it has a full-length figure of the deceased above an inscribed panel ; sometimes the standing figure is replaced by a figure lying on a couch and served with food and drink at

---

FIG. 44.—BUILDING INSCRIPTIONS.

(a) (Caerleon.) Valerian, Gallienus and Valerian junior "restored from the ground centurial barracks for the Seventh Cohort, by Desticius Juba, senator, imperial propraetorian legate, and Vitulasius Laetinianus, legate of the Second Augustan Legion ; work in charge of Domitius Potentinus, prefect of the said legion."

(b) (Ravenscar.) " Justinianus, praepositus (and ?) Vindicianus (a blundered phrase) built this fort from the ground."

(c) (Lanchester.) Gordian " restored the headquarters and armouries, fallen into disrepair, by Maecilius Fuscus, imperial propraetorian legate ; work in charge of Marcus Aurelius Quirinus, prefect of Gordian's Own First Cohort of Lingones."

(d) (Risingham.) Severus " Adiabenicus Parthicus Maximus," consul three times, and Caracalla, consul twice [and Geta, whose name is erased]. " The first cohort of Vangiones, a thousand strong and furnished with a contingent of cavalry, with its commanding officer Aemilius Salvianus, .tribune, restored from ground-level this gate and these walls, decayed through age, under the superintendence of Oclatinius Adventus, procurator of our lords the Emperors."

a little table, the so-called "sepulchral banquet" scene (Figs. 46, 47). Occasionally in Britain, and often on the Continent, the head and shoulders of the deceased are alone represented, and there are other varieties of funeral portraiture. Symbolic elements often appear in the sculpture ; a lion, signifying the destructive power of death, is sometimes shown devouring a human head ; sometimes a bird is held in the hand of the deceased. A mounted soldier may be represented, in a common Greco-Roman fashion, riding victoriously over an enemy (Fig. 45).

The inscription generally begins with the formula *Dis Manibus*, " to the gods of the underworld." Then follows the name of the deceased in the nominative, genitive, or dative ; then his age. This is the usual simplest form. In place of *Dis Manibus* we may find *memoriae* or some other initial formula ; the name may be supplemented by various descriptions and titles ; the age is often meticulously given in years, months, and days ; we may be told who put up the stone, a widow or a son or an heir or a freedman, or even the deceased himself in his lifetime ; a phrase of commendation may be added (" to his beloved wife," " to his deserving master," or the like), and the whole may conclude with a phrase like H.S.E. (Fig. 43 *e* ; *hic situs est*, common in the first century and disappearing soon after A.D. 100), or S.T.T.L. (*sit tibi terra levis*).

Tombstones are fairly common which record a large number of names, often of one family or one burial-club. These were no doubt erected on large tombs ; they do not necessarily indicate simultaneous death in an epidemic or the like.

When the deceased is a Roman citizen, he is often given his full name ; *Q. Valerius, C.f.* (= *Gaii filius*) *Maec.* (= *Maecia tribu*), and his birthplace may be added. But this practice dies out at an early period. In the case quoted there is no *cognomen* (*cf.* Fig. 43 *e*) ; this also is an early characteristic, and the cognomen is generally present after about A.D. 70. The formula then runs thus : " *L. Caiatius L. F. Gal. Sextinus Lug.*" (Lucius Caiatius Sextinus, son of Lucius, of the Galerian tribe, from Lyons). A soldier's tombstone gives, beside his rank, the length of his service in the army, under the heading *stip(endiorum) XX*, or the like, " he served twenty years."

PLATE II

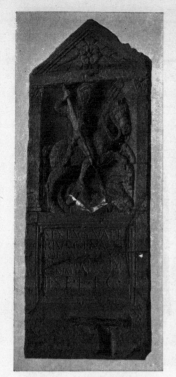

FIG. 45
TOMBSTONE AT CIRENCESTER

FIG. 46
TOMBSTONE IN THE YORKSHIRE MUSEUM,
YORK

PLATE III

FIG. 47
TOMBSTONE AT SOUTH SHIELDS

FIG. 48
MILESTONE FROM STAINMORE

At a late period the use of stone sarcophagi became fashion-
able, and these tended to oust the earlier tombstone. The inscriptions upon them are constructed in the same manner.

§ 8. OTHER CLASSES OF INSCRIPTIONS

Official documents recording legal enactments, etc., are
hitherto unknown in this country ; but the military diploma
is a type of inscription directly emanating from the emperor.
This is a double plate of bronze, to be folded up and worn on
the person, recording the grant to time-expired auxiliary soldiers
of citizenship " and the right of marriage with the wives whom
they had at the time of the said grant, or whom they should,
if then unmarried, thereafter marry, provided one man marry
one woman only." The diploma was dated and bore the name
of the emperor and the regiments to which the grant was made ;
each copy further bore the name of the individual soldier to
whom it was issued.

Equally official are the stamps on pigs or ingots of metal,
recording the name of the emperor under whom the mine concerned was being worked as crown property ; to this is sometimes added, on the pigs of lead which were produced in great
numbers in Britain, the legend *Brit. ex arg(entariis)*, " British
lead, from the silver-works," indicating that the silver had been
extracted from it, and sometimes the name of the district :
e.g. Degeangli, the Flintshire lead-mining region, or Lutud.,
an abbreviated form of a place-name (Lutudarum) somewhere
near Matlock. Ingots of silver have been found bearing stamps
beginning *Ex of(ficina)*, " from the workshop of so-and-so " ;
several inscribed bronze ingots have been found in North Wales,
and some tin ingots stamped with the name Syagrius and the
Chi-Rho monogram of Christ, from the Thames near Battersea,
are in the British Museum. At Truro is another tin ingot,
found near Mawgan-in-Pydar, bearing an emperor's head of
fourth-century type and the letters DD.NN. (" our Lords," the
Emperors).

Small plates of metal with inscriptions are fairly common.
Some are charms or curses (Fig. 49 *a*) ; there are two at Bath,
one inscribed with an elaborate curse, written backwards,
apparently against somebody who " stole Vilbia from me,"
and the other scrawled with meaningless scratches by a person

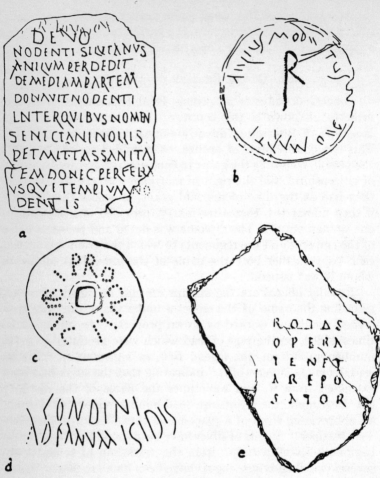

FIG. 49.—INSCRIPTIONS, NOT ON STONE.

(a) (Lydney.) Curse, on a metal tablet. "To the god Nodens. Silvianus has lost a ring, and dedicated half (*i.e.* of its value) to Nodens. Among those who are called Senicianus, permit no health until he bring it to the temple of Nodens."

(b) (Bosence.) Pewter cup, inscribed, "I, Aelius Modestus, dedicate this to the god Mars." In the centre, R.

(c) (Caerleon.) Leaden disk, to be nailed on a box or the like. "Century of Vibius Proculus."

(d) (London.) Graffito on jug. "London, at the temple of Isis."

(e) (Cirencester.) Square word, scratched on wall plaster. "Arepo the sower holds the wheels carefully."

who wanted to utter a similar curse but could not write. Some
are dedications to deities ; others objects to be fastened upon
leather jerkins and bearing the name of the soldier who owned
them. There are also small bronze castings with pierced or
openwork lettering, sometimes merely wishing " good luck "
to the owner of the object decorated, sometimes with legends
less easy to understand.

Seals bearing the owner's name are sometimes found, and
we have great numbers of leaden sealings, stamped with legends
generally identifiable as the names of military units, which
may have served to seal up regimental property. Weights
often bear numerals, and a legend like *Caes. Aug.* may be present,
showing that the weight has been tested by government in-
spectors. The same government testing is recorded in the case
of the large bronze measure from Carvoran now at Chesters,
bearing the name of the Emperor Domitian and a certificate
as to its weight and capacity—the latter incorrect.

Fibulae, knives, and various domestic utensils are often
stamped with the maker's name ; and this fact, especially in
the case of pottery, affords evidence of the utmost value for
the state of manufacture and trade under the Empire. The
enormous distribution of such things as the lamps of Fortis,
an Italian potter, the brassware of the Cipii and Ansii, Cam-
panian manufacturers, and the red-glaze " Samian " pottery
first of Tuscany and then of Gaul, can only be mentioned in
passing. It is of interest, in connection with the question how
far education was diffused, to consider the vast number of
graffiti scratched on such objects by their owners, sometimes
consisting of a name, sometimes of a cross or other mark of
identification.

A special class of inscriptions is the stamps with which
apothecaries marked cakes of ointment for use on the eyes.
These " oculists' stamps " are little square tablets of stone
with the inscriptions cut neatly on the four edges : *Q. Iuli
Murrani melinum ad claritatem*, " Quintus Julius Murranus's
honey ointment for clearing the eyes " ; *L. Val. Latini evodes
ad cicatrices et aspritudin(em)*, " Lucius Valerius Latinus's
scented ointment for scars and roughness."

Tiles are stamped by the maker, whether a legion, an auxiliary cohort, the public authorities of a city, or a private firm ;

they also often bear unofficial inscriptions by the workmen who made them—*fecit tubulum Clementinus*, " Clementinus made this box-tile " ; . . . *puellam*, something about a girl ; *Primus fecit x*, " Primus has made ten tiles " ; *satis*, " enough ! " ; or a date or a name, or a bit of an alphabet ; or a tag of verse, or a comment on a fellow-workman's habits : *Austalis dibus xiii vagatur sibi cotidim*, " Austalis has been going off on his own every day this fortnight." Sometimes wet tiles were used in school, it seems, for writing-lessons, or else writing-lessons occupied the work-men in the tileries during the lunch hour ; at Caerleon some-one has written *Bellicianus* on a tile, and three other people of varying degrees of illiteracy have carefully copied it underneath. Scrawls on wall-plaster are not unknown ; at Caerwent some one scribbled something, now illegible, which moved some one else to write beneath it *puniamini*, " for shame ! " And at Cirencester a " square word " (Fig. 49 *e*) has been thus scratched. Its Roman date has been doubted, because this square word was a charm in the Middle Ages ; but the lettering is Roman enough. It seems to mean " Arepo the sower guides the wheels carefully." [1]

§ 9. CHRISTIAN INSCRIPTIONS

Archaeological evidence of Christianity in Roman Britain is exceedingly scanty. So far as inscriptions are concerned, we have nothing but a few examples of the Chi-Rho monogram (*e.g.* on various lamps ; on a stone in Chedworth villa ; on a mosaic pavement at Frampton ; on tin ingots from Battersea ; on a silver bowl from Corbridge ; [2] it is common on coins of the middle and late fourth century), and a few tombstones, recognised as Christian by the presence of distinctive formulae, notably the statement that the deceased lived " so many years, more or less " (*plus minus*), as if the exact length of his earthly pilgrimage were a matter of indifference. Curiously, the pagan

---

[1] *Clementinus, E.E.*, ix, 1292*b* ; *puellam, C.I.L.*, vii, 1259 ; *Primus, E.E.*, vii, 1143 ; *satis, E.E.*, ix, 1292*c* ; *Austalis, E.E.*, vii, 1141 ; *Bellicianus, C.I.L.*, vii, 1255 ; *puniamini, E.E.*, ix, 1015 ; *Arepo, ibid.*, 1001. For writing-tablets and examples of inscriptions on them, see ch. xvi.

[2] Some alleged cases are due to error. Thus, one supposed example on a piece of bronze at York is in fact a division on a scale marked with the numeral X.

formula *Dis Manibus* is not at first dropped ; but at a later period—after the Roman evacuation of Britain—it was supplanted by *Hic Jacet* or the like. One such stone is at Carlisle, another at Brougham, and a third comes from Risingham. There are no others. But there are very many belonging to the post-Roman period, when the Latin language and a certain amount of Roman civilisation survived in the country, pushed gradually westward by the Anglo-Saxon settlements. They are mostly found in Wales ; but there are several in Cornwall and the south-west, and two in Galloway. Only one has ever been found at a Roman site in the proper sense of the term, namely at Chesterholm close to Hadrian's Wall. Many of these post-Roman tombstones are bilingual, having a Celtic inscription cut in ogams along the edge ; but only one ogam inscription has been found at a true Roman site, namely at Silchester.[1]

§ 10. Inscriptions in Greek

Greek was much spoken and written by educated persons all over the Empire, and there are naturally some Greek inscriptions in Britain. Of those now to be seen in the country some have been imported from abroad by modern collectors ; but the following are quite certainly relics of Roman Britain : a tombstone from Brough-under-Stainmore (*E.E.*, vii, 952), altars from Chester (*C.I.L.*, vii, 8), Lanchester (*C.I.L.*, vii, 431 ; bilingual), and Corbridge (*C.I.L.*, vii, 97, Fig. 40*f*), a slab at Maryport (*ibid.*, p. 85), a pavement at Aldborough (*ibid.*, p. 66), a pair of bronze votive tablets at York (*ibid.*, p. 62), a scrap of bronze from near Charlbury (*E.E.*, ix, 1003), and a few rings and domestic utensils. A strip of gold from Carnarvon has a magic inscription upon it, part of which is Greek (*Segontium*, 130).

---

[1] Hübner, *Inscriptiones Britanniae Christianae*, is the only general account, but a bad one. Haverfield, " Early Northumbrian Christianity " (in *A.A.*³, xv, 22). Risingham : *C.I.L.*, vii, 1021. Carlisle : *E.E.*, ix, 1222. Brougham : *L.S.*, 814. Chesterholm : Haverfield, *op. cit.* Silchester : Haverfield, *Romanisation*, p. 82, with references.

§ 11. Abbreviations used in Inscriptions [1]

A	Adiutrix, ala, amicus, animo, annus, aprilis, ara, arma, Augustus, Aulus, Aurelius (-a), avus.	B	bene, beneficiarius, bonus.
AAVVGG	Augusti (2).	BB . FF	beneficiarii.
AC, ACT	actarius.	BB . MM	bene merentes.
AD(I)	Adiutrix.	B . COS	beneficiarius consularis.
ADIAB	Adiabenicus.	B . F	beneficiarius.
ADL	adlectus.	B . F . COS	beneficiarius consularis.
ADN	adnepos.	B . M	bene merenti.
AE(L)	Aelius (-a).	B . PR	beneficiarius praefecti.
AED	aedes, aedilis.	B . Q	bene quiescat.
AEDIF	aedificavit.	BR	Breuci, Brittones, Britannia.
AEM	Aemilius (-a).	BRAC	Bracaraugustani.
AEQ	eques.	BRIT	Britannicus.
AER	aera (= stipendia).	B . R . P . N	bono rei publicae natus.
AET	aeternus.	BVC	buccinator.
AN(N)	annus.	C	Caesar, Gaius, calendae, castra, circiter, civis, civitas, Claudius (-a), cohors, colonia, condidit, coniux, consul, cuneus, custos.
A . N	Augustus noster.		
AN(I)	Aniensis.		
ANT	Antonius.		
AP(P)	Appius.	C . A	curam agens, custos armorum.
AP(R)	aprilis.		
AQ	aqua, aquarius, aquilifer.	CAES	Caesar.
		CAM(IL)	Camilia.
AQV	aquarius, aquilifer.	CC	Caesares, Gaii.
AR, ARM	armorum (custos).	C . C . A	cuius curam agit.
AR(N)	Arnensis.	CC . NN	Caesares nostri.
ARAB	Arabicus.	CC . VV	clarissimi viri.
ARC	architectus.	C . D	consulto decurionum.
ARMEN	Armeniacus.	C . E	coniux eius, curam egit.
A . S	a solo.	C . F	coniux fecit.
ASC	ascia.	C . F . C	coniux faciendum curavit.
AST	Astures.		
AV	Aulus, Aurelius (-a).	CHO	cohors.
AVG	Augustus (-a), augustalis.	CIV	civis, civitas, civitate.
		C . K	coniux carissimus.
AVGG	Augusti (2).	C . L	Gaii libertus.
AVGGG	Augusti (3).	CL	clarissimus, Claudius (-a).
AVG . L	Augusti libertus.		
AVG . N	Augustus noster.	CLA	Claudia, classis.
AVR	Aurelius (-a).	CL . BR	classis Britannica.

[1] A fuller list may be found in Cagnat, *Cours d'Epigraphie latine;* or Dessau, *Inscriptiones Selectae,* vol. iii, part i.   I have here given those likeliest to be useful.

C . N	Caesar noster.
CO	cohors, coniux.
COH	cohors.
COL	collina, collegium, colonia.
COLLIB	collibertus.
COMMIL	commilito.
CON	coniux.
CON . KAR	coniux carissimus.
CONS	consecravit, conservator.
CONS . P	consularis provinciae.
COR	cornicer, cornicularius, corona.
COS	consul, consules, consularis.
COSS	consules.
C . P, C . P . EST	cui praeest.
C . Q . V	cum quo vixit.
C . R	civis Romanus.
C . V	clarissimus vir.
CV	cura, curator.
CV . AR	custos armorum.
CVI . PR	cui praeest.
CVR	cura, curator, curavit.
CVR . AG	curam agens.
D	dat, decem, december, decretum, decurio, designatus, deus, dies, dignus, divus, Dolichenus, dominus, domo, donat, donum, duplicarius.
DAC	Dacus, Dacicus.
D . D	dono dedit, dedicavit, dii deae, domus divina.
DD . NN	domini nostri (2).
DDD . NNN	domini nostri (3).
DEC	december, Decimus, decretum, decurio.
DELM	Delmatae.
DIS . M	dis manibus.
D . M(.S)	dis manibus (sacrum).
D . N	dominus noster.

DO	domus, donum.
DOL	Dolichenus.
D . P	de pecunia, donum posuit.
D . P . S(.D)	de pecunia sua (dedit).
D . S	deus sanctus, deus Sol.
D . S . D	de suo dedit, de sententia decurionum.
D . S . F	de suo fecit.
D . S . P	de sua pecunia, de suo posuit.
DVPL	duplicarius.
E	eius, est, evocatus.
EE . QQ	equites.
EE . VV	egregii viri, eminentissimi viri.
EE . MM . VV	eminentissimi viri.
EM	emeritus.
EM . V	eminentissimus vir.
EQ	eques, equitata.
EQQ	equites.
EV	evocatus.
E . V . S	ex voto suscepto.
EXAC	exactus.
EX . AD . CAS	exactus ad Castoris.
EX . ARG	ex argentariis.
EX . AVCT	ex auctoritate.
EX . FIGL	ex figlinis.
EX . OF	ex officina.
EXPL	exploratores.
EX . T(EST)	ex testamento.
EX . V	ex voto.
F	fecit, faciendum, felix, fidelis, filius, fit.
FAB	Fabius (-a), fabri.
FAC	faciendum, faciebat.
FAC . CVR	faciendum curavit.
FAL	Falerna.
F . C	faciendum curavit.
FE	februarius, fecit.
FEC	fecit.
FEL	felix.
FI	filius.
FID	fidelis.

FL, FLA	Flavius (-a).	I . O . M(.D)	Iuppiter Optimus Maximus (Dolichenus).
F . M	filius matri, filio mater.		
F . P	filio piissimo, filio posuit, filius posuit, filius patri.	IVL	Iulius (-a).
		IVN	iunior.
		K	kalendae, karus, karissimus, koniux.
F . S	fecit sibi, filius suus.		
F . S . ET . S		L	legio, lex, libertus, librarius, locus, Lucius.
	fecit sibi et suis.		
G	Gaius, Galeria, genius.	L . A	libens animo.
GAL	Galeria.	L . D, D . D	
GER(M)	Germania, Germanicus, Germanus.		libens dat, dono dedit.
		L . E	libertus eius.
GN	Gnaeus.	LEG	legatus, legio.
G . P . R	genius populi Romani.	LEG . AVG	legatus Augusti.
G . R	Germani Raeti.	LEG . LEG	legatus legionis.
GR	Graecus.	L . ET . L	liberti et libertae.
G . S	Germania superior.	LIB	libertus, librarius, libens.
H	habet, heres, hic.		
HADR	Hadrianus.	LIBB	liberti.
HAS	hastatus.	LIB . COS	librarius consularis.
HAS . P	hastatus prior.	L . L	legatus legionis, libens laetus.
HAS . PO	hastatus posterior.		
H . D . S . P		L . L . M	laetus libens merito.
	heres de suo posuit.	L . M(D, F, P, S)	
HER	heres.		libens merito (dat, fecit, posuit, solvit).
H . E . T . F			
	heres ex testamento fecit.	L . P	libens posuit, libertus posuit.
H . ET . L	heredes et liberi.	L . S	libens solvit.
H . F . C	heres faciendum curavit	M	manes, manus, Marcus, maritus, Mars, mater, Matres, maximus, menses, Mercurius, merens, miles, militavit, mille, Minerva, minus, Mithras, moneta, monumentum, mortuus, mulier.
HIS(P)	Hispania, Hispani.		
H . L	hic locus, hoc loco.		
H . M	hoc monumentum.		
HON	honoratus.		
HORR	horreum, horrearius.		
H . P	hastatus prior, heres posuit.		
H . S . E	hic situs est.		
I	ianuarius, invictus, Iulius (-a).	M . A	militavit annos.
		MAEC	Maecia.
ID	idus.	MAG	magister.
IM(A)	imaginifer.	MAR	maritus.
IMP	imperator.	MAT	mater.
IMPP	imperatores.	MATR	Matres.
IN H . D . D		MAX	maximus.
	in honorem donus divinae.	M . C	mater castrorum, mater carissima.
INS	instante.	M . E	merita eius.

MED	medicus.	ORD	ordinarius.
MEN	mensis.	OVF	Oufentina.
MES	mensis.	P	pagus, parens, passus,
MET	metalla.		pater, patronus, pe-
M . F	mater fecit, monumen-		cunia, pedes, per,
	tum fecit.		pius, pondo, popu-
M . F . P	mater filio posuit.		lus, posuit, pro, pro-
MIL	miles, militavit, milia,		vincia, publicus.
	milliaria.	PA(R)	parentes.
M . L	miles legionis.	PA(T)	pater, patronus.
MON(IM)	monumentum.	PAL	Palatina.
M . P	mater posuit, mille	PANN	Pannonia, Pannonii.
	passus.	PAP	Papiria.
M . S	Moesia superior, merito	PART(H)	Parthicus.
	solvit.	P . E	parentes eius, posteri
M . S . P	monumentum sibi		eius.
	posuit.	PEC	pecunia, pequarius.
M . V . F	monumentum vivus	PED	pedatura, pedes,
	fecit, maritus uxori		pedites, peditata.
	fecit.	PET	Petriana.
N	natio, natus, nepos,	P . F	pater fecit, parentes
	noster, numerus,		fecerunt, patri filio,
	numen.		pia fidelis, pius
NA(T)	natio, natus.		felix.
NARB	Narbonensis.	PF	praefectus.
N . AVG	numen Augusti.	PIL . PR, POST	
NEP	nepos.		pilus prior, posterior.
N . EXPLOR		P . L	patrono libertus, pa-
	numerus exploratorum.		tronus liberto, pro-
N . M	numerus militum.		vincia Lugdunensis.
N . M . Q	numen maiestasque.	P . L . L	posuit laetus libens.
NN	nostri.	PO(B, P)	Publilia.
NOB . CAES		POM(P)	Pomptina.
	nobilissimus Caesar.	POP	populus.
NON	nonae.	PORT	porticus.
NOR	Norici.	POS	posuit.
NOT	notarius.	P . P	parentes piissimi, pater
NOV	november.		patriae, pater piis-
NVM	numen, numerus.		simus, pater posuit,
NVM . AVG			piissimo posuit, prae-
	numen Augusti.		positus, praeses pro-
O	officina, optio.		vinciae, primus pilus,
OB . M . E	ob merita eius.		primipilaris, publi-
OCT	october.		cani provinciae, pro
OF	Oufentina, officina.		pietate.
O . M	ob memoriam, optimus	P . P . AVGG	
	maximus.		perpetui Augusti.
OP(T)	optimus, optio.	P . R	populus Romanus.

PR	praefectus, praetor, pridie, primus, princeps, pro, procurator, provincia.	ROM	Romanus, Romilia.
		R . P	respublica.
		S	sacrum, sanctus, salve, scripsit, se, semis, servus, sextarius, Sextus, signifer, singularis, situs, sol, solvit, stipendia, sunt, suus.
PRA(EF)	praefectus.		
PRI	primus, princeps.		
PRID	pridie.		
PRIN	princeps.		
PRO	proconsul, procurator, provincia.		
		SAB	Sabatina.
PROB	probavit, probante.	SAC	sacer, sacerdos, sacravit.
PROC	proconsul, procurator.		
PRON(EP)	pronepos.	S . AC . D	sub ascia dedicavit.
PRO . PR	pro praetore.	SACER	sacerdos.
PRO . S	pro salute, pro se.	SACR	sacrum.
PR . M	praepositus militum.	SAG	sagittarii.
PROV	provincia.	SARM	Sarmaticus.
PR . POS(T)		S . AS . D	sub ascia dedicavit.
	princeps posterior.	S . C	singularis consularis, sub cura.
PR . PR	praefectus praetorio, praeses provinciae, princeps prior, pro praetore.		
		S . D . N	salus domini nostri.
		SEN	senatus, senior.
		SEP(T)	september, Septimius.
P . S	pecunia sua, proprio sumptu, pro salute, pro se.	SER	Sergia, Servius.
		S . ET . S	se et sui.
		SEX	Sextus.
P . S . D . N		SIG(N)	signifer, signum.
	pro salute domini nostri.	SING	singularis.
		S . L . M	solvit libens merito.
P . S . ET . S		SOL	solvit.
	pro se et suis.	SP	spectabilis.
P . S . F. P	pecunia sua fecit, posuit.	S . P	sua pecunia, sumptu publico.
P . S . S	pro salute sua.	SPL	splendidus.
PVB(L)	publicus, Publilia.	S . P . Q	senatus populusque, sibi posterisque.
PVP	Pupinia, pupillus.		
Q	quaestor, que, qui, Quintus, Quirina, quondam.	S . S	sumptu suo, susceptum solvit.
		S . S . L . L . M	
Q . C . A	quorum curam agit.		susceptum solvit laetus libens merito.
Q . D	quaestor designatus, quondam.		
		ST	Stellatina, stipendia.
QVI(R)	Quirina.	STIP	stipendia.
R	restituit, Romanus.	S . T . T . L	sit tibi terra levis.
R . C	reficiendum curavit.	S . V . F	sibi vivus fecit.
REF	refecit.	S . V . L . A, M	
REIP	reipublicae.		solvit votum libens animo, merito.
RES(T)	restituit.		

S . V . T . L	sit vobis terra levis.
T	terra, tesserarius, testamentum, tiro, titulus, Titus, tribunus, tumulus, turma.
T . C	titulum curavit.
TER	Teretina.
TES(SERA)	Tesserarius.
T . F	testamentum fecit.
T . F . C	titulum, testamento, faciendum curavit.
TI(B)	Tiberius.
TIT	titulus.
T . M . P	titulum memoriae posuit.
TORQ . ARMIL . PHAL	torquibus armillis phaleris.
T . P	titulum posuit, tribunicia potestas.
TR	tribunus, Tromentina.
TRA	Traianus, Traiana.
TRE(V)	Treviri.
TRIB	tribunus.
TRIB . P(OT)	tribunicia potestas.
TRO	Tromentina.
TR . P(OT)	tribunicia potestas.
TVB	tubicen.
TVM	tumulus.
TVNG	Tungri.
V	vale, Valerius (-a), Venus, verna, veteranus, vexillarius, Victoria, victrix, vir, Virtus, vivus, Voltinia, votum, vovit, uxor.
V . A	vixit annos.
VAL	Valerius (-a).
V . B	vir bonus.
V . C	vir clarissimus.
VE	Velina, veteranus.
V . E	vir egregius.
VER	verna.
VERED	veredarii.
VET	veteranus.

VEX	vexillatio, vexillarius.
V . F(S)	vivus fecit (sibi).
VFEN	Oufentina.
V . H	vir honestissimus.
V . I	vir inlustris.
VI	vixit.
VIC	vicit, victoria, vicus, vicani, victor, victrix.
VICT(R)	victrix.
VIK	vicani.
VIL	villicus.
VIX	vixit.
V . L	veteranus legionis, vir laudabilis.
V . L . M . S	votum libens merito solvit.
VLP	Ulpius (-a).
V . L . P(M)	votum libens posuit (merito).
V . L . S(M)	votum libens solvit (merito).
VLT	Voltinia.
VOL(T)	Voltinia.
VOT	votum, Voturia.
V . P	vir perfectissimus, vivus posuit, votum posuit.
V . Q . F	valeat qui fecit.
V . S	votum solvit, voto soluto, vir spectabilis.
V . S . L . A	votum solvit libens animo.
V . S . L . L	votum solvit libens laetus.
V . S . L . L . M	votum solvit libens laetus merito.
V . S . L . M	votum solvit libens merito.
V . S . M	votum solvit merito.
V . S . P	vivus sibi posuit.
V . S . P . S . S	votum susceptum pecunia sua solvit.

V . SS . LL . MM

    votum solverunt liben-
tes merito.

V . S . S . L . M

    votum susceptum solvit
libens merito.

V . V   Valeria Victrix, Ulpia
Victrix, Venus Vic-
trix, virgo Vestalis.

VV . CC   viri clarissimi.

VV . EE   viri egregii.

VX   vixit, uxor.

Symbols

Ɔ, 7, >   centurio, centuria.

∞   mille, millia, milliaria.

IIVIR   duovir.

IIIVIR   triumvir, etc.

CHAPTER XII

COINS [1]

§ I. COINS AS ARCHAEOLOGICAL EVIDENCE

General Principles.—The study of coins may be approached from many different points of view. In the first place, every coin is an *objet d'art* whose date and place of origin are fixed with relative accuracy ; consequently the historian of art finds in the coinage of a given period a mass of unusually precise and reliable evidence concerning its plastic art. Secondly, every coin is a vehicle of exchange-value, a link in the network of trade ; and the economic historian can draw important conclusions from the distribution and character of coin-finds relating to the period under review. Thirdly, every coin is an official document, bearing the stamp of the issuing authority ; and it can be used to convey messages of various kinds from this authority to the people who are going to use it. By analysing the symbolism of coin-types and the statements contained or implied in coin-legends the political historian can often obtain information of great value.

Here we are concerned with none of these things, but only with coins as archaeological evidence. The principle which governs this use of coins is in itself simple, but its application is complicated by various subordinate principles and points of detail. It is this : a place inhabited for an appreciable time by people using coins almost always contains coins which they have accidentally lost or purposely buried there ; these coins

---

[1] Mr. H. Mattingly has very kindly read this chapter in MS. and made a number of observations, some of which have been worked into the text, to its great improvement, while others seemed more proper for addition to the text in the form of footnotes. These notes are distinguished by the initials H.M. I am also indebted to Dr. G. F. Hill for reading the chapter in proof.

were in circulation during the period of inhabitation, and therefore give a clue to the date and length of that period.

In order that this principle should be of any practical value, it must first be conceded that people are in the habit of losing an appreciable proportion of the coins they possess. In this connection it may be instructive to quote the following case. About 1820 a cottage in a Berkshire village was burnt down, and has never been rebuilt. The writer owned the site of this cottage, which formed part of his kitchen garden, from 1921 to 1928. During that time his gardener, in digging over the site, picked up and gave him 18 coins : two of Charles II, two of William III, one of Anne, one each of George I and II, three of George III, and three illegible : also four foreign pieces, namely a sixteenth-century Nuremberg jetton, a French eighteenth-century coin, a Prussian silver piece of 1791, and a Belgian nickel of 1916. Similar results are found wherever a long-inhabited site, occupied by people in the habit of using coins, is turned over ; and it is probable, on the analogy of well-known statistical facts, that out of every thousand coins used a fairly constant number are lost. Doubtless this number is very small, but it mounts up in the course of time.

A normal site, therefore, inhabited by coin-using people, yields to careful excavation a representative series of coins in use during the period in which it was occupied. Stray coins may have been dropped on the site before or after this period ; but they can be detected, when the excavation is scientifically carried out, by their context : they are found in surface soil or underneath the lowest occupation-levels. In the absence of scientific excavation they can often be diagnosed as strays by their relation to the rest of the series. Thus, in the above case, the total absence of Victorian coins shows that the Belgian nickel is a stray. But this can be asserted with confidence only because the total number of coins in the list is fairly large. If it had consisted, say, of three pieces, one Charles II, one George III, and the Belgian nickel, the description of this last as a stray would have been far less firmly based. This shows that any addition to our coin-list not merely adds a new fact to those already known, but also throws new light on these other facts. If a hundred coins are found on a site, each one tells us more than if only ten had been found. This is partly because all evidence has a negative as well as a positive aspect. If a site yields two coins separated by a gap of a hundred years, the gap is a mere gap in our knowledge ; but if it yields two hundred coins, forming two groups separated by a gap of a hundred years, the gap represents not a lack of evidence, but the evidence of a lack—evidence that coins were not reaching the site during that century, and that therefore it was perhaps not occupied.

The Life of Coins.—But before we can use coins except for the roughest kind of dating, we must not only have a large number of them and work according to sound general principles, we must also know how long they were in circulation : that is, what interval must be assumed between the time when they were minted and the time when they were lost. In my pocket at the present moment (in February, 1929) are a dozen coins, the earliest minted in 1902 and the latest in 1928. If I lost one of these in the garden, it might be the worn penny of 1902, the very much worn halfpenny of 1905, or any of the others down to the almost unworn half-crown of 1923 or the very slightly worn penny of 1928. Thus there is a very rough indication of the interval elapsed between minting and loss, in degree of wear ; and hence the " condition " of coins must always be carefully studied. The indication is very rough because a particular coin may have lain idle in a hoard and not been subjected to wear ; or for some other reason two coins of the same year may have worn very differently. But these erratic sources of error cancel out when large numbers of coins are examined. A single penny of 1860 may be less worn than one of 1890 ; but a dozen pennies of 1860-70 will be on the average more worn than a dozen of 1890-1900.

The life of a coin—the length of time during which it re-mains in circulation—varies so much that no universal rule can be laid down. Experience alone can determine, when a given coin is found on a given site, what length of life can be assigned to it. But experience shows that certain generalisa-tions, though admittedly rough, hold good in the main for British finds, and these we shall now try to state. They are based, it may be explained, on analysis of the coins found at four classes of sites : (*a*) pre-Flavian (mostly in the south of England) ; (*b*) Flavian, first in Wales and later in the north ;

(c) Hadrianic, on Hadrian's Wall, and (d) Antonine, on the Wall of Pius.

1. *Republican Silver*, sometimes dating from quite a long time B.C., circulates freely until late in the first century A.D. It was probably valued for the good quality of its metal, and could hardly have escaped being " driven out " according to Gresham's Law unless it was accepted at a premium. Be that as it may, we find it in sites first occupied about the year 75 ; but a very short time after this it seems to vanish or at any rate to become abruptly rarer, and in sites ascribed to Agricola (c. 78-84) it is less common, and seems to disappear before A.D. 100.[1]

2. *The Silver of Mark Antony* was very much debased, and hence, according to Gresham's Law, survived the purer silver of the early emperors and lasted in use down to c. A.D. 250.

3. *Imperial Coins Earlier than Claudius* are rare in Britain, and are practically confined to pre-Flavian sites. On later sites they occur only where the total number of coins found is very large. Thus, in Coventina's Well at Carrawburgh on Hadrian's Wall, which must have begun accumulating its huge hoard in Hadrian's time, there are three coins of Antony, no Republican coins, and only eight Imperial coins before Claudius, out of a total of about 15,000. At Newstead, a Flavian site, out of 113 silver coins, there are nine Republican coins and eight of Mark Antony, as against only two of Augustus and Tiberius. At Corbridge, another Flavian site, early Imperial coins are almost wholly absent, though there are many of Mark Antony, and a fair amount of Republican silver. Pre-Claudian Imperial coins, therefore, were rarely in circulation after Nero's reign. The silver, at any rate, was melted down.

4. *Coins of Claudius, Nero*, and others before Vespasian, are fairly common in the south, at places occupied before the Flavian period. At sites founded during the Flavian period they form

---

[1] (a) As long as the Republican denarius was not worth more *as metal* than $\frac{1}{25}$ aureus, there was no very strong draw on the more worn specimens. It would pay the Government to melt it down and coin it into debased Neronian denarii, but not the ordinary citizen.

(b) Vespasian countermarks a number of Republican denarii. It looks as if he called in the more worn ones, while countermarking others for continued use.

(c) Trajan called in the old coinage c. A.D. 107.—H.M.

a small and rapidly-dwindling fraction of the whole. After the
turn of the century, coins of this period became decidedly rare.

5. *Flavian Coins* seem to have rapidly ousted previous
issues,[1] and greatly predominate over them at sites founded
in the Flavian period. Thus at Newstead there are thirty-
three Flavian silver and sixty-three Flavian brass as against
seven pre-Flavian Imperial silver and three pre-Flavian brass.
Moreover, Flavian coins lasted in circulation a long time. In
the reign of Hadrian, and even later, there was a good deal of
Flavian money about ; and most second-century sites yield a
few pieces of this period.

6. *Coins of Trajan* have a long life. In the middle of the
second century they were practically as common as those of
Hadrian.

After this time, there is no longer sufficient evidence to
enable us to do more than guess at the length of life enjoyed
by various issues in Britain. During the greater part of the
third century the life of coins was generally short, because the
tendency of the age was one of depreciation. On the other
hand, in the fourth century coins lived longer ; and coins of
the Constantinian age were even imitated in the fifth century,
which seems to show that they were still widely current.

Rate of Travel.—How long did coins take to come into
currency at a given place, that is, to travel from the mints
into (for instance) a remote corner of a distant province ? It
has recently been stated[2] that Roman coins travelled slowly
from hand to hand, and " drifted " by degrees outwards from
the centres of Imperial life to the fringes of the Empire, so
slowly that a round figure of thirty years may be given for
the minimum interval between a coin's being struck on the
Continent and its reaching the north of Britain. If this could
be proved it would be an extremely important principle, and
would entail serious reconsideration of many arguments based
—as most chronological arguments concerning the Roman
period and depending upon archaeological material are based,
at least in part—on the evidence of coins. But although it is

---

[1] The " restored " issues of Titus and Domitian seem to show that about
A.D. 80-81 a great deal of worn *aes* was withdrawn from circulation. The
" restored " types commemorate the vanishing coinage.—H.M.

[2] By Mr. Edward Foord, in *The Last Age of Roman Britain.*

true that an occupation always lasts until a date later than the striking of the last coin lost in its debris, this difference of date cannot be estimated, in normal circumstances, at anything like so high a minimum as thirty years. Thus, on Romano-British sites known to have been founded during the Flavian period we find few pre-Flavian coins ; on Hadrian's Wall the earliest coins normally found are coins of Trajan, with a few Flavian pieces ; on the Antonine Wall the same is, broadly speaking, true. The fact seems to be that, although at a given date many coins thirty years old, and more, were circulating in these remote frontier districts, newer pieces were mixed with them.

Criticisms of the " coin-drift " theory (*e.g.* in *J.R.S.*, xv, 114 ; *Eng. Hist. Review*, April, 1926 ; *History*, x, 327), have been mostly based on the facts of coin history in the earlier Empire, where it is easiest to check the theory by correlations between historical events like the campaigns of Agricola and the building of the two Walls, and the coin-finds at places concerned in these events. These correlations show that, for the first and second centuries, the theory is quite untenable. But it was originally propounded in connection with the fourth and fifth centuries, in support of the view (for which *cf.* Bury in *J.R.S.* x, 146 *seqq.*), that Britain was not, as the ancient historians say, abandoned by the Roman central government about A.D. 407-410, but held for another twenty or thirty years. This view would be supported by the existing coin-evidence if the " coin-drift " theory were sound. It has been shown, however (Salisbury, "Richborough Coin-Problems," in *Num. Chron.*, 1927 ; *cf.* also *Ant. J.*, vii, 268-277 ; *Richborough*, ii, 112), that the mint-history on which the theory depends for this period is mistaken.

At the same time, the fact that Roman coins almost entirely ceased to flow into Britain about A.D. 395 must not be used without serious qualification to prove that the traditional date for the Roman withdrawal is correct ; for about that time the Gallic mints ceased work and the main source of supply was therefore cut off.

Hoards.—Strictly speaking, coin is being hoarded whenever it is not being spent. The money in one's purse or pocket, or in the till of a shop, is a hoard, even if none of it was there

yesterday and none will be there to-morrow. This is recognised by archaeologists, who would certainly treat a lost purse,
or a pocketful of loose cash, as a hoard ; but in a special sense
the word is used of a quantity of coin put by in a safe place,
the owner's reserves, not his floating cash balance. In this
narrower sense, hoards have certain special characteristics to
which we shall return, after considering the characteristics
belonging to all hoards.

Every hoard consists of a number of coins possessed at one
time by one owner, individual or corporate. These coins have
been added to the hoard successively, over a period of time
which may have been long or short, but which must have ended
before the hoard was " deposited " or lost. The date of de-
position or loss is therefore not earlier than the date of the
latest coin in the hoard, and may be later. If the latest coin
is much worn, a considerable interval is implied. But on the
other hand, a coin may, in some circumstances, remain in fresh
condition for a long time.

Where a hoard consists, not of floating cash, but of reserves or savings, some of its contents may have been withdrawn from circulation for many years; and if, as often happens,
the owner has selected good specimens for hoarding, every coin
in the hoard may be in fresh condition, however long a time
elapsed between its being minted and lost. A hoard of this type,
unlike a hoard of floating cash, will represent not the average
state of the currency at the moment of loss, but the financial
history of its owner. Thus, a floating cash hoard will generally
consist, for the most part, of recent coins, and will include a
diminishing proportion of older pieces. A savings hoard, on
the contrary, will generally contain a more evenly-spaced selec-
tion : there is no reason why recent coins should preponderate
in it, and in general those coins will be most frequent which
were most commonly current at the times when he was best
able to save.

In actual practice, the majority of hoards partake of both
natures. They are, as a rule, savings ; but savings which have
been drawn upon from time to time, so that there has been
a constant tendency for the earlier coins in them to disappear.
In this connection it is useful to remember that the more
valuable a coin is, the less often it is carried about loose, or

passed from hand to hand. Therefore a gold hoard generally conforms more to the type of savings, a copper hoard more to the type of floating cash. And for the same reason, the relation between age and worn condition is steadiest in the case of copper and least constant in the case of gold. Gold passes so seldom, relatively speaking, from hand to hand, that it may still be very fresh a long time after minting; and in a gold hoard the condition of the coins is almost always relatively good.[1]

Where there is no well-established banking system, savings must always be hoarded, short of investing them; and there is no doubt that at any given moment an appreciable percentage of the existing Roman currency was being hoarded in this form. Certain economic conditions would, from time to time, accentuate this tendency. When the value of money is falling sharply, users find that it will not buy as much as they are accustomed to think it should; they therefore allow it to hang on their hands, and thus hoards everywhere tend to accumulate. This happened in the depreciation of the third century, which reached its climax in the financial disaster of Gallienus's reign. The result of these events is to be seen in the great numbers of hoards assignable to about the years 260-280 and containing vast quantities of debased silver and silver-washed copper.

Normally, any hoard of savings is ultimately broken up and spent, either by the owner or by his heirs. Those which we find are the exceptions to this rule. There may be two reasons why a given hoard of savings should remain unspent for the archaeologist to find : either it becomes worthless, or it is lost. We have seen that a large class of hoards in the late third century consisted of coin which had become, relatively or absolutely, valueless. The loss of a hoard means that the person who deposited it did not live to reclaim it either by his own hand or by that of his heirs; and that would be likeliest to happen if he met with a sudden death. When a countryside is disturbed by warfare or raiding, the number of hoards does not increase—for these conditions do not cause people in general to have more savings—but the proportion of hoards

---

[1] But, contrary to current statements, the Corbridge second-century gold hoard [*Num. Chron.*[4], xii, 1912] shows a good gradation of wear from Nero down to Antoninus.—H.M.

that are lost increases with every increase in the intensity of the disturbance.

If, then, the archaeologist knows of an unusually large number of hoards dated to a certain period, he may regard this as evidence either of economic crisis or of political unrest. If it is a widespread phenomenon, it probably points to grave depreciation in the currency; if a local, to destruction of life and property through war.

§ 2. HISTORY OF ROMAN IMPERIAL COINAGE [1]

Mints.—Under the Republic, coinage was issued by authority of the Senate, the mint being controlled by the *tresviri aere argento auro flando feriundo* (*III viri a . a . a . f . f .*) or, for short, *tresviri monetales.* Late in Republican history, generals commanding troops in the provinces began striking coins at provincial mints, in virtue of their *imperium.* Augustus, after a long series of experiments, divided the work of issuing money between himself and the Senate, by opening a mint of his own at Lugdunum (Lyons) to strike gold and silver, and assigning to the Senate the duty of striking copper at Rome. Caligula transferred the emperor's mint to Rome, and, apart from a few local issues, Rome remained the source of currency, both imperial and senatorial, until late in the second century.

The civil wars of the closing years of that century stimulated the revival of several provincial mints; and though this revival did not lead to their permanent establishment, it seems to have shaken the supremacy of Rome and made it easier for a policy of decentralisation to assert itself from time to time. The Lyons mint, revived by Clodius Albinus in 196-197, was reopened once more by Gallienus about 255. When Gallienus lost Gaul, and Britain with it, in 258 or 260, Lyons became the mint of the Gaulish emperors. Gallienus retorted by setting up a new mint at Milan, which under Aurelian was moved to Ticinum. It was in Gallienus's reign, too, that the mint of Siscia on the Danube seems to have been opened. This multiplication of provincial mints led to the virtual disappearance of the senatorial brass coinage.

---

[1] The reader will understand that the following outline ignores everything that does not affect the monetary history of Britain.

The reorganisation of the coinage by Diocletian involved the closing of some mints and the opening of others. On his accession, he found at least two mints at work in Britain. London was given a mint by Carausius (286-293) ; this continued at work until about 324-326 (G. F. Hill, in *Roman London*, pp. 187-188). Carausius had a second mint at a place whose name began with C, which has been identified with Colchester (Webb, *The Reign and Coinage of Carausius*, p. 46) ; but Mr. Mattingly points out to me that the legend CL, which is also found, suggests rather Clausentum (Bitterne), which would be convenient for a fleet based on the Isle of Wight. In any case, this mint was closed in 296 when Allectus was overcome by Constantius Chlorus. There is also a possibility that Carausius had a mint at Wroxeter (G. F. Hill, " A Mint at Wroxeter ? " in *Num. Chron.*, 1926). Diocletian left the London mint working. In Gaul, he struck coins at Trier and Lyons ; in Italy, at Rome, Ticinum, and Aquileia. But early in the fourth century a new mint was opened at Arles, and shortly afterwards Ticinum was closed down about the same time as London. Throughout the early and middle fourth century, Trier was the main source of the coins used in Britain, followed by Lyons ; coins of Arles were also common, and a fair number came from Siscia. After the close of the Constantinian period, Trier ceased to be the chief source of bronze for Britain ; and after about 364 Arles and Lyons become the chief sources, especially Arles, which in the last quarter of the century supplied Britain with about half its total importation of coins [1] (Salisbury, *Num. Chron.*, 1927, pp. 112-113). The London mint was revived by Magnus Maximus (383-388) but did not remain at work after his fall. [2] About 395 the issue of bronze in Gaul ceased, and that of gold and silver was transferred to Milan.

[1] Salisbury shows that the very numerous late fourth-century coins (Valentinian I to Arcadius and Honorius) at Richborough are divided among mints roughly as follows : Arles, 47 per cent. ; Lyons, 20 per cent. ; Arles or Lyons, 2 per cent. ; Aquileia, 14 per cent. ; Rome, 9 per cent. ; Trier, 6 per cent. ; Siscia, 1 per cent.; Cyzicus, 0·5 per cent.; Antioch, Constantinople, Milan, Nicomedia, Alexandria, Thessalonica, Heracleia, an insignificant fraction each.

[2] A series of coins of Valentinian I, Valens, and Gratian, with mint-mark SMLAP, formerly ascribed to London (*cf. Num. Chron.*, 1915, pp. 482 *seqq.*) are now assigned to Lyons (*ibid.*, 1924, pp. 69-74).

Mint-Marks.—In the late Republican period, coins are freely marked with symbols serving sometimes to identify a particular die, sometimes to show in what *officina* or workshop of the mint the coin was made, etc. (Mattingly, *Roman Coins*, p. 37). These symbols, however, are not strictly comparable with the mint-marks proper which begin to appear in the reign of Gallienus. These consist of various elements :—

(i) The number of the *officina* or workshop, of which there were as a rule several in a mint. This may be written in various ways : (*a*) I, II, III, IIII, . . . or OF I, OF II, etc. (*b*) PRIMA, SECVNDA, TERTIA, QVARTA, or P, S, T, Q. (*c*) A, B, Γ, Δ, Є, S, Z, H. N is used for NONA.

Early mint-marks, especially of Rome, often consist of nothing except the *officina* number.

(ii) A prefix to the mint-name : *e.g.* P(ecunia), M(oneta), S(acra) M(oneta).

(iii) The mint-name itself. Those which are most likely to be found at a site in Britain are the following :—

Alexandria : AL, ALE.	Rome : R, RM, ROM, ROMA.
Amiens : AMB, AMBI.	Serdica : SD, SERD.
*Aquileia : AQ, AQVI.	Sirmium : SIR, SIRM, SM.
*Arles : AR, ARL, CON, CONST.[1]	*Siscia : S, SIS, SISC.
Colchester or Clausentum : C.	Thessalonica : TE, TES, TH, ⊕ES.
*London : L, LN, LON, AVG.[2]	Ticinum : T, TI.
*Lyons : L, LD, LG, LVG, LVGD.	*Trier : TR, TRE.
Milan : MD, MED.	

The vast majority of mint-marks found in Britain belong to the half-dozen mints marked *, especially common being those of Trier, Lyons, Arles, and (towards the end of the third century), London.

(iv) Marks of value. Of these the commonest is XX. I, which was introduced by Aurelian ; its signification is not established beyond controversy.[3]

(v) Marks denoting a metal : OB(ryziacum), for gold, and P(u)S(ulatum), for Silver.

[1] Arles was called Constantina after about A.D. 325.

[2] London was called Augusta after about the middle of the fourth century.

[3] Mr. Mattingly rejects the idea that XX. I indicates an *antoninianus*, and suggests to me that Aurelian's unit was a double *sestertius* containing 20 *libellae*.

With these facts in mind, we can read most of the mint-marks that are commonly found in this country. Here are a few examples :—

Aquileia, first officina.	SMAQP.
,, *second officina.*	SMAQS.
Arles, first officina.	PARL, PCON, PCONST.
,, *second officina.*	SARL, SCON, SCONST.
,, *third officina.*	TCON.
,, *fourth officina.*	ARLQ.
London.	ML, MLXXI, PL, PLON, PLN.
Lyons.	PLG, PLVG, LVG, PLN.
,, *first officina.*	LVGP.
,, *second officina.*	LVGS, LVGPS, SLVG, SLG.
Trier.	PTR, TR.
,, *first officina.*	TRP, PTRE, PTR.
,, *second officina.*	TRS, STRE, STR, TRPS.

There are some mint-marks which do not fall into the above classification ; of these, the one most interesting to British students is the RSR of Carausius, which probably stands for *R(ationalis) S(ummae) R(ei)*.[1]

Metals and Denominations.—The rough-and-ready classification of Roman coins into gold (N), silver (R), and first, second, and third brass (Æ 1, 2, 3), is a good way of beginning, but no more. We shall take the three main divisions in turn and trace their history in outline.

N. The *aureus*, the standard gold coin of the early and middle Empire, was $\frac{1}{42}$ of a pound in weight under Augustus (*i.e.* 121·5 grains). Nero reduced its weight to $\frac{1}{45}$ (113·5 grains). This remained its nominal weight until the early third century, when Caracalla reduced it to $\frac{1}{50}$ (100 grains). During the third century no standard weight was even approximately adhered to ; and when Diocletian reformed the coinage in 296 he fixed the weight of the *aureus* at $\frac{1}{60}$ of a pound. Constantine, however, finding further reforms necessary, abolished the *aureus* in 312, and struck a new gold piece, the *solidus*, at $\frac{1}{72}$ of a pound (*c.* 70 grains). This was henceforth the standard Roman gold coin.

[1] Mattingly and Sydenham, *Rom. Imperial Coinage*, i, 1 *seqq.* ; *ibid.*, v, part i, 15 *seqq.* ; lists of coins in excavation reports, *e.g. Wroxeter*, 1912-14 and *Richborough*, i, ii.

Pieces forming multiples or fractions of the standard unit were also struck at various times ; but the only ones in regular use were the half-*aureus* (or *quinarius aureus*, the *aureus* being properly called *denarius aureus*) in the early and middle period, and the piece weighing one-third of a *solidus* (*triens* or *tremissis*) in the late.

Æ. The standard silver coin in the early period was the *denarius* (properly *denarius argenteus* to distinguish it from the *denarius aureus*). Augustus found it weighing $\frac{1}{84}$ of a pound, the same as the half-*aureus* (61·39 grains), and kept it at this, striking also a silver *quinarius* or half-*denarius* at 30·69 grains. The *aureus* was tariffed at 25 *denarii*. Nero reduced the *denarius* to 52·64 grains ($\frac{1}{96}$ of a pound), and at the same time further decreased its silver content by alloying it with about 10 per cent. of copper. After Nero, both weight and quality continued to deteriorate. Under Trajan the alloy amounted to 20 per cent. ; Marcus Aurelius increased it to 25 per cent. ; Commodus to about 30 per cent. ; and under Septimius Severus it amounts to as much as 50-60 per cent.

A new coin, distinguished by the " radiate " crown on the emperor's head, was the *antoninianus*, introduced by Caracalla in A.D. 214. It was made, like the *denarius*, of debased silver, and its original weight seems to have been 78·75 grains. This might suggest that it was tariffed at $1\frac{1}{2}$ *denarius ;* but Mr. Mattingly points out that a simpler hypothesis is that it was a coin of inflation, a double *denarius* struck deliberately much too light. It is more likely that a new coin should be issued with a value of two *denarii* than with the strange value of one and a half, and on this view it is easier to understand the ratio between the *antoninianus* and the *aureus*, and also to see why the new coin competed with the *denarius* and finally vanquished it.

When this happened, the *antoninianus* became the only silver coin in general circulation (after A.D. 242). In the reign of Gallienus the " billon " or debased silver of which it was made declined even further in purity, and the latest *antoniniani* may easily be mistaken for copper coins when somewhat corroded. Thus the *antoninianus* became the symbol of the financial disasters of the third century, and was abolished. Aurelian, *c.* A.D. 272, demonetised the inflation issues of his predecessors and established a new coinage based on the unit marked XX. I, *i.e.* probably a double *sestertius* for a double *denarius*, but Diocletian abolished this and introduced a silver issue based on a pure silver coin, the *milliarense*, which, according to the generally accepted view, was tariffed at 1000 to the gold pound, *i.e.* 20 to the *aureus* of $\frac{1}{50}$ pound. Some time after 340, after the introduction of the gold *solidus*, a new silver coin was struck, the *siliqua*, tariffed at 24 to the *solidus* and weighing 42 grains. Towards the end of the fourth century, the silver coinage consisted of *siliquae* and half-*siliquae* with a few *milliarensia* used as double *siliquae*. The half-*siliqua* begins to appear in the time of Gratian (*Num. Chron.*, 1915, p. 478).

Æ. The popular classification of Roman coins lumps under this head two different metals, brass and copper.[1] Brass or *orichalcum* is a yellow metal containing about 75-85 per cent. copper, and the rest zinc with some tin or lead or both. In the orichalc of the third century, lead predominates over everything else except the copper.

The earliest Imperial coinage contained two orichalc pieces, the *sestertius* (popularly called " First Brass ") of 421 grains, and the *dupondius* of 210·5 grains. These were worth, respectively, $\frac{1}{4}$ and $\frac{1}{8}$ of a *denarius*. There were also two copper coins, the *as* of 175·4 grains, $\frac{1}{16}$ of a *denarius* in value, and the *quadrans* of 43·9 grains, worth a quarter of an *as*. This is popularly called " Third Brass," and the *dupondius* and *as* are confused together under the name of " Second Brass." These brass and copper coins were struck by the Senate, and bore in consequence the letters S(enatus) C(onsulto) in the field on the reverse.

Nero introduced an elaborate system with five different orichalc coins (*sestertius, dupondius, as, semis, quadrans*) and three copper coins (*as, semis, quadrans*) ; but this was an unnecessary complication, and was abandoned by his successors, who reverted to the old system, and even dropped the copper *quadrans* (Sydenham, *The Coinage of Nero*).

In the third century, owing to alloy in the metal and variation in the weight, *dupondii* and *asses* are difficult to distinguish.

[1] Dr. Hill recommends the use of the term *aes* when it is desired to refer to brass and copper without distinguishing between them.

The *sestertius*, during the same period, was always tending to lose weight. In the reign of Commodus it falls to about 400 grains; in that of Septimius Severus, to 375, and by the time of Gallienus it has gone down to 200-250. Soon after Aurelian's reign it disappears and billon takes its place as small change.

Diocletian in 296 introduced a bronze coinage washed with silver, in three denominations: the *follis*, a large coin about 25 mm. in diameter and weighing 150 grains; a coin weighing about 60 grains with a radiate head on the obverse; and a small coin of about 20 grains with a laureate head. The Diocletianic *follis* is the regular copper coin of the beginning of the fourth century; but it fell rather rapidly in weight as time went on, and the various denominations become somewhat confused in a general depreciation which reached a climax after 330.

About 348 Constantius and Constans introduced a new coin of 80 grains, but this in turn began to fall in weight between 350 and 360. After 361 there are four bronze coins in regular use: (1) a coin of 120 grains, corresponding to the Diocletianic *follis*, struck by Julian, Jovian, Valentinian I, and Valens; (2) a coin of 80 grains, corresponding to the coin introduced in 340, struck by Gratian, Valentinian II, and Theodosius I; (3) a coin of 40 grains in general use after Julian; (4) a coin of 20 grains struck especially towards the end of the century by Theodosius, Arcadius, and Honorius (Mattingly, *Roman Coins*, p. 224). Finally, a word must be said of the "minimi" which are very common in British sites of the late fourth century. They are probably an emergency local coinage of that period, reproducing in a debased version and on a small scale types of the Constantinian period or even earlier (Mattingly, *op. cit.*, p. 236); and it is probable that they went on being struck and used considerably after the end of the Roman occupation of Britain.[1]

---

[1] General references for this section: Marquardt, *röm. Staatsverwaltung*, ii, 25-34. Mommsen, *Geschichte d. röm. Münzwesens*. Mattingly, *Roman Coins*. Mattingly and Sydenham, *Roman Imperial Coinage*, i, 23-32. Hill, *Handbook of Greek and Roman Coins*.

CHAPTER XIII

SAMIAN WARE OR TERRA SIGILLATA [1]

POTTERY forms by far the commonest group of finds on any Romano-British site, and within the last generation it has become possible to date large classes of it with considerable accuracy. The most important class for this purpose is the bright red glazed ware which English antiquaries, confusing it with the pottery mentioned under that name by Pliny, long ago took to calling " Samian." None of it comes from Samos, and for this reason other names have been sought. " Terra sigillata " is current on the Continent, but this only applies properly to one section of it, that bearing moulded decorations. " Gaulish red-glaze " is inaccurate, because it did not always come from Gaul. We shall keep the traditional name and call it Samian.

Samian is easy to recognise. Its paste and glaze are both red, whereas imitations have a paste of some other colour. Its shapes belong to a fairly definite series of identifiable forms ; this is due to mass-production at great industrial centres, where standard articles were produced for a large export trade. It frequently bears the name of the maker, impressed as a rule by means of a small stamp, or sometimes, in the case of decorated ware, interpolated among the decorative motives. A great many makers can be identified as having worked at a certain place and a certain time ; the shape of any given vessel

[1] This chapter has been revised throughout, and corrected in many points of detail, by Dr. T. Davies Pryce. Not content with this, Dr. Pryce, on my consulting him as to the desirability of including a selected list of the commonest potters' names with their dates and localities, gave me much invaluable help in drawing up such a list, which I have included in this chapter as § 4.

also has chronological value; its fabric hardly less so, though this is a subject that cannot be learnt from books; and finally, in the case of decorated ware, the details of the decoration are highly significant. But the last is a subject demanding masses of detail, and cannot be even touched upon in a book like this.

§ 1. DISTRIBUTION AND CHRONOLOGY OF SAMIAN POTTERIES

Italy.—Red glazed ware of this type was being made in the first century B.C. in Italy, chiefly at Arretium (Arezzo), but also elsewhere. In this area, which produced a great abundance of beautiful pottery, the flourishing period of the industry belongs to the late first century B.C. and the early first century A.D. It thus falls into the Augustan period of artistic activity, and shares the characteristics of that period. By the time of the conquest of Britain, Arretine ware was no longer being regularly exported to the provinces. The very rare specimens found in this country are therefore either late pieces brought over at the conquest or very soon after, or else relics of trade between the Empire and Britain before the conquest. In the latter case they are of great interest, but rather in connection with pre-Roman than with Roman Britain.

South Gaul (Ruteni).—La Graufesenque, the greatest manufacturing centre for South Gaulish Samian, must have begun to work before A.D. 20, and continued to about A.D. 100-110. Here, especially in its later phases, systematic mass-production resulted in the building-up of an enormous export trade, and vast quantities of pottery from this centre are found in Britain. Less important centres were at Montans and Banassac, the former having about the same life as La Graufesenque, the latter beginning about 40 and ending about 110.

Rutenian ware is generally rather dark-red or cherry-red— as opposed to orange—with very glossy glaze and a hard well-fired paste.

Central Gaul (Arverni).—Lezoux (near Clermont-Ferrand), was the chief Arvernian pottery. It was probably in existence by about A.D. 40, but during the first century it was overshadowed by the Rutenian factories, and did not export very largely. In the second century it takes the leading place, and finds its chief market in Gaul and Britain, most of whose second-century Samian comes from Lezoux. The fabric is usually more orange in colour than that of South Gaul, and the glaze is in general less glossy ; as time goes on, both design and fabric tend to deteriorate. Minor Arvernian centres at Lubié, Vichy, St.-Bonnet, St.-Rémy, etc., have, with the exception of Vichy, little interest for the British student. Lezoux ceased work about the year 260.

East Gaul, etc.—A large number of potteries engaged in making Samian existed in an area west of the Rhine between Bale and Cologne and extending as far west as the upper Oise. Work in this area began towards the end of the first century. The potter Satto, whose place of residence is unknown, was one of the pioneers, and the industry was established at Luxeuil, near Belfort, and Heiligenberg, near Strasburg, shortly before the year 100. The former factory lasted till about 200, the latter till about 160. La Madeleine, near Nancy, began about the same time and had a short life to about the end of Hadrian's reign. It was largely responsible for the introduction of Arvernian patterns into East Gaul. A group west of Verdun (Avocourt, Les Allieux, Lavoye, with an outlier at Compiègne) was active in the middle of the second century, and Ittenweiler, in Alsace, during the reigns of Trajan and Hadrian. A northern group centres round Trier : here work began early in the second century and went on until the middle of the third century, when Trier was one of the chief sources of Samian. South of Trier are Eschweilerhof (mostly Antonine), and Blickweiler (mostly Hadrianic) ; north, on the Rhine, Remagen and Sinzig, late derivatives of Trier. An eastern group has its centre at Rheinzabern, near Karlsruhe, which must have begun work about 120 and produced plain and moulded ware down to the beginning of the third century, when barbotine decoration took the place of moulded ; in the late second century offshoots grew up at Kräherwald on the Neckar, and Westerndorf on the Inn. Finally, there was a Swiss group working at Bregenz, Baden-in-Argau, and Windisch in the late first and early second centuries.

East Gaulish ware naturally predominates in the forts of the German frontier, but its importance in Britain is not so great as that of La Graufesenque and Lezoux. There is, however, no doubt that a good deal of supposedly Lezoux pottery really comes from Luxeuil and Blickweiler in East Gaul, and perhaps Vichy in Central Gaul ; and this may be true at times even of wares found in Britain.

§ 2. METHODS OF DECORATING SAMIAN WARE

Moulded Ware.—The makers of decorated Samian in its earliest form were copying the decoration on silversmiths' vessels ; this they found could best be done by preparing a hollow mould and pressing clay into it to form the bowl. The decoration had to be formed in negative on the inside of the mould, and the easiest way of making it was by stamping the mould with various ready-made decorative units—figures, animals, vegetable and formal motives, positively modelled on separate stamps. Since one stamp could be used any number of times, a single signed bowl is a source from which we can identify others, by identity of the stamps used, as coming from the same factory. An invaluable collection of these stamps has been made by Déchelette (*Les Vases céramiques ornés de la Gaule romaine*), and the most valuable portions of the evidence concerning their chronology are given by Oswald and Pryce. All " decorated Samian," in the ordinary sense of the words, is moulded ware.

Appliqué Ware.—Here a plain vase is first made, and then separate decorative motives, modelled or, generally, stamped in the same clay, are applied to it. In this way a bolder relief could be achieved, and a vessel could be decorated, if required, all over a globular surface. The method is used in Arretine ware, and Gaulish specimens are found which must date about the end of the first century ; but it only becomes really common in the late second and early third centuries, when it almost entirely replaced moulded technique in Central Gaul. In Britain, *appliqué* ware is not often found, except for the *appliqué* lion's head spout on form 45.

Stamped Ware.—The last degradation of decorated Samian consisted in the practice of stamping designs, mostly of a crude geometric type, direct on the vessel. This practice seems to begin late in the third century, and produces a type of ware known as Marne bowls, which is found in fourth-century British sites in the south and east. Various other stamped fabrics more or less imitating Samian are common in the fourth century.

Barbotine.—This is a style of ornament made by laying clay when wet on the surface of a vessel, forming it into patterns by using a funnel or tube exactly as in decorating an iced cake. Apart from its restricted use as on forms 35 and 36, it is rare on Samian found in this country, though very familiar on Castor ware. It is freely used by late East Gaulish potters in the last phases of the industry, but their products hardly reached Britain. In late Lezoux ware it is sometimes used for subordinate details in moulded designs.

Painted Ware.—Samian ware painted with patterns in thin white slip, a method of decoration already familiar in other fabrics, was made in the third century and later, but is hardly found in Britain.

Incised Ware.—Here the decoration is cut on the wheel, exactly as in cut glass. It seems to begin about the middle of the second century, especially on form 72 ; the best examples come from Lezoux and were made in the late second and early third centuries ; but the technique continues into the fourth century, with marked deterioration.

Roulette Decoration or Runnering.—A runner is the English trade name for a toothed wheel revolving freely on a spindle and brought into contact with a vessel spinning on the wheel, so as to produce a belt of tooth marks. In French this instrument is called a *roulette*, and archaeologists use the word rouletting to describe the decoration which is made by its means. This decoration is always found on the rim of form 29 ; frequently in a ring on the floor of forms 18 and 31 ; and sometimes instead of the ornament on forms 30 and 37—a practice which is more particularly characteristic of second-century East Gaulish potters. It is also used on various plain shapes other than 18 but less common, notably the small bowl, form 24/25.

Marbled Ware.—This is covered with a yellow glaze veined with streaks of red ; a technique used by Arretine potters and copied in South Gaul. As made there, it seems to be a pre-Flavian product, and in Britain it is found rarely and only on very early sites. Another so-called marbled ware, not Samian, in which a yellow ground is speckled with red, was made in

Germany at a later date (end of first century and first half of second), but very seldom reaches Britain.

§ 3. SAMIAN FORMS AND THEIR CHRONOLOGY

The forms of Samian ware have been distinguished and numbered by Dragendorff (*B.J.*, xcvi, 18-155 ; xcvii, 54-163, 1895-96) ; additional numbers have been added to his list by Déchelette (*Les Vases céramiques ornés de la Gaule romaine*, 1904), and Walters (*Catalogue of Roman Pottery . . . in the British Museum*, 1908). These numbers are now recognised as standard, and the complete series may be found in Walters's *Catalogue*. Other forms have been distinguished by other writers, *e.g.* Curle (*Newstead*), Ritterling (early shapes ; *Das frührömische Lager bei Hofheim im Taunus*, 1913), and Ludowici (late shapes ; *Rheinzabern*, i *seqq.*). A classified and illustrated conspectus of all known shapes, with evidence as to their dating, is given in Oswald and Pryce, *Terra Sigillata* (1920). In the following pages, thirty selected forms are illustrated which are likely, between them, to account for practically all the Samian ware found on an ordinary site in Britain.

A. Decorated Ware

29. Carinated bowl, with rouletting below the lip, and below this two zones of decoration separated by a narrow plain moulding. It lasted throughout the first century, but appears rarely in the early years of the second. The outward slope of the rim, and the sharpness of the carination, are accentuated as time goes on, the earlier specimens being more nearly hemispherical. But accurate dating depends on details of decoration (see O. and P., Chapter V, and literature there quoted).

37. Hemispherical bowl, with plain band below the lip, separated by an ovolo from the decoration. The latter is variously arranged : (*a*) in two friezes, a style which is especially characteristic of an early date (Vespasian—early Domitian) and due originally to the influence of 29 ; (*b*) in a continuous scroll (at all periods) ; (*c*) in panels or " metopes " separated by upright divisions, sometimes containing circular medallions (at all periods) ; (*d*) in the so-called free style, in

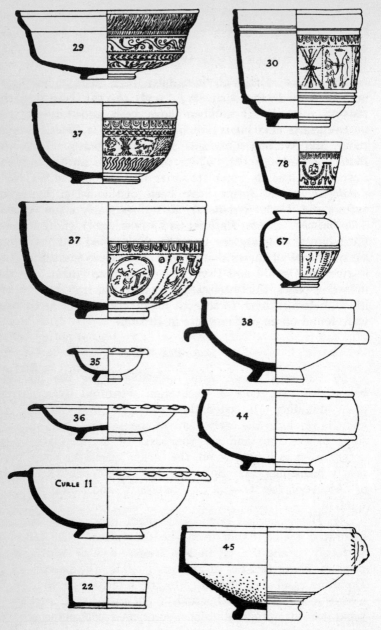

FIG. 50.—SAMIAN POTTERY ($\frac{1}{4}$).

which various motives are scattered over a field without divisions (at all periods) ; or (*e*) in an arcade (in the first century ; but also, and especially, at a late period). This form begins in Nero's reign and soon drives out 29 ; by A.D. 85, 29 has become the exception and 37 the rule ; a few years earlier, the reverse is the case. It persists till the end of the Samian manufacture. Flavian specimens generally have a narrow plain band above the ovolo ; those of the Antonine period almost invariably have a much wider one ; *cf.* the illustration, where the upper specimen is Flavian and the lower Antonine.

30. Cylindrical bowl. This begins early in the first century and lasts somewhat beyond the middle of the second. The decoration is arranged very much as in 37. The form is not so common as 29 and 37 ; it is common in the pre-Flavian period and again in the Antonine period, but less so during the intervening years, when its place is largely taken by the derivative form 78 (see below).

The illustration of form 30 shows features of both first and second-century examples of this bowl. Thus, the decoration is of second-century type, while the internal fluting below the rim is characteristic of the first century. In the second century this fluting is usually represented by one or two narrow grooves or is altogether absent.

78. This is developed out of the earlier type of 30 ; but differs in having no definite lip or foot-stand, and in the more pronounced slope of its wall. It belongs to the reigns of Vespasian—Domitian, and there is no evidence that it ever survived later than Trajan.

67. This globular vessel is the least rare of the remaining decorated forms. It is found at Flavian sites (the example illustrated is from Newstead), and extends into the reign of Trajan but not, apparently, later.

B. Plain Ware

35, 36. Round-sided cups, deep and shallow respectively, with barbotine leaves on a curved rim ; 35 is mainly Flavian ; 36, though frequently found in the Flavian period, is also common in the second century, tending to get larger and coarser as time goes on.

Curle 11. Mortarium-like bowl with flattish rim bearing barbotine leaves. The form, which resembles mortaria of the first century, is especially found on Flavian sites and lasted into the reign of Trajan.

38. Hemispherical bowl with overhanging flange about half-way down. This seems a later development of Curle 11, and does not appear before the time of Hadrian. It is common in the middle and late second century and lasts to the end of the Samian period. Occasionally it has been used as a mortarium, and it is very often copied in coarse ware.

44. Bowl resembling 38, but with the flange reduced to a slight ridge. It appears in the middle and late second century, and imitations go on longer.

45. Samian mortarium with upright side (wall-sided) and lion-head (or sometimes bat-head) spout. This is one of the two common Samian mortaria, the other (earlier and less common type, late second century) having a flange turned so steeply down as externally to resemble the wall-sided type; 45 begins in the late second century, and is especially characteristic of the early third.

22. Small cylindrical bowl. A first-century form, occurring in the Flavian period and before. A wider and shallower form (23) is mainly pre-Flavian.

15/17. Platter with quarter-round moulding inside at the junction of the wall and floor. A corresponding external hollow is generally, but not always, present. In its true form, as in the upper of the two illustrations, it is shallow and has a flat floor, a slight rise or kick in the centre (sometimes absent), and a rather steep wall. The specimen figured is Claudian. After this, the vessel becomes deeper and more bowl-shaped; the wall becomes less steep and the floor less flat; and thus is produced the Domitian-Trajan variety of the lower illustration. But in the meantime it has become less common, and in the Flavian period it is being superseded to a considerable extent by 18.

18. Platter with flat floor, rising gently to the centre in many early examples, more steeply in later; curved and rather steep wall; bead lip. This is the commonest plain form of the late first century. In the Claudian period (see upper illustration) it is shallow and flat in general effect; in

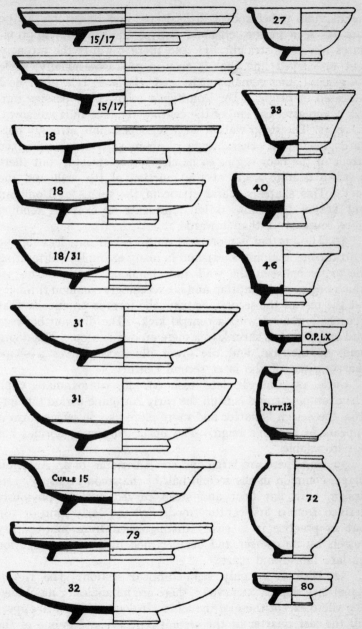

FIG. 51.—SAMIAN POTTERY (*continued*) (¼).

the Flavian, it becomes a little deeper and the profile of the floor (as seen in the left-hand half of the drawing) approximates less to a straight line and more towards the strongly bent or curved line that is seen in 31. Occasionally, while the general lines remain unchanged, the wall is a good deal increased in height. By Domitian's reign, 18 is passing into 18/31, and after the end of the century the true 18 is unknown.

18/31. The steep wall of 18 here slopes more strongly outwards, reaching a general angle of about 45° ; the bend in the profile of the floor begins to be clearly perceptible ; but there is still a definite angle at the junction of the wall and the floor. This shape is characteristic of the reigns of Domitian and Trajan. The illustration represents an example tending more towards 31 than towards 18.

31. The bottom is more and more dished out, leaving the central cone standing sharp and in many examples obliterating the angle between the wall and the floor. In the true 31, which begins with Hadrian and is exceedingly common throughout the rest of the second century, the form is practically that of a shallow bowl with a central kick. The division between wall and floor has shrunk to a mere groove or step. The depth tends to increase, and the lower illustration gives a shape characteristic of the later second century.

Curle 15. Campanulate dish (*cf.* 46, campanulate cup). The example figured is from the early Antonine period ; before this, the design is flatter and more plate-like, in which form it appears in Trajan's reign. The upturned rim is normal but not invariable.

79, 80. These are large and small varieties of an Antonine shape, common in the second half of the second century. Its design, with flat floor and steep curved wall, is obviously derived from a first-century model (*cf.* the early form of 18), but in practice it is easily distinguished from first-century vessels by its coarser and heavier modelling, not to mention its late fabric and glaze.

32. Dish of roughly semi-elliptical section. The rim is sometimes slightly incurved ; there are no angles or mouldings anywhere except those of the foot. It does not seem to appear till the last quarter of the second century, and is one of the characteristic shapes of the third.

27. Cup with profile like a trefoil arch upside down. This is the ordinary plain cup of the late first century; very common in that period, it lasts well into the second century though in diminishing quantities. The specimen figured is Domitian-Trajanic; before the Flavian period, the rather heavy rounded rim is absent, and in its place is a smaller rim, often keeled at the outside. An internal groove close to the lip, and a small groove surrounding the foot-stand, are almost universally present in first-century examples. After that time, both these features are generally absent.

33. Conical cup. The example figured is Antonine. The external groove and the slightly campanulate shape are normal from the latter years of the first century; earlier, down to about the time of Domitian, the sides are usually straight and the groove is generally absent; in Claudian specimens the sides are slightly convex externally. The normal form as here illustrated has a very long life with very slight variations, lasting to the end of Samian manufacture; but it only becomes really common in the Hadrian-Antonine period, and for practical purposes it may be said to supersede 27 in the reign of Hadrian.

40. Small hemispherical bowl. This form, like 32, which it much resembles, is commonly a product of the East Gaulish potteries, dating from the late second and early third centuries. It was, however, also made in the early second century at Lezoux, and develops out of a similar but lighter and more graceful Claudian form.

46. Campanulate cup, whose heavy out-curved rim distinguishes it from 33. The example figured is Antonine. The form, in a less clumsy design, seems to establish itself about Trajan's time; but the mid-second century is its main period and it does not seem to have outlasted the end of the century. A form (Curle 16) intermediate between 46 and 33 has been found in the period 140-180.

O.P. 60. Dish or bowl with flat rim terminating in an upturned edge. The specimen figured is a bowl, but the diameter varies, and wide dish-like specimens are found (cf. the relation between 80 and 79). The junction of wall and floor may be curved or angular. It is most commonly found in the Antonine period.

Ritterling 13. Ink-pot. With variations, these appear throughout the period.

72. Globular vase. As a plain form, this is early, first appearing in the first century ; but it lasts into the second century, and similar forms with incised and barbotine ornament survived to the end of that century and beyond.

§ 4. POTTERS' STAMPS

Samian potters frequently signed their work. Their names are impressed on their vessels by means of a stamp giving, in the majority of cases, an easily legible signature. In the case of many hundreds of potters, it is now possible to say something of the period and place at which they worked ; and therefore an index of potters' names containing this information, where it exists, is essential to the archaeologist who is using this type of pottery. No index of the required kind has ever been published ; but the student may be referred to the " Index of Potters " in *O. and P.* as the nearest approach to such a thing. Here, in accordance with the general plan of this book, a short selected index is given.

The names are here given in the nominative. This is seldom the form in which they occur in the actual stamp ; as a rule, a potter called Lucius (for instance) would stamp his vessels either LVCIVS F(ecit), or LVCI M(anu) or MA(nu), or LVCI O(fficina) or OF(ficina), or OF(ficina) LVCI. Sometimes these various formulae can be used to discriminate between potters of the same name ; but often the variations have no such significance, and in any case they form a complication that would lead us far beyond the scope of this book.

SELECTED LIST OF POTTERS' STAMPS

Where it is probable that two or more potters worked under the same name the fact is indicated, as (i), (ii), or (iii).[1]

C.G. = Lezoux and Central Gaul. E.G. = East Gaul.

The potters are grouped in the periods of their *chief* activity.

I. FIRST-CENTURY POTTERS

(a) *Early or Pre-Flavian Potters*

All South Gaulish except ATEPOMARVS.

ABITVS	CELER	ONCPA
ACVTVS (i)	COCVS (i)	PAVLLVS (i)
ALBINVS (i)	DAMONVS	POTITVS
AMANDVS (i)	DARIBITVS	PRIMVS (i)
AQVITANVS	DARRA	REGENVS
ARDACVS	FIRMO (i) =	ROGATVS
ATEPOMARVS (C.G.)	FIRMO . FE	SALVE
AVE VALE	GALLICANVS	SCOTIVS
BALBVS	GENIALIS (i)	SCOTTIVS
BASSVS	INGENVVS	SENICIO
BILICATVS	LABIO	SENO
BIO (i)	LICINIANA	SILVANVS (i)
BOLLVS	LICINVS	STABILIO
CANTVS	MACCARVS	SVCCESSVS
CAPITO (i)	MASCLVS (i)	VALERIVS
CARVS	MELVS (i)	VAPVSO
CASTVS (i)	MODESTVS (i)	VOLVS
CATLVS	NAMVS	VRVOED

(b) *Early Potters whose activity was continued (to varying extents) into the Flavian Period*

All South Gaulish.

ALBINVS (ii)	FELIX (i)	MVRRANVS
ALBVS (i)	L. C. CELSVS	NIGER
BASSVS and COELIVS	MANERTVS	NIGER and AVDACVS
CABVCA	MASCVLVS (ii)	(NIGRI AVD)
CELADVS	MATVGENVS	PASSENVS }
CRESTIO (i)	MOMMO	PASSIENVS }
CRESTVS	MONTANVS (i)	SECVNDVS (i)

[1] In some instances, it may be surmised that the same *officina* was producing work of a different character at varying periods.

(c) Flavian Potters

All South Gaulish except PRIMVLVS. Some of these potters, such as GERMANVS and VITALIS, began to work in Nero's reign ; the activity of others, such as L. COSIVS, L. COSIVS VIRILIS, BIRACILLVS, M. CRESTIO, CRVCVRO, NATALIS, was probably prolonged into the first decade of the second century.

ACVTVS (ii)	IBERTVS (? C.G.)	PATRICIVS
AVITVS (i)	IVLLINVS (i)	PAVLLVS (ii)
APER	IVSTVS	PRIMVLVS (C.G)
BIRACILLVS	L. COSIVS	PRIMVS (ii)
CALVS	L. COSIVS. VIRILIS	PONTIVS or
CALVVS	LOGIRNVS	PONTEIVS
CARILLVS	L. TER. SECVNDVS	PVDENS
CENSOR (i)	LVCCEIVS	ROPPVS
COSIVS RVFVS	MANDVILVS	RVFINVS
COSIVS RVFINVS	MANSVETVS	SABINVS
COTTO	MARTIALIS	SASMONOS
CRISPVS	MASCVS or MASCVVS	SECVNDVS (ii)
CRVCVRO	M. CRESTIO (ii)	SEVERVS
DAGOMARVS	MEDDILLVS	SILVANVS (ii)
DOMITVS	MEMOR	SILVINVS (ii)
FELICIO	MERCATO	VANDERIO
FIRMO (ii) =	NATALIS	VERECVNDVS (i)
OF FIRMONIS	NEQVRES	VIRILIS
FRONTINVS	NICEPHOR	VIRTVS
GERMANVS	NIGRINVS	VITALIS (i)

II. SECOND-CENTURY POTTERS

(a) Trajan-Hadrian

Some of these potters, such as BIGA and RANTO, may have commenced work in the late first century. The activity of others, such as AVSTRVS, may have extended into the reign of Antoninus Pius.

Where not stated, the potters worked at Lezoux and other localities in Central Gaul.

ALBILLVS (E.G.)	IANVS (E.G.)
ARCANVS	IOENALIS (C. or E.G.)
AVSTRVS	LIBERTVS
BIGA	PVTRIV
BIRRANTVS	RANTO (E.G.)
BONOXVS	REGINVS (E.G.)
BVTRIO	SATTO (E.G.)
CARANTINVS	SECVNDINVS
CENSORINVS	TALVSSA
DONNAVCVS, who used the ꟾOꟾ monogram (C. or E.G.)	VIDVCVS or VIDVCOS (S.G. and E.G.)
ꟾOꟾ potter of Blickweiler	VERECVNDVS (ii)
IANVARIS	

(b) *Hadrian-Antonine*

Lezoux or Central Gaul where provenance is not stated.

ADVOCISVS
ALBINVS (iii)
ALBVCIVS
ATENICVS
ATILIANVS
ATTIANO
AVENTINVS
AVITVS (ii) (C. or E.G.)
AVITI . F (iii) (E.G.)
BANVILLVS
BELLINICVS
BELSVS (E.G.)
BORILLVS
CALETIVS
CAMBO (E.G.)
CAMBVS
CARATILLVS
CATIANVS
CERIALIS (ii) (E.G.)
CIBISVS (E.G.)
CINNAMVS
CINTVSMVS (C. and E.G.)
CIRIVNA (E.G.)
COBNERTVS (E.G.)
DIVICATVS
DIVIXTVS

DOECCVS, who used the large
ꓷꓷꓷ monogram
FIRMVS (E.G.)
GEMINVS (ii)
LATINNVS (E.G.)
LAXTVCISSA
LVTAEVS (E.G.)
MAIOR (E.G.)
MVXTVLLVS
NAMILIANVS
PATERNVS (i)
PAVLLVS (iii)
PRIMITIVS (E.G.)
PRISCVS
QVINTVS (ii) (C. and E.G.)
REBVRRVS (ii)
REDITVS
REGALIS (E.G.)
RITOGENVS
SACRILLVS
SATVRNINVS
TITTIVS
TITVRO
VERECVNDVS (iii)
VICTOR (E.G.)
VICTORINVS (E.G.)

(c) *Antonine Potters whose activity was prolonged into the First Half of the Third Century*

ALPINIVS (E.G.)
Q. ALPINIVS (E.G.)
CENSOR (iii) (E.G.)
COMITIALIS (E.G.)
CRICIRO (E.G.)

DEXTER (E.G.)
IVLIVS (ii) or (iii) (E.G.)
MAIAAVS (E.G.)
TORDILO (E.G.)

CHAPTER XIV

COARSE POTTERY

§ 1. INTRODUCTORY

THE purpose of this chapter, dealing with wares other than Samian, demands a word of explanation. The reader is offered a series of nearly a hundred numbered and dated pottery-types, followed by notes on one or two special fabrics. The types selected for discussion are strictly confined to types (*a*) found in this country, because types do, and dates may, vary from one country to another ; (*b*) found in circumstances which absolutely fix their date, either because they have been found in the course of scientific excavation or because they come from a site with a known and short period of occupation ; (*c*) properly published, so that the reader can check the writer's statements and is not asked to take or leave his *ipse dixit*.

The task of dating a number of types by this method has been undertaken in the belief that the time is ripe for a first attempt at something of the sort. Twenty years ago, hardly a shred of the material used in this chapter was in existence. Ten years ago, only about half of it existed. To-day it exists in such profusion that to consult it in its entirety is difficult, and to extract provisional conclusions from it permissible. Some of these conclusions, as they affect the dating of individual types, are stated here, chiefly with the intention of giving the beginner a trustworthy introduction to a very important and difficult subject. Attention is concentrated on the shape of vessels, not because it is the only thing worth studying, but because it is the only thing that can be, to some extent, learnt from books.

As this chapter is not intended to be a substitute for the actual handling of pottery, so it is not intended to replace the use of books not here quoted, in which further types and other instances are illustrated and discussed. The reader will find no references to museum catalogues and foreign publications, not because he need not study them, but because such references would not promote the end of this particular chapter.

Before proceeding to the discussion of the individual types, it is well to explain what is meant by a type. These pots—often very rough pieces of work made by people with little training and under conditions little favourable to uniformity either of pattern or of quality—show only feeble and inter-mittent tendencies towards standardisation. Each potter did much what he pleased, and each pot was a new thing. The archaeologist who begins to collect and classify the forms of coarse pots soon finds that he is dealing with an infinite variety of fluctuating shapes each passing over into others by gradations that are at first hardly perceptible. It is impossible to draw up a complete list of these shapes ; it is impossible even to do for coarse pottery what Dragendorff did for Samian, and draw up a list complete enough for practical purposes. All one can do is to select, out of the welter of forms, a number of more or less recognisable fixed points, and use these as trigonometrical stations for a more detailed survey whose complication must be very great.

The types here offered are of this kind. Few specimens will be found corresponding exactly to any one of the illus-trated types ; a great many will be found with a fairly close resemblance to one or other, or intermediate between two ; for instance, jar-rims intermediate between 64 and 72—they might be called 64/72—are very common ; so are examples that might be called 65/72, and so on.

The beginner will, for this reason, find that a good deal of experience is needed before he can use these types freely for dating purposes. He may find a pot which by his unaided efforts he would assign to one type, when an expert would assign it to another, perhaps to one with quite different chrono-logical associations. It is not a question of merely looking a form up and seeing what its date is ; it is a question of using your judgment as to the significance of this or that resem-blance connecting the specimen which you are studying with this or that type.

In spite of these difficulties, it is hoped that this chapter may be a help to the beginner ; and also that it may be of some value to the trained archaeologist to have a series of types, however incomplete, to which he may refer in reporting upon his discoveries, instead of having to choose between, on the one hand, publishing much unnecessary description and many unnecessary illustrations, and, on the other, saying nothing about the vast majority of his finds.

§ 2. DATED TYPES

1-16. Mortaria. The *mortarium*, or *pelvis*, is a stout bowl, shaped internally like a segment of a sphere and studded with particles of hard grit, which was used for triturating food. It has a heavy rim, to resist the cracking, beginning at the edge, to which a bowl so used is liable. In the first and second centuries it has a bead-and-roll rim (1-10) ; by the fourth century this has given way in the south to the flanged (12), and in the north to the hammerhead (13-14) type. Exactly how and when these changes took place we do not yet know. Out of the great variety of mortarium-forms, many of them confined to a quite small district, a few of more or less general interest have been selected for discussion.[1]

1. Thin horizontal rim, hardly curved at all. A first-century type, not very common anywhere in Britain, but becoming decidedly rare after 100 (Bushe-Fox, 10 ; Hardknot).

2. Thick horizontal rim, very slightly curved. A first-century type (Newstead), lasting rarely into the first half of the second. It is found as late as the Antonine period (Balmuildy), but even at early second-century sites (*e.g.* Gellygaer) it is generally absent.

3. Upward-sloping rim, curved over at the end. Late first and early second century (Slack, Hardknot) ; seldom so late as Hadrian ; isolated specimens occur as late as Pius (Balmuildy).

4. Upward-sloping rim, hooked at the end. First-century type (Newstead), lasting into the early second century (Hardknot).

---

[1] The fundamental work on Romano-British mortaria is Bushe-Fox's series of numbered types published in *Wroxeter*, 1912. It is here referred to as " Bushe-Fox," followed by a series-number.

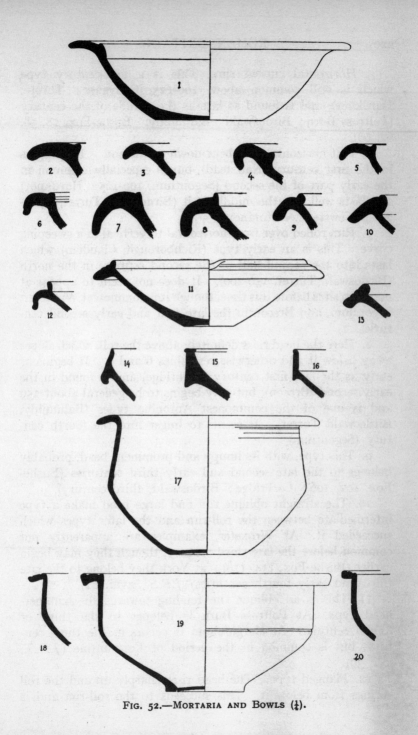

FIG. 52.—MORTARIA AND BOWLS (¼).

5. Horizontal curved rim. This is a first-century type which is still common about 100-125 (Gellygaer; Throp; Hardknot), and is found as late as the middle of the century (Poltross Burn; Birdoswald; Balmuildy. Bushe-Fox, 18, 58, 62, 66).

6. Flat horizontal rim, bent down at the end. This begins in the first century (Newstead), but is especially common in the early part of the second (Segontium, 100-125; Hardknot) and lasts well into the middle of it (Birdoswald Turret, 150 ?-200; Newstead, Antonine).

7. Rim rolled over from horizontal to vertical in a sweeping curve. This is an early type (Richborough, Claudian) which lasts into the second half of the second century in the north (Birdoswald Turret, 150-200). It does not seem to appear at northern sites before this time, though it is common at Wroxeter, Segontium, and Brecon in the late first and early second centuries.

8. Here the bead rises definitely above the roll, which slopes away below it and otherwise resembles 6 and 7. It begins as early as the late first century (Corbridge) and is found in the early second (Brecon), but only begins to be general about 150 and is one of the commonest Antonine types (Balmuildy, Birdoswald Turret). It seems to linger into the fourth century (Segontium).

9. This type, with its lumpy and prominent bead, probably belongs to the late second and early third centuries (Bushe-Fox, 102, 106; Corbridge; Birdoswald, third century).

10. The straight oblique rim and large bead make a type intermediate between the roll-rim and the later types which succeeded it. At Wroxeter, examples are apparently not common before the late third century, though they may begin earlier (Bushe-Fox, 114, 118); at York they belong to the late third and early fourth centuries (*J.R.S.*, xviii, 82).

11. This is an oblique rim tending towards the hammer-head type. At Poltross Burn it belongs to the third or fourth century. At Margidunum it occurs in the third century, but is common in the period of Constantine (*J.R.S.*, xvi, 39).

12. Flanged type. The bead rises sharply up and the roll springs from below it. This succeeds to the roll-rim and is

the standard third and fourth-century type throughout the south and midlands. Rarely it appears in the second century (Caerleon, Hadrian-Antonine; Balmuildy, Antonine). In the north it is never more than a rare visitor; a few examples occur in Yorkshire, practically none on the two Walls. For the dating of its varieties we have no evidence.

13-14. The hammer-head type succeeds to the roll-rim in the north, as the flanged does in the south, but at a later date. At Wroxeter and in North Wales both types are found, but at southern sites like Silchester the hammer-head occurs only as a very rare stray. It has not been proved to exist before about 270, but its presence and the absence of earlier types in a deposit of 220-300 at Margidunum (*J.R.S.*, xvi, Pl. VI, 11, 12), suggest that it may have been current for a considerable part of the third century, though it seems to have become common only in the fourth. Already in the late second century, however, a type verging towards it had begun to be made (Limestone Bank; *A.A.*³, ix, 66). Whether it went on to the end of the fourth century is uncertain; it fails to appear at Huntcliff (*J.R.S.*, ii, 225). No data exist for the chronology of its varieties; it will suffice here to point out that the slope of its side may vary from 30° to 60°, and that the rim may be plain or reeded.

15. The vertical-sided mortarium came into use about the end of the second century (Corbridge, 150-200; Bushe-Fox, 218-238; Caerleon about 200; Birdoswald, third century). It is no doubt influenced by Drag. 45, and, like many imitations of Samian shapes, it outlasts its original, for it is said to be mainly a late type, though I cannot quote evidence of this.

16. This is a definite imitation of Drag. 45, and is common in the third and fourth centuries (Bushe-Fox, 242; Rich., types 107, 115).

17-34 are bowls. 17-22 are carinated bowls, *i.e.* their sides are angular in profile. This is one of the most useful types for dating. It passes through a regular series of changes from Claudius to Hadrian, after which it merges in other types. The rim, which is flat, tends especially in the first century to be delicately modelled and reeded on the upper surface; and, especially after the end of the century, the carination may be softened into a curve without materially changing the type.

There is also a late carinated bowl (Rich., 162 ; Segontium, late third and fourth centuries), and others faintly similar are found in the late New Forest stamped ware ; there is also the late type No. 31 ; but it is easy to avoid confusing these with the types now under review.

17. In the middle of the first century the sides of the bowl " tumble home " from the carination, and as a rule the rim bends slightly downwards (Richborough, 20, Claudius).

18. A variety with down-turned rim seems generally to belong to the first century, but lasts into the second (Caerleon ; *A.*, lxxviii, 180 ; but also Brecon, Poltross Burn, Limestone Bank, Birdoswald, the last three Hadrianic).

19. The standard type, with vertical sides and horizontal rim, is mainly Flavian (Newstead, Caerleon, Corbridge), but it lasts into the reign of Trajan and, though not very freely, into that of Hadrian (Poltross Burn, several specimens).

20. A variety with upturned rim seems to be always later than 100 (Gellygaer, Hardknot, Haltwhistle Burn, Brecon, Caerleon, Birdoswald ; *A.*, lxxviii, 180), but does not appear to last later than No. 19.

21. Under the influence of No. 44, the carinated bowl takes a new form during the first half of the second century. The lattice pattern which is sometimes present, the pie-dish rim, and the sloping side, are borrowed from No. 44, but the carination remains. This type is already found before 140 (Brecon, Slack) and in the Hadrian-Antonine period on both Walls. It lasts into the second half of the century (Appletree Turret, 150 ?-200 ; Corbridge, 150-200).

22. A similar bowl, but with bead rim instead of pie-dish rim, also betrays the influence of second century-dish types, and is found perhaps as late as the third quarter of the second century (Appletree Turret, 150 ?-200). It is possible that here and in No. 21 a reminiscence of Drag. 29 should be seen.

23. This is a variety of 21 with the carination receding towards the bottom of the vessel, leaving a mere chamfer. It is a deep version (bowl instead of dish) of No. 45, and, like that, is found as early as 100-120 (Brecon), but is for the most part Antonine (Balmuildy ; Corbridge, 150-200), and lasts well into the third century (Margidunum ; *J.R.S.*, xvi, Pl. VI, 30).

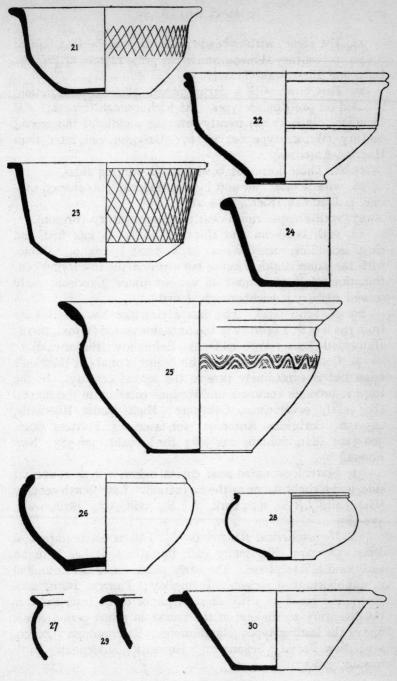

Fig. 53.—Bowls (½).

24. The same, with a bead-rim, occurs in the first half of the second century at Slack, and in the years 125-200 at Poltross Burn and Birdoswald Turret.

25. This bowl, with a flaring mouth above a constriction, is based on pre-Roman types. At Richborough (type 14) it is Claudian ; it lasts apparently into the middle of the second century (Wrox., type 62, 80-120 ; Caerleon, not later than Hadrian-Antonine).

26-28. Three forms of bowl with in-curving sides.

26, with a bead rim and high-shouldered pear-shaped outline, is Claudian (Rich., type 18).

27, with oblique rim, is early second century (Brecon).

28, with bead-rim and elliptical profile, is late first and early second centuries (Wrox., 12, 80-120 ; Hardknot). Bowls with the same elliptical curve but without the in-curving continuation of it are found at various times (Caerleon, early second century ; Richborough, fourth).

29. Roll-rim bowl. This has a rim like No. 5. It lasts from the late first century to the Antonine period (Wrox., 16-18 ; Haltwhistle Burn ; Poltross Burn ; Balmuildy ; Birdoswald).

30. Conical flanged bowl. This begins in or about Hadrian's reign but is exceedingly rare in the second century. In the third it becomes common, and remains common in the fourth. (For early occurrences, Gellygaer ; High House Milecastle, 125-150 ; Corbridge, Antonine ; for later, *e.g.* Poltross Burn, 300-330 ; Margidunum, 220-300 ; Birdoswald, 376-383 ; New Forest.)

31. Flattish carinated bowl, conical below, with short upright side, and a slight flange at the carination. Late fourth century (Huntcliff, *J.R.S.*, ii ; York, *J.R.S.*, xviii, 97 ; Birdoswald, 376-383).

32. Hemispherical flanged bowl. This is an imitation of Drag. 38 ; and, like many such imitations, it has both an early and a late phase. The early phase (Hadrian-Antonine) is unimportant (Caerleon ; Balmuildy ; Poltross Burn, 200-300) ; the great majority of such pieces occur from the late third century to the end of the fourth, in which period this is one of the leading types (Margidunum ; Richborough ; Pevensey ; New Forest ; Segontium ; Huntcliff ; Mildenhall ; Birdoswald, 376-383).

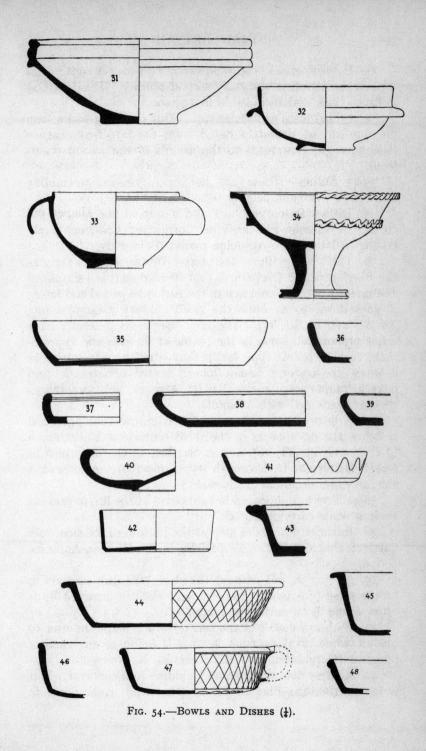

FIG. 54.—BOWLS AND DISHES ($\frac{1}{4}$).

33. Hemispherical bowl with drooping rim. A continental type of the late first and early second century. It appears at Poltross Burn and Birdoswald in 125-200.

34. Frilled tazza or incense cup. This probably had a long life ; it can be definitely dated from the late first century (Richborough, Newstead) to the middle of the second (Caerleon).

35-45. Dishes. These are flat open vessels, resembling bowls but with less height.

35. Dish with curved side and a step at the foot of the curve. A common Flavian type (Corbridge ; Caerleon) rarely lasting as late as the Antonine period (Balmuildy).

36. The same, without the step. This appears as early as the Flavian period (Newstead), but most often it is a simplified and later form of 35, common in the Antonine period and later ; it goes down to at least the third century (Margidunum ; *J.R.S.*, xvi, Pl. VI, 15). The later specimens generally have a less pronounced curve in the profile of the side and approximate to the conical type (41) ; they often have a lattice or a wavy line outside, and a looped scrawl underneath, and have a rudimentary carination (*cf.* Nos. 41, 46) ; sometimes they are provided with a handle.

37. A heavy type with an external groove running round it below the lip appears in the third century at Margidunum (*J.R.S.*, xvi, Pl. VI, 26), and is ascribed to the late third or fourth century at Richborough (types 167-168). A somewhat similar vessel occurs at Birdoswald in 376-383.

38-40 have a pronounced inward curve at the lip, to prevent spilling while carrying liquids.

38. Incurved lip, and a step at the bottom of the side. At Caerleon this form belongs especially to the Hadrian-Antonine period.

39. As No. 38, but without the step ; the date appears to be the same (Caerleon), though a very slightly incurved lip is often found both earlier and later.

40. With a " kick " in the centre, which helps the user to hold it while drinking from it, this is found in the time of Claudius (Margidunum ; *J.R.S.*, xiii, Pl. X, No. 5).

41. Rimless dish with straight oblique (conical) side. This is found from the Flavian period (Newstead) right down to

the fourth century (York). In the second and third century it may have a trellis or a wavy line scored outside it, and merges into contemporary forms of 36 ; like them, it may have a rudimentary carination, as shown in the figure ; but this is absent in the fourth century.

42. Rimless dish with almost vertical (cylindrical) sides. This seems to be a first-century form (Newstead, type 34).

Nos. 43-48 are dishes with rims. There are two types of rim, the flat or pie-dish rim, and the bead rim.

43-45. Pie-dishes, with narrow, flattish rims. These are derived from a Continental form of the Augustan period ; but in Britain they only occur sparingly in the first century, mostly towards the end of it, and begin to appear in considerable numbers only at early second-century sites like Gellygaer and Slack and in pre-Hadrianic deposits at Corbridge. They are very common indeed about the middle of the second century ; but on the Antonine Wall a tendency is already at work to replace the pie-dish rim by the bead-rim.

43. Early form of pie-dish with straight or concave side and a reeded rim. Early second century (Gellygaer) ; not found after Trajan.

44. Pie-dish with curved side. This is No. 36 with a pie-dish rim added. It is found from about 120 (Haltwhistle Burn) to at least the middle of the century, and generally has a trellis on the side.

45. The same with straight (conical) side. This and the foregoing merge into one another in such a way that the line between them is not easy to draw, but this is decidedly the commoner, and lasts from Trajan or Hadrian (Gellygaer) to late in the second century. Apart from the rim it is just like 41.

46-48 have a bead-rim. This does not seem to begin so early as the pie-dish rim ; it is absent from Gellygaer and rare at Hardknot and Slack ; its chief period is the late second century.

46. Dish with curved side (as No. 35) and bead-rim. A common type in the Antonine period. It generally has a rudimentary carination, as shown in the figure, and a trellis ornament.

47. Like 46, but with a handle (Segontium, 100-125). The rim of this specimen is intermediate between the pie-dish rim

and the bead-rim proper, and shows how the latter developed out of the former—perhaps for convenience in drinking, as the handle suggests.

48. Dish with straight side (as No. 41) and bead-rim. This is hardly ever found in the second century ; at that date such dishes almost always have a slight curve in the rim and belong to No. 47. In the fourth century, however, it does appear (Poltross Burn, York).

49-56. Flagons. This may be described as a jug with a narrow neck, or alternatively as a flask with a handle. It is one of the many foreign types which were naturalised in Britain as a result of the Roman Conquest. The early examples are therefore all imported, and native styles do not greatly affect its development.

49-51 are so-called " screw-neck " flagons. The term is inaccurate, because the mouldings on the neck are not a screw-thread but separate rings ; but no more convenient name has been suggested. The type begins in the reign of Tiberius, and lasts until the middle of the second century.[1] It is a curious fact that on the Continent this type is very common at Trier, and practically unknown elsewhere.

49. In the reign of Claudius this flagon has a peaked handle (Rich., type 33).

50. Later in the century the handle becomes more square in profile (Flavian period ; Newstead, Corbridge).

51. In the second century the top moulding tends to assert itself at the expense of the others, which dwindle into insignificance. In this form the type lingers into the third quarter of the second century, though it is rare after about 140 (Poltross Burn, Birdoswald Turret, 125-200 ; High House Turret, 150-200 ; Balmuildy, 140-200 ; Corbridge, 150-200).

52-53. Flagon with double-ring lip. This begins before the " screw-neck " (which is in fact a development of it), lasts alongside of it, and survives it as the standard type of the second century.

52. The earlier varieties are more sharply modelled than the later ; they have a more cylindrical neck, which passes more abruptly into the curve of the body.

[1] A third-century revival of the "screw-neck" is accompanied by features which obviously betray its late date ; Caerleon (*A*., lxxviii, 185, po. 58), Richborough type 148:

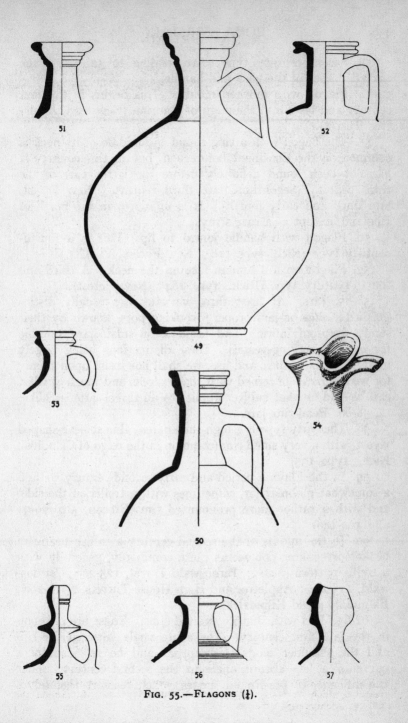

FIG. 55.—FLAGONS (¼).

53. Second-century type corresponding to 52. Note the curved shapes of the neck and handle.

54. Flagon with pinched mouth. This begins in the first century and lasts into the reign of Hadrian (Newstead, Appletree Turret).

55. The flagon with a ring round the middle of its neck is common on the Continent before 250, but in this country it has not been found definitely before the latter part of the third century (Segontium, late third century; New Forest, late third and early fourth). It is unknown in the north of England, except as a rare stray.

56. Flagon with handle joined to lip. This is a fourth-century type (Rich. type 118; New Forest, Pl. IX).

57. Flagon with a human face on the neck. A third and fourth-century type (Rich., type 184; New Forest).

58-85. Jars. At least three varieties are usually distinguished: *ollae* or jars proper; cooking pots, known by their sandy fireproof fabric; and beakers, or small jars suitable for use as drinking-vessels. These distinctions being largely matters of size, fabric and use, we shall not insist upon them; for we are here concerned with shape alone, and much of what can be said on that subject applies to all three varieties alike.

58-60. Bead-rim jars.

58. The early type is a high-shouldered, almost pear-shaped vessel, with a very small rim (common in the reign of Claudius; Rich., type 135).

59. In the Flavian period and early second century we find a somewhat globular jar, sometimes with a trellis on the side, and with a rather more pronounced rim (Brecon, A.D. 70-90 and 100-140).

60. In the middle of the second century a tallish bead-rim beaker or cooking-pot occurs quite commonly, generally with a trellis pattern (Slack; Birdoswald Turret, 125-200; Birdoswald, 125-200; Appletree and High House Turrets, 150 ?-200; Balmuildy; Old Kilpatrick).

61-63. Jars with sharply everted rims. These are common in the late first century. The acute angle between the rim and the shoulder tends to disappear and be replaced by a curve or a less abrupt angle in the second century, under the influence of pre-Roman tastes, which reassert themselves

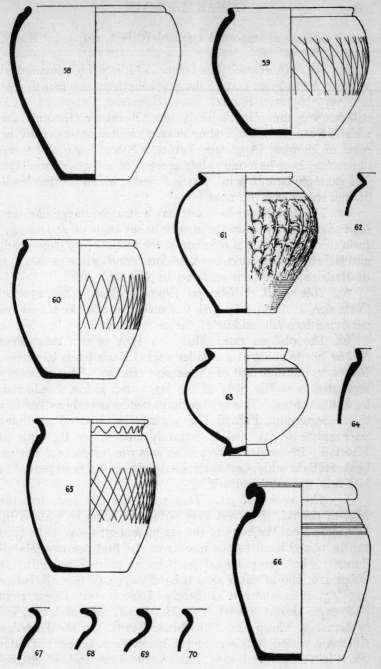

FIG. 56.—JARS (¼).

at the expense of imported fashions (*C.W.*², xiii, 343 ; *Wrox.*, 1912, p. 69).

61. Jar with everted bead-rim. This is a high-shouldered jar with a head-rim turned sharply back from the mouth. It is a very common Flavian form (Newstead, Corbridge, etc.), still fairly common in the early second century (Throp, Halt-whistle Burn, etc.), and lasting in very small quantities into the reign of Hadrian (Appletree Turret, 125-200). An odd scrap or two may even be found as late as the time of Pius (Balmuildy). The example figured is in " rustic " ware, which is often made in this shape and the next.

62. This is like the last, but has a straight flange-like rim, bent sharply back from the mouth at an angle of at least 45° from the vertical. It is common in the first century (Newstead) and lasts into the second, but is seldom found as late as the reign of Hadrian, when it is replaced by No. 64.

63. This small globular jar (Poltross Burn, A.D. 125-200 ; Corbridge, A.D. 150-200) is an instance of a rim like the above surviving into the middle of the second century.

64. The oblique rim. This is a type of rim resembling No. 62 but inclined at a smaller angle, which tends to replace No. 62 in the first half of the second century. It is generally separated from the body of the jar, which is low-shouldered, by a slight ledge. This type perhaps begins as early as Trajan's reign (Segontium, Fig. 76, No. 30, may be regarded as almost an example of it), and is certainly current by the time of Hadrian ; in the Antonine period it is the commonest rim for beakers (Balmuildy, Corbridge, etc.). It has not been proved to last into the third century.

65. The neck-rim jar. This resembles the last, but the edge of the rim is turned over outwards, so as to make a lip separated from the body of the jar by a short neck. The type can be traced back to the middle of the first century (Margi-dunum) ; but for practical purposes it only comes into use about 110, and at many sites it hardly appears, if at all, before 125 (*e.g.* it is common at Brecon, 100-120, but absent from Gellygaer, almost absent from Hardknot, rare at Slack, ex-ceptional at Throp and Haltwhistle Burn). In the Hadrian-Antonine period it is one of the commonest types, but after 200 it is replaced by No. 72. The vessel is generally a cooking-

pot in sandy grey-black ware with a trellis pattern round the body. The neck is often decorated as shown in the figure, with a wavy line ; this feature seems to be commonest quite early in the history of the type (*Brecon*, p. 218), and, though far from rare in the middle of the second century (Balmuildy), becomes less common after 150 (*C.W.*², xiii, 376).

66. A special kind of neck-rim jar is characteristic of "Huntcliff ware" (see below, § 3), and is the commonest shape in which that ware is found. The rim is grooved for a lid, and is bent over in a heavy drooping lip ; the jar is hand-made. This shape belongs to the late fourth century (Yorkshire coastal signal-stations), beginning perhaps about the middle of the century.

67-70. Recurved rim, sweeping round in an outward curve answering the inward curve of the shoulder. This type goes back to the Claudian period (Richborough) and reappears in almost every subsequent generation (*e.g.* Newstead, Flavian ; Wroxeter, 80-120 ; Throp and Haltwhistle Burn, early second century ; Balmuildy, Antonine ; Poltross Burn, 200-270, 270-330 ; Segontium and Huntcliff, late fourth century).

68. A variety with a ledge at the base of the neck.

69. A variety with an offset at the base of the neck.

70. A variety with an offset in the middle of the neck. All these varieties reappear at widely differing dates.

71. Cordon jar. This is a variety of the recurved-rim jar. Cordons, or raised ridges running horizontally round a vessel, are very common in pre-Roman pottery. After the Roman conquest they still appear, especially round the base of the neck. The earliest examples (Claudian ; Margidunum, Rich. type 1), so far resemble their predecessors as to stand on a pedestal foot. In the Flavian period (Newstead, type 38), the cordon jar still retains a tendency to a high-shouldered pear shape. In the early second century (Brecon, Gellygaer) and the Hadrian-Antonine period (Benwell, Appletree Turret, Poltross Burn, Balmuildy, Wroxeter) the pear shape is disappearing, and in the third century the type still lingers on, but has sunk into a comparatively globular shape (several at Margidunum, 220-300 ; *J.R.S.*, xvi, Pl. V, 1, 3-5).

72. Jar with cavetto rim. This rim rises from the body of the jar almost vertically at first, and then sweeps round in about

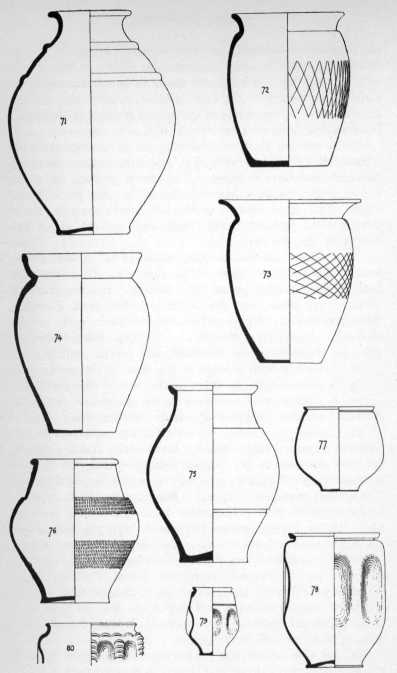

FIG. 57.—JARS (*continued*) (¼).

a quarter of a circle, forming a cavetto moulding. This kind of rim is found as early as Claudius (see No. 81, Margidunum ; *J.R.S.*, xiii, Pl. X, 8), but only becomes common when the type is re-developed out of 64 by substituting a curved rim for a straight one. This development does not definitely set in until the reign of Pius, when the " earlier cavetto," as figured, begins to appear. On the Antonine Wall this is one of the regular types, especially for cooking-pots (*e.g.* Balmuildy) ; late in the second century it is gradually superseding 64 and 65.

73. The later cavetto rim, which belongs chiefly to the first half of the fourth century, is wide-spreading and generally wider than its own height. The jar, on the other hand, becomes narrower as the rim becomes wider ; often the diameter of the rim is a good deal greater than that of the jar itself. With this late cavetto rim is associated a new type of trellis, obtuse-angled instead of acute-angled (*Wrox.*, 1913, p. 53 ; New Forest, Pl. XVIII ; Brecon, *c* 73 ; Segontium, No. 56 ; *J.R.S.*, xviii, 82 ; Birdoswald, 300-376).

74. Bell-mouth jar. This has a hollow rim to hold a lid. It appears at Margidunum in the reign of Claudius (*J.R.S.*, xiii, Pl. X, 1), and in the late first or early second century at Slack ; but it is still common in the third and fourth centuries (Margidunum ; *J.R.S.*, xvi, 40). It is also a fourth-century Continental type. So far as Britain is concerned, it seems to be made only in a hard grey gritty ware whose centre of distribution is at or near Derby.

75. The butt-beaker. This is a pre-Roman jar which survives into the Roman period. One at Segontium is probably of the first century ; one at Wroxeter is Antonine (Wrox., type 71).

76. This is a third-century example (Rich., type 142) which is intermediate between the foregoing and No. 85 ; its body is becoming more bulbous, its neck more conical.

77. A little beaker with an everted bead-rim, having its greatest girth well below the middle, and granulated or roughcast externally, extends from the Flavian period (Newstead) to the Antonine (Balmuildy, Corbridge, Newstead, Poltross Burn, Birdoswald). After this time a kindred form, with a longer foot and narrower mouth, is one of the standard types for Castor ware.

78-80. The folded beaker has large shallow indentations in its sides. It is sometimes rough-cast or decorated with scales ; it is also one of the commonest Castor forms, but in that ware it approximates in shape to the bulbous beaker (No. 85).

78. In the first century it has a stiff angular profile with upright, oblique or everted rim (Rich., types 12, 55 ; Newstead, type 31).

79. A variety shaped like No. 77 appears in the reign of Hadrian (Caerleon).

80. In the third century the rim is recurved and loses its angular profile (*J.R.S.*, xvi, Pl. VI, 16).

81. The pear-shaped jar, with its profile recalling the pre-Roman pedestal urn, is an early type. It is common in the middle of the first century (Margidunum, *J.R.S.*, xiii, Pls. X, XI), and the Flavian period (Newstead, type 28) ; after this it occurs only sporadically (*e.g.* Corbridge, 150-200). Its rim is always of an early type, generally Nos. 61 or 62 ; in the example figured, note the Claudian cavetto rim referred to under No. 72.

82. The beaker with a constricted shoulder is a reminiscence of pre-Roman shapes. It is found in the first century with a rustic surface (Brecon) ; it is fairly common in the early second century (Gellygaer), and occurs as late as Hadrian (Poltross Burn).

83. Carinated beaker. A pre-Roman type which reappears in the early and middle second century (Rich., types 75-77, first half of the second century ; Appletree Turret, 150 ?-200).

84. A straight-sided conical beaker, shaped like an ordinary tumbler, belongs to the first half of the second century (Brecon, 100-120 ; Haltwhistle Burn ; Poltross Burn, 125-200 ; Birdoswald Turret, 125-200). It is not found after Hadrian (*C.W.*[2], xiii, 347).

85. Bulbous beaker, with a globular body and tapering conical neck. On the Continent this begins before the middle of the third century, but though Britain has third-century examples (*J.R.S.*, xvi, Pl. V, 8) most of the dated specimens belong to the fourth century (Wrox., type 81 ; Rich., type 96). It is a common south-country form, but seldom penetrates so far north as Wroxeter and York, and never farther.

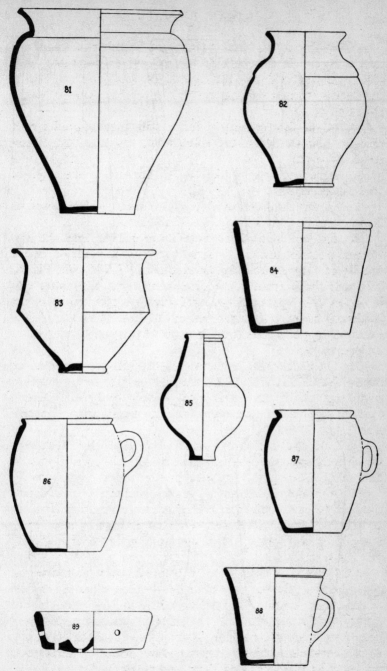

FIG. 58.—JARS, MUGS, STRAINER (¼).

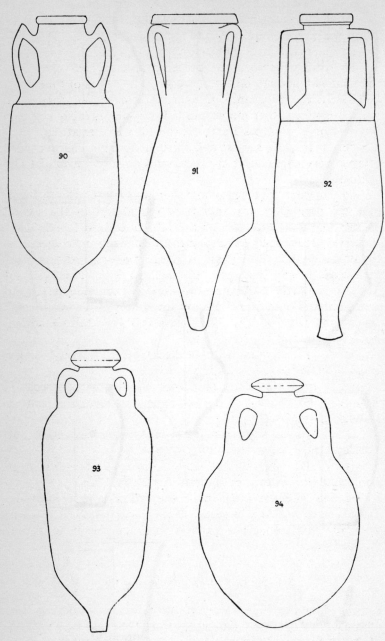

FIG. 59.—AMPHORAE (ABOUT $\frac{1}{12}$).

86-88. The mug is a beaker with a handle. It is a northern form, which never appears in the south (*Rich.*, i, 89) ; little jugs found at Silchester do not belong to this type.

86. The earliest example (Brecon, A.D. 70-90) has convex sides and the handle high on the shoulder ; the rim is of type 59.

87. In the Hadrian-Antonine period a beaker of type 64, with a handle rather more than half-way up, is fairly common in the north (Poltross Burn, Newstead, Old Kilpatrick).

88. In the late second and third centuries a concave-sided mug is very common at Wroxeter and already appears at Old Kilpatrick.

89. Strainer. This is an article in use, apparently, throughout the period, at any rate from the middle of the second century (Wrox., type 38) to the late third and fourth (New Forest). It is explained as a press for making little cheeses.

90-94. Amphorae. These are large two-handled jars, used like casks for the transport of wine, oil, etc. Fragments of them—thick, pale-buff potsherds—are very common on Roman sites, but whole examples are not often found. They all come from abroad, and fall into two main types : a tall cylindrical type (90-93), and a globular (94).

90. A tall amphora with peaked handles is found in the reign of Claudius (Rich., type 25).

91. A type with long handles, set close to the neck, is Claudian, but persists to the beginning of the second century (Caerleon, type 78).

92. A type like 91, but with square handles, occurs at Caerleon (type 80) in the years 90-130.

93. A tall amphora with loop handles is a first-century type still found in the reign of Hadrian (Caerleon, type 81).

94. The globular amphora is the ordinary type from the early second century onwards (Newstead, Bar Hill), though the tall type sometimes persists into the Antonine period (Balmuildy).

§ 3. Notes on Certain Fabrics

The distinctions between different fabrics cannot be discussed briefly in print ; differences which are easy to point out orally, in the presence of examples, are difficult if not impossible

to describe in a book, and in general the subject is best left to
personal instruction and experience. It would, no doubt, be
possible in a book to discuss the best-known wares, such as
Castor and New Forest ; but this would soon pass beyond the
limits of space available in the present volume, and it must
suffice to give a few references.

Castor ware, which is a ware with a blackish lustrous glaze,
consisting mostly of thin-walled beakers, especially folded and
bulbous beakers, and often decorated in barbotine with running
animals and curvilinear vegetable motives, or with rouletting,
was made both on the Continent and (among other wares) in
the Castor district, where the production seems to have begun
in the late second century and to have lasted until about the
end of the Roman occupation. The *locus classicus* for a description of the pottery district is Artis, *Durobrivae* (1828) ; a
general account of the industry is given in the Victoria County
Histories of Northamptonshire and Huntingdonshire.

New Forest ware, or rather New Forest wares, for more
than one type of pottery was made in the New Forest, are less
easy to match by Continental parallels. The New Forest industry has been best studied by Mr. Heywood Sumner, and
described in his *Excavations in New Forest Roman Pottery Sites*
(1927). The industry belongs to the late third and fourth
centuries ; its most characteristic products are a hard grey
ware coated with a purplish or brownish metallic glaze, and
a creamy ware with a red slip ; both frequently stamped or
painted with various ornamental motives.

Apart from these two important fabrics, we know little as
yet about the local styles in Romano-British pottery. Desig-
nations like " Upchurch " and " Salopian " have been
abandoned because we no longer believe that they correspond to any really localised industry ; and all we can do
at present is to point to a few monographs on the produce of
particular establishments, *e.g.* Mr. T. May's article in *A.*,
lxxii, on " The Pottery from the Waste Heap of the Roman
Potters' Kilns discovered at Sandford, near Littlemore, Oxon."
(1922) ; or Mr. P. Corder's book on *The Roman Pottery at Cram-
beck, Castle Howard* (York, 1928) ; or the brief note on the
legionary factory at Holt, Flintshire, in Haverfield's *Roman
Britain in* 1914. The explorer of this site died without pub-

lishing any of his results; but the material which he left behind him is to be published in the near future. It is now in the National Museum of Wales, at Cardiff.

In conclusion, it may be of service to add notes on two important and easily-recognised fabrics, both of wide occurrence and both of definite chronological significance. These are the so-called rustic ware and the late fabric for which the name of Huntcliff ware is here proposed.

Rustic Ware.—This is decorated with barbotine, treated in a peculiar way. As a rule, barbotine is allowed to dry naturally, and accordingly forms itself into smooth shapes; in rustic ware it is roughened by manipulation with the fingers while wet, so that it forms ridges and points of an irregular kind. The method is to lay the finger on the wet barbotine and then lift it vertically off; the wet clay follows the finger and rises into a point.

This kind of ornament is found on little Continental bowls of the early first century; but the British rustic decoration is probably derived not from these but from the " herring-bone " barbotine ornament examples of which came into this country in the middle of the first century and reached the north at an early date (*J.R.S.*, xiii, Pl. XI, 14, 16). It is in the north that the British rustic ware began to be made not very long after this. The characteristic British ware has irregular ridges of rustication running, as a rule, vertically; sometimes there is an attempt at a more formal kind of pattern, which vaguely resembles the herring-bone or scale ornament of first-century Continental wares (see *e.g.* Slack, Fig. 43 *b*), but this is exceptional. Other types of rustication, *e.g.* in dots (*Segontium*, Fig. 76, No. 24; *Brecon*, Fig. 95, *c* 7, Fig. 96, *c* 18) are found outside northern Britain, and may be regarded as varieties, on the one hand, of the Continental fabrics already mentioned, and, on the other, of the common British dotted barbotine ware (*Wrox.*, 1913, Pl. XV, 13); but the irregularly ridged pattern, though it is common as far south as Wroxeter (*Wrox.*, 1913, p. 49), never seems to travel into the south of England or into Wales, and nothing like it is found on the Continent. It belongs to the Flavian period, and its shapes are the ordinary Flavian shapes for jars (especially Nos. 61, 62). Early in the second century it begins to disappear; for though examples occur in the earliest strata on Hadrian's Wall they are relatively rare, and on the Antonine Wall only one tiny scrap has been found, namely at Old Kilpatrick.

Huntcliff Ware.—This new name is suggested for a well-known fabric of the fourth century, first adequately studied in connection with the signal-station at Huntcliff (Yorks.; *J.R.S.*, ii, 227-230). It was on that occasion called "black pitted ware," but its colour sometimes varies to a smoky reddish or greyish-brown. It has been called "vesicular," but the little holes in it are not bubbles, and other fabrics have similar holes. It has been called "pitted calcite ware," but the calcite fragments which it contains are found in many British fabrics, and their disappearance by solution, leaving pits that show where they have been, is a chemical accident. Since all these names have actually caused confusion in the past, I propose that in future it be called Huntcliff ware.

It is a peculiar development of the calcite-loaded ware, brownish as a rule, and somewhat soapy to the touch, which was made in pre-Roman Britain and lingered on, unaffected by Romanising influences, throughout the Roman occupation. This ware is always liable to become "vesicular," or, properly speaking, pitted, when the fragments of calcite are dissolved in acid liquids. Late in the Roman period this native fabric began to reassert itself ; no longer confined to the un-Romanised native settlements, it began to invade the centres of Roman life, but always in very small quantities. In the north, however, it underwent a remarkable development. Probably about the middle of the fourth century, Huntcliff ware begins to be made ; this differs from the earlier calcite ware in being hard and gritty, instead of soapy, in texture, and predominantly black, instead of predominantly brown, in colour. Late in the fourth century it became enormously common all over the north of England. The chief shapes are a peculiar neck-rim jar (no. 66) ; a jar with an oblique rim a little like no. 64 ; and a jar with a plain recurved rim. Exactly the same types are found in all parts of northern England, but this ware never travels to the south, or to central England, or Wales ; the examples mentioned in *Segontium* (p. 167, nos. 41-45), for instance, are not Huntcliff ware.

CHAPTER XV

BROOCHES

BROOCHES or fibulae are less valuable to the archaeologist than pottery as evidence of date, because they are far less common ; but they are quite common enough to deserve more attention than they generally get. In many cases their chronology is clearly enough determined to make them hardly less useful than pottery on this score ; and their artistic possibilities make them interesting in themselves, which pottery of the Roman period seldom is, and lead to far-reaching inferences about the cultural and artistic history of the peoples who used them.

The purpose of this chapter is to put forward a classification of the standard types of Romano-British brooch, with notes, where possible, on the dating and distribution of each group. For the present purpose it is necessary to simplify the classification as much as possible, and accordingly I have omitted a number of types which because of their rarity are unlikely to demand the reader's attention ; I have also refrained from multiplying references, and from illustrating and describing more than a very few types in each group, although the variety of such types is nearly always large and always worth studying. These omissions are inevitable in a handbook like the present ; but since the subject has never before been systematically dealt with, this chapter will at any rate partially fill a gap in archaeological literature.

All the brooches here to be discussed are ultimately derived from a simple wire brooch resembling a safety-pin. But long before our period begins, the original safety-pin had developed in various ways and differentiated itself into various forms which it is the business of prehistoric archaeology to describe.[1]

---

[1] *A.*, lv, 179 ; Déchelette, *Manuel d'archéologie* ; *B.M. Guides, Early Iron Age*, 41-53, *Roman Britain*, 50-61 ; *A.A.*³, xxi, 175-178.

Here it is only important to bear in mind that, by the time the Romans conquered Britain, the conquerors on the one hand, and the conquered on the other, were using brooches of many different kinds. Spring pins and hinge pins, bow brooches and plate brooches, simple patterns and elaborate patterns—all these were already in use ; and therefore it would be idle to attempt to trace, within the history of the Romano-British brooch, any such evolution as might lead from any single one of these, by itself, to any other. The brooches we are to examine do in a sense grow out of each other, but their growth is a complicated matter. A new type is never produced as it were by parthenogenesis from a single parent ; the new modifications arise through reminiscences of one type being combined with imitation of another. In the offspring we can detect the likeness of both parents, and often, if we look close enough, of grandparents, uncles and aunts. Thus the groups which it is the business of this chapter to distinguish are related to one another like a number of families all inhabiting the same district, which intermarry and produce unexpected combinations of facial likeness, armorial bearings, and landed property.

Most Romano-British brooches belong to the general class called the bow brooch. We shall therefore begin with this class, dividing it, since it is very large, into groups each labelled with a letter of the alphabet.

Group A.—One-piece brooch, early pattern (1, 2). The one-piece brooch is made of a single piece of wire, worked at one end into a point and at the other into a catch-plate. In the middle it is twisted into a spring. The bow may be left a mere rod of metal (1, rod-bow) or it may be hammered flat (2, strip-bow) ; or it may be flattened in one place only, being there expanded into a disc. The catch-plate, again, may be a solid plate of metal (2), or it may be pierced by an opening (1). But in spite of these variations, the profile is fairly constant : it is always elongated, never humped in the middle. Brooches of this type begin before the Roman invasion, and are mostly found on quite early sites where the native element has not yet been overlaid by Roman influence.[1]

---

[1] *A.*, lxxi, 190 ; *Lowbury*, Plate VIII, p. 32 ; *Glastonbury*, i, 190 ; *W.A.M.*, xliii, 390.

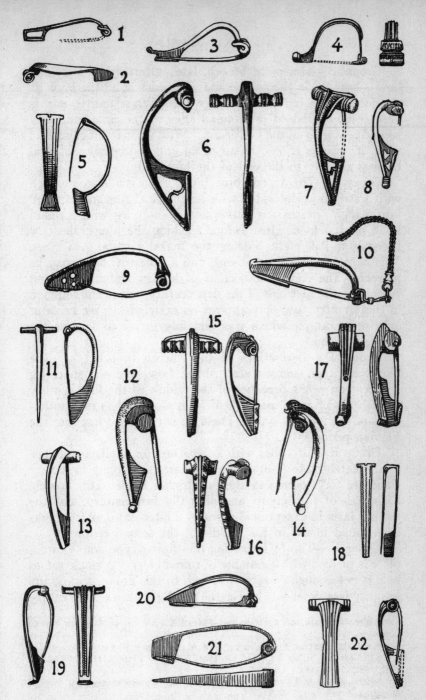

FIG. 60.—BROOCHES, GROUPS A–K (½ SIZE).

A (1, 2) ; B (3) ; C (4) ; D (5) ; E (6-8) ; F (9) ; G (10) ; H (11-17) ; J (18) ; K (19-22).

Group B.—One-piece brooch, late pattern (3). Here the bow is humped in the middle and often ends in a little knob at the foot. This pattern is foreign rather than native, and is very common indeed on Roman sites of the first and early second centuries on the Continent. With us, it is not common ; when it appears it has the air of an import from abroad, and belongs roughly to the end of the first century.[1]

Group C.—The Aucissa brooch (4). This is a hinged brooch with a strip bow decorated with longitudinal ribs and humped into a high semicircular curve, and a short leg with a round knob on the foot. Just before reaching the hinge, the bow becomes a flat plate bearing the maker's name AVCISSA. This name is sometimes absent, and a different name may be present. The Aucissa brooch is of foreign manufacture and belongs to the first half of the first century. It is not common in this country, and only appears on early sites. We know of only one example which was certainly in use as late as the Flavian period.[2]

Group D.—Derivatives of the Aucissa brooch (5). The hinge, the high semicircular ribbed bow, and the short leg reappear on a few brooches of the middle of the first century in such a way as to make them seem more or less rude imitations of the Aucissa type. These do not seem to last into the Flavian period.[3]

Group E.—Brooches with key-pattern (or similar) piercings in the catch-plate (6-8). The key-pattern piercing in a very elaborate form occurs in the pre-Roman Polden Hill brooch. Examples of this group are normally first-century, but the feature lasts in exceptional cases to a later date, and one has been found in use in the middle of the second century.[4]

Group F.—This (9) is another pre-Roman type, whose catch-plate is pierced with a number of round holes. A single round hole is not enough to refer a brooch to this group, and occurs in fairly late types—as late as the middle of the second century

---

[1] *Wroxeter*, 1914, no. 1 ; *Newstead*, Plate LXXXV, no. 1 ; *Caerleon*, no. 1 ; *Lowbury*, 32.

[2] *A.J.*, lx, 236 ; *A.J.*, lxii, 265 ; *W.A.M.*, xli, 279 ; *Wroxeter*, 1912, no. 5.

[3] *Richborough*, ii, no. 2 ; *Woodcuts*, Plate XI, 1, 3 ; Plate XIII, 3 ; *W.A.M.*, xliii, 181 ; xliv, 138.

[4] *B.M. Guide R.B.*, 52 ; *Wroxeter*, 1914, no. 5 ; *Richborough*, ii, no. 3 ; *Newstead*, lxxxv, 4 ; *C.W.*[2], xi, 442.

(*cf.* 28, 30) ; but two or more holes show that the brooch belongs to the middle of the first century or not much later.[1]

Group G.—The plain rod-bow (10). This group resembles F in profile but has a solid catch-plate. It belongs to the first and second centuries; the later specimens are generally stumpier and heavier than the early, and those with a hinge pin are later than those with a spring. There may be a little ornament on the fore-edge of the bow. The example figured was in use in the first half of the second century.[2]

Group H.—Dolphin brooches (11-17). This is a convenient name for a pattern in which the bow is humped forward over the junction of the arms, like the forehead of a conventional dolphin. The feature is seen in the Polden Hill brooch, and runs through a large family of brooches extending throughout the first century and the first half of the second, and belongs in the main to the southern Britain. The bow may be ornamented in various ways, often with a plain or beaded keel along the fore-edge (13). The arms are generally short, but may be long (15) ; the pin is generally on a spring, but sometimes, perhaps in late specimens only, hinged (11). Like many of the commonest British groups, this is practically unknown on the Continent.[3]

Group J.—Flat strip bow (18). Here the bow is hardly a bow at all in the literal sense, being a mere flat strip of metal. It is a rare pattern and only appears on the earliest sites.[4]

Group K.—Segmental strip bow (19-22). Here the bow is still a mere strip of metal, but it is curved into a flattish segment of a circle. This is largely a Continental group and is related to groups C and W. The bow may be plain or ribbed longitudinally ; the pin may be hinged or sprung ; but all types are early, and the group tends to die out by the Flavian period.[5]

[1] *Swarling*, Plates XI-XV ; *Richborough*, i, no. 1 ; *Rotherley*, Plate XCVII, no. 4 ; *A.*, lxxi, 191.

[2] *Woodcuts*, Plate XIV, no. 8 ; *Rotherley*, Plate XCVIII, nos. 1, 3, 11, 13 ; *Richborough*, ii, nos. 4, 5 ; *A.A.*[3], xxi, Plate VIII.

[3] *Rotherley*, Plate XCVIII, nos. 2, 4, 10, 12 ; *Isca*, Plate XXXI, no. 5 ; *Lowbury*, pp. 37-38 ; *Saalburg Jahrb.*, iii, 18.

[4] *Woodcuts*, Plate XIII, nos. 4, 9 ; *Rotherley*, Plate XCIX, 2, 3 ; Plate C, 3, 10, 12 ; *W.A.M.*, xliii, p. 180.

[5] *Wroxeter*, 1914, no. 2 ; *Devizes Mus.*, no. 331, 763 ; *Woodcuts*, Plate XI, 10 ; *S. Ferriby*.

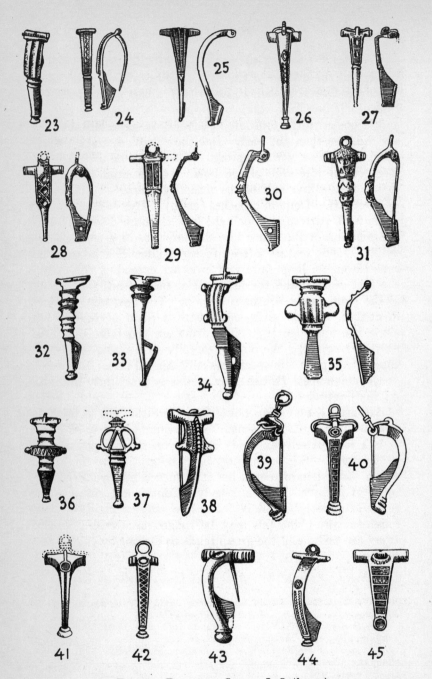

FIG. 61.—BROOCHES, GROUPS L-Q (½ SIZE).

L (23, 24); M (25-27); N (28-31); O (32, 33); P (34-38); Q (39-45).

Groups LMN (nos. 23-31).—These show the development of a type with a segmental strip bow not unlike group K, becoming naturalised on British soil, especially in south-western England.

Group L.—Strip bow, half decorated, half plain (23-24). The upper half of the bow forms a more or less rectangular panel decorated in various ways ; it is divided from the lower half, which is left plain, by an emphatic transverse moulding. This pattern is common on the Continent in the reigns of Augustus and his successors, but though an example has been found in Germany with a coin of Hadrian, this is an exceptional case, and they seem to have been already becoming rare in the Flavian period. In this country they are almost always found on pre-Flavian sites.[1]

Group M.—Tapering bow (25-27). Here the bow begins in a wide strip and tapers to a narrow foot. The upper part of the bow is generally decorated, which produces a certain resemblance to group L ; and it would seem that M, which belongs to the late first and early second centuries, is a British development of L under the influence of certain types of H.[2]

Nos. 26 and 27, which plainly belong to group LMN, may be regarded as special forms of M. No. 26 (from Twabléy, near Malmesbury) has a lozenge stud on the upper part of the bow (cf. group Q) ; it occurs in the south-west, and probably belongs to the late first century ; late examples at Caerleon (*Caerleon*, nos. 7, 8) are ascribed to the early second century.

No. 27 (*Caerleon*, no. 9) is not later than A.D. 125. It represents the link between M and N.

Group N.—Similar to the last, but with cast head-loop (28-31). The division of the bow into a strip-shaped and decorated upper, and a plain lower, portion is a legacy from the Continental group L ; but British influences appear in the fact that the ornament on the upper portion is generally enamelled, and in the presence of a head-loop, a feature which is very common in British brooches but apparently never found in brooches made elsewhere. It was used for the attachment of a

---

[1] *R.F.H.*, iv, Plate IX, no. 14 ; *Wroxeter*, 1914, no. 3 ; *P.S.A.*, xxiii, 500 ; *W.A.M.*, xliii, 328 ; *B.J.*, cxii, 83.

[2] *Wroxeter*, 1914, no. 4 ; *Caerleon Amph.*, nos. 4-6 ; *Lowbury*, nos. 43, 44 ; *Woodcuts*, Plate X, nos. 6, 8, 11.

chain, connecting a pair of brooches. In this group the head-loop is cast solid with the brooch, a relatively late characteristic. These brooches belong to the middle and late second century. They are especially found in the lower Severn valley, and extend as far east as Berkshire and Oxfordshire. Their design and workmanship are on a low level, and this is never more painfully evident than when (*e.g.* 30, 31) they imitate the acanthus mouldings of group R. Their enamelled patterns are of the poorest, consisting of mere triangles, lozenges or rect-angles of inferior enamel.[1]

Group O.—Cross-ribbed bow (32, 33). This is decorated with a varying number of transverse ribs. It has a hinged pin, and generally a pierced catch-plate. It is a foreign type, found at Continental sites of the early and middle first century ; in this country it is rare, and occurs only at early sites. It does not last into the Flavian period, and seems never to have been made in Britain.[2]

Group P.—Winged bow (34-38). This is very much like the last, but has little knobs or wings projecting laterally from the middle of the bow. Sometimes (*e.g.* 37) there are loops as well as wings. These brooches are fairly common in the south of England, but they are confined to pre-Flavian sites and evidently did not last much beyond the reign of Claudius. They are essentially Continental, and the only British-made brooches that could possibly be referred to this group are a few (*e.g.* 38, from Woodeaton) whose resemblance to the rest is a mere far-off reminiscence.[3]

Group Q.—The head-stud brooch (39-45). This is a rather stout heavy brooch with its bow humped almost into a semi-circle. A strip of enamelled ornament, rectangles or lozenges, generally runs along the fore-edge. The foot expands into a projection not unlike a seal ; and at the head is a stud, generally enamelled, which served originally to secure the end of the hook which confined the chord of the spring. This is one of the commonest British types. It was chiefly made, like all the

---

[1] *Woodcuts*, Plate X, no. 2 ; Plate XI, no. 9 ; *Lowbury*, no. 45 ; *Isca*, Plate XXXI, 10 ; *Caerleon*, nos. 10, 13 ; Wright, *Uriconium*, 281.

[2] *Hofheim*, no. 247. Examples from Colchester (B.M.), Woodeaton (Oxford ; *J.R.S.*, vii, 109, no. 44).

[3] *Coll. Ant.*, vi, iii; Scarth, *Aquae Solis*, Plate L, 8 ; Wright, *Uriconium*, 281 ; *B.M. Guide R.B.*, 52 ; *J.R.S.*, vii, 107, Fig. 7.

more artistic Romano-British brooches, in the north ; and is
derived from a pre-Roman Brigantian brooch (39) which lacked
the head-stud. In the south the examples tend to be shoddy
imitations, often visibly late in date (*e.g.* 44, 45). The pin may
be sprung or hinged ; the former is the earlier pattern, and is
as a rule combined with finer workmanship. The head-loop
may be of wire or cast solid with the brooch ; again the former
is the earlier, and the hinge pin is not very often combined
with a wire loop. Some late and degraded specimens have no
head-loop at all ; there are some of these (closely resembling
45) on the Continent, which may possibly have been made
abroad as local imitations of the British type. In some,
generally late, specimens, the enamelled ornament is absent
(43) ; in one case, which does not look late, it is replaced by
a plait of wire (41 ; Antonine period). In some cases there
is a row of little knobs down each side of the bow. These
brooches appear to have been first made in the early second
century. The best of them probably belong to the first half
of that century, and the degraded types to the middle and later
part of it.[1]

Group R.—The trumpet brooch (46-60). This is the best-
known of all Romano-British brooches, and many names have
been suggested for it. Perhaps their various partisans can
agree to accept a letter of the alphabet. One leading characteristic is the trumpet-mouth or blunderbuss-mouth which
forms the head of the bow. This is derived from a pre-Roman
brooch known in this country as the Aylesford type, and has
affinities with many widespread Continental patterns. In itself, however, it is a perfectly original production, never found
outside Britain except for a few obvious strays, and never
made except for a limited space of time in the Roman period.
It is artistically inferior to the pre-Roman metal-work of the
Britons, but it represents the high-water mark of Romano-
British art ; it developed in the north of England after the
Roman conquest, and flourished during the first half of the
second century.

The typical brooch of this group has round the waist of the

---

[1] *P.S.A.*, xxii, 57 ; *Corbridge*, 1910, p. 40 ; *Newstead*, lxxxvi, nos. 19-22 ;
Wroxeter, 1914, no. 10 ; *B.M. Guide R.B.*, Figs. 61, 63 ; *Traprain*, 1919,
Fig. 12 ; 1920, Fig. 12, Fig. 21 ; 1923, Fig. 9.

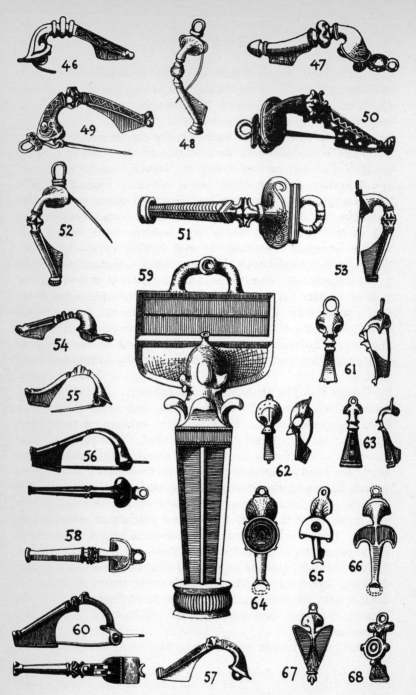

FIG. 62.—BROOCHES, GROUPS R–S ($\frac{1}{2}$ SIZE).

R (i) (46-48) ; R (ii) (49-53) ; R (iii) (54-56) ; R (iv) (57-60) ; S (i) (61-63) ; S (ii) (64-67) ; S (iii) (68).

bow a complex moulding formed by a central ball, or disc, or cushion, embraced by two members each consisting of an acanthus. The waist-knob is pre-Roman, and the Aylesford brooch already combines it with a rudimentary trumpet head ; and this combination is found in the Flavian period, especially in the north of Britain, in brooches like 46-48, which form sub-group R (i).[1] These are unlike anything found on the Continent, and are the immediate precursors of the fully-developed trumpet type, which came into existence when, apparently about the year 100, some genius borrowed the classical acanthus and added it to the waist-knob of a brooch, thus producing a pattern like 49-53, forming sub-group R (ii).[2] Brooches of this pattern, sometimes richly enamelled (49), sometimes plain (52), sometimes ornamented in relief (51), are extremely common in the north of Britain in the first half of the second century. In the true Celtic spirit, the ornament on the trumpet head is often made with eyes and nostrils, to resemble the head of an animal ; but however the brooch is finished in detail, it is almost always a masterpiece both of design and of manufacture. Traces of the workshops in which these brooches were made have been found at Brough-under-Stainmore and Kirkby Thore in Westmorland, and at Traprain Law in Haddingtonshire. They were used throughout England, but their diminishing numbers in the south make it clear that they were not made there. It is easy to distinguish south-country imitations of them ; examples may be seen in 30, 31, 56, 58, 60.

In some examples the moulding is not carried all round the waist of the bow, but only round the fore-edge and sides, the back being left plain. In this case, if the acanthus is absent (54-56) the brooch belongs to sub-group R (iii) ; if present (58-60) to R (iv). Typologically, these ought to be later than (i) and (ii), but the facts are more complicated. No. 54, though falling in sub-group R (iii), is derived not from R (ii) but directly from its predecessor R (i) ; and no. 54 is actually dated to A.D. 110-130 (*Wrox.*, 1912, no. 7). But in the very same deposit an example of R (iii) was found whose cast head-loop and degraded trumpet seemed to mark it as typologically late

---

[1] *Newstead*, lxxxv, no. 8 ; *Segontium*, Fig. 54 ; *A.C.*, lxxxiv, 112 ; *Traprain*.
[2] *A.A.*[3], xxi, 173 ; *P.S.A.*, xxii, 12 ; *Newstead*, lxxxv, 9-12, lxxxvi, 13-16 ; *C.W.*[2], iii, 70 ; *Saalburg Jahrb.*, iii, 19.

in the whole group. This implies that cheap and inferior imitations of the trumpet brooch, in which the acanthus has been left out, the spring pin and wire loop replaced by hinge pin and cast loop, and the trumpet flattened into a bowed strip, were already current in southern and central England before the middle of the second century. How long they lasted we do not know ; probably not until the end of the century.[1]

Sub-group R (iv) has the half-round mouldings of the last, but the acanthus is present. The fact that this sub-group almost always has a hinge pin and often a cast head-loop makes it possible to say that on the whole R (iv) is later than R (ii) ; but certainly the two types were for the most part of their history contemporaries. No member of either group can be confidently said to have been made before 100 or after 200.[2]

A variety of this sub-group (59, 60) has a large rectangular plate inserted between the head and the head-loop. This type is rare and there is little evidence for its date ; but it is best to assume that it belongs to the same period as the main part of group R, the first half of the second century. The best-known example, from Aesica (59), is eccentric and hideous, but not debased ; and it was finally lost about A.D. 197, having been hoarded for an unknown period previously.[3]

Group S.—Other trumpet-headed brooches (61-68). In this group certain types are united which agree in having a trumpet head but lack the other features of group R. Sub-group S (i) (61-63) has a trumpet head and ends in a fan-tail. Specimens corresponding to this description are found on the Continent ; but (in addition to some other differences) almost all our examples have the typically British head-loop, while almost all the Continental examples lack it. In some cases (*e.g.* 61) the design has been visibly influenced by the example of group R, even the acanthus moulding being sometimes present. The date is probably early and middle second century.[4]

---

[1] *Wroxeter*, 1912, nos. 7, 8 ; 1913, no. 5 ; *Segontium*, 133 ; *Lowbury*, no. 53 ; *Caerleon*, no. 15.

[2] *A.A.*[3], xxi, Plate VII, 1, 2 ; *Traprain*, 1914, nos. 1, 2 ; *Caerleon*, no. 14 ; *W.A.M.*, xliii, 180 ; *Lowbury*, no. 52 ; *R.F.H.*, ii, 40.

[3] *A.*, lv, 179 ; *A.A.*[3], xxi, Plate X ; *Woodcuts*, Plate XIII, no. 10.

[4] *C.W.*[2], xix, 13, no. 19. Other examples, B.M., Ashmolean.

Sub-group S (ii) has a trumpet head and a plate, generally circular (64) or semicircular (65) or pelta-shaped (66), lying flat on the waist of the bow. This pattern is fairly common in Britain but hardly ever occurs on the Continent (*O.R.L.*, *Stockstadt*, vii, 20 ; *R.F.H.*, vol. ii, No. 57). A special variety (67) has the plate shaped like the wings of a fly.[1]

S (iii) combines the fan-tail and the disc on the waist (68).[2] A similar brooch with a T-shaped head instead of the trumpet, and lacking the head-loop, was probably made on the Continent. These two sub-groups belong mainly to the middle of the second century.

Group T.—The P-shaped brooch (69-76). This name is suggested for brooches in which the bow is short and humped, and combined with a long straight leg. Throughout the Roman period, brooches of this shape are very common on the Continent. We have already seen an example of the profile in group B, which is a stray from Continental sources, and soon disappears. How largely British industry supplied its own market from the Flavian period to the late second century, may be judged by comparing the incidence of P-shaped brooches on the Continent (*cf. O.R.L.*, *Zugmantel*, Pl. IX) and in Britain respectively. Apart from two or three of group B, the only early P-shaped brooches in this country are one or two eye-brooches (69 ; *B.M. Guide R.B.*, Fig. 65), a type very common on the Continent, and one or two isolated specimens (*e.g.* 70, 71), perhaps imported before the Roman invasion, of Continental types belonging to the first half of the first century. Even when we come to the late second century, the characteristic P-shaped brooches of that date on the Continent are almost wholly absent from Britain. It is not until the first half of the third century that this pattern begins to make its presence felt. A few examples of a P-shaped brooch with a row of knobs along the bow (73) are dated about A.D. 220 ;[3] about the same time the earlier types of crossbow brooch (74, 75) begin to appear in small numbers, and the fully-developed

---

[1] Wright, *Uriconium*, 280, 282 ; *C.W.*[2], xix, 13, no. 16 ; *Newstead*, lxxxvi, no. 25 ; *Segontium*, 132.

[2] *Newstead*, lxxxvi, 24 ; *Wroxeter*, 1913, no. 3 ; *P.S.A.S.*, xxxv, Plate A, no. 4.

[3] Corbridge : *A.A.*[3], vii, 184 ; *Caerleon*, no. 17 ; *O.R.L. Faimingen*, 38 ; *R.F.H.*, ii, Plate III, 59.

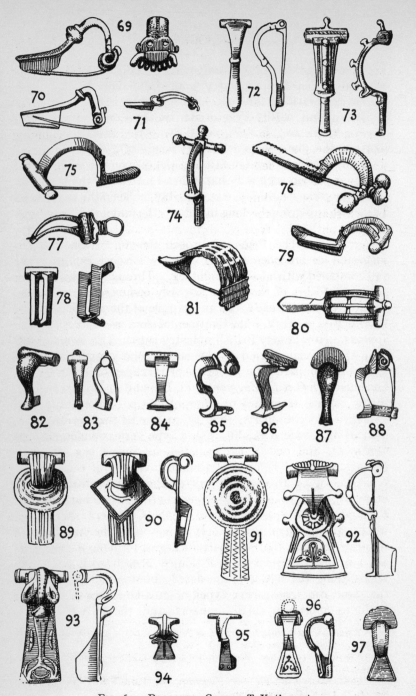

FIG. 63.—BROOCHES, GROUPS T–X (½ SIZE).

T (69-76) ; U (77-81) ; V (82-88) ; W (89-91) ; X (92-97).

crossbow type, with large heavy knobs (76), which belong to the fourth century, are fairly common.[1]

Group U.—The divided bow (77-81). This is another group common on the Continent and rare in Britain. One type, with an Aucissa-like profile (81), belongs to the beginning of the Roman occupation ; others, P-shaped (79, 80), are dated about 180-260 ; others again, with no leg (77, 78), are probably of the same period.[2]

Group V.—The knee brooch (82-88). This is a small bow-brooch shaped like the lower part of a leg with the knee bent. It is a Continental type which found its way into this country about the middle of the second century and became popular here, some types being largely made at local workshops. The type with angular contours (84, 86, 88) was probably never made in Britain. The head is sometimes cylindrical, sometimes a flat semicircular plate ; in the latter case the Central European affinities of the type are very clear.[3]

Group W.—The thistle brooch (89-91). This is in profile P-shaped except when, as in No. 91, it lacks the bow ; but its peculiarity lies in the fact that its broad ribbed bow is separated from its flat tail by a round or lozenge-shaped plate. It is a Continental type, beginning in the first century B.C., and in common use at Augustan sites in north-western Europe. In Britain it seldom appears, having gone out of common use before the time of Claudius ; a few specimens are found at early sites.[4]

Group X.—The bow and fan-tail (92-97). This is a derivative of the foregoing. The ribbed decoration has vanished or been greatly modified ; the plate has in general disappeared as a separate member, though it may still be present as a circular expansion at the root of the tail (92) ; and finally we are left with a little P-shaped brooch with a fan-tail (96, 97). The magnificent " Aesica " brooch is an example of this type, and has been described by a high authority as one of the most

---

[1] *B.M. Guide R.B.*, Fig. 68 (earlier), Fig. 69 (later type).

[2] *Corbridge*, 1908, Fig. 19 ; *Richborough*, ii, 11-13 ; *C.W.*², xix, 7, nos. 5, 5a ; cf. *O.R.L.*, *Osterburken, Wiesbaden*, etc.

[3] *Corbridge*, 1910, nos. 14-19 ; *Newstead*, lxxxvii, nos, 28-33 ; *O.R.L.*, *Zugmantel, Osterburken*.

[4] *B.M. Guide R.B.*, Fig. 66 ; *Coll. Ant.*, vii, Plate XXI ; *Devizes Mus.*, no. 761 ; *A.U.H.V.*, ii, xii, Plate III.

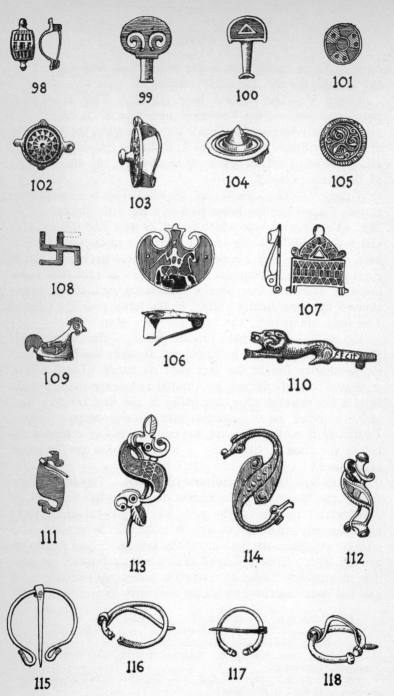

FIG. 64.—BROOCHES, GROUPS Y–Z, AND MISCELLANEOUS (½ SIZE).

Y (98); Z (99, 100); Disc (101-105): Other shapes of plate (106-108):
Animals (109, 110): S-shaped (111-114); Penannular (115-118).

fantastically beautiful things that have come down to us from antiquity. It was made in the north of England or in Scotland, and in the light of our present knowledge it must be dated to the first half of the second century.[1]

Group Y.—Bow-fronted brooches (98). These were derived from Nos. 4 and 5, and are intermediate between a bow brooch and a plate brooch. They have a strip-bow which has developed into a broad half-hoop, decorated with enamel or other work. They are found rarely in Britain, and often on the Continent, and occur in the early second century.[2]

Group Z.—Plate and leg (99, 100). These consist of a plate brooch, generally pelta-shaped or semicircular, with a leg to hold the catch-plate. Typologically they might be regarded as intermediate between group S (ii) and the plate brooch ; but their date is the middle and late second century, and crescent, disc, and other forms of plate brooch were already current in the middle of the first.[3]

Disc Brooches.—Of these there is a great variety, with and without enamel or other ornament. In one form or another they are found throughout the Roman period, and many of the chief types are found widely distributed. The space here available does not permit even the briefest account of the main varieties ; we can only say that many are of Continental origin, and that they occur more commonly in the second century than at any other time ; 101-103 are enamelled and probably all belong to the second century, though some or all of them may have lasted to a later date. No. 104, with a coloured glass cone in the centre, dates from about A.D. 250 to the end of the Roman period and beyond. No. 105, in repoussé metal work, may be of the third century.[4]

Other Plate Brooches.—Crescent and pelta (106) brooches are fairly common ; so are a number of types made of two triangles or two discs or the like, which run into great variety and

---

[1] *A.*, lv, 179 ; *P.S.A.*, xxiii, 407 ; *W.A.M.*, xxxv, 404 ; *Wroxeter*, 1912, no. 3 ; *Ant. J.*, iv, 153 ; *P.S.A.S.*, xxxv, 403 ; *Richborough*, i, no. 4 ; *B.M. Guide R.B.*, Fig. 67, Fig. 71.

[2] *Isca*, Plate XXXI, 7 ; *Coll. Ant.*, vii, Plate XX ; *Caerleon*, no. 19 ; *A.*, lxix, 29, Figs. 29, 30.

[3] *Richborough*, ii, no. 10 ; *Newstead*, lxxxvii, no. 27 ; *O.R.L.*, *Osterburken*.

[4] *B.M. Guide R.B.*, Fig. 73 ; *Wroxeter*, 1912, nos. 1, 2, 9 ; 1914, nos. 11, 12 ; *Lowbury*, p. 36 ; *A.J.*, lxii, 268 ; *Corbridge*, 1908, Fig. 22.

which it would be tedious to enumerate. These enamelled plate brooches are common to Britain and the Continent, but most of them were probably made in or near Belgium. Special forms of plate brooch are the swastika (108), the chatelaine (107), with a rod on which were suspended tweezers and other toilet utensils, the animal brooch, representing a fish or a dog or the like, the boot-sole, and the horse and rider. Animal brooches in the round also occur (110). The most interesting of these is one in the form of a sitting hen (109), enamelled, which is a specially British type and mostly found in the eastern counties.[1]

The S-Brooch.—This is a form of plate brooch calling for special treatment. Beginning, perhaps in the middle of the first century, as a plain metal plate with an arm at the top for use as a hinge and another at the bottom to serve as a catch (111), it develops first into a rich piece of formal design (112), and later, with the usual Celtic tendency to turn everything into animal-forms, into a dragon with a head at each end (113). In this fully-developed shape, which it achieves early in the second century, or perhaps earlier, it is one of the finest examples of Romano-Celtic art. Such brooches were made in the north, and are sometimes found also in the south of Britain; very rarely they have been found on the Continent also. We have no evidence of their survival to a late date in the century. Probably they disappeared earlier than group R, and still earlier than group Q.[2]

The Penannular Brooch.—This, which some Continental scholars prefer to call a buckle, was a fairly common form of brooch throughout the Roman period in Britain.[3]

[1] *B.M. Guide R.B.*, Figs. 73 to 76; *P.S.A.*, xxiii, 500; *V.C.II. Somerset*, i, 357; *Richborough*, i, no. 8; Fox, *A.C.R.*, Plate XXII; *P.S.A. Scot.*, xxxv, Camelon, Fig. 37; *P.S.A.*, xxiv, 224; xxv, 156; *W.A.M.*, xliii, 181.

[2] *V.C.H. Derby*, i, 239; *Segontium*, 133; *P.S.A.*, xxii, 59; *Corbridge*, 1908, 116; *Wroxeter*, 1914, no. 9; *Traprain*, 1914, 1919, 1921; *B.J.*, lxxxvi, 176, Plate IV, no. 29.

[3] *B.M. Guide R.B.*, Fig. 64; *Newstead*, lxxxviii, no. 17; *O.R.L.*, *Wiesbaden*, 94.

CHAPTER XVI

WEAPONS, TOOLS, AND UTENSILS

§ 1. Arms and Armour

To give a complete account of the equipment of the Roman soldier, even in outline, would take us far beyond the limits of this book. All we can do is to describe the main types of object that are likely to be found in excavations or observed in museums. These we shall classify under a few headings.

The Sword.—The legionary foot-soldier of the early Empire was armed with the *gladius* (Fig. 65 *b*), a short heavy sword chiefly used for stabbing. Many auxiliaries were armed with the same weapon ; but it began to go out of use in the second century and seems to have disappeared in the third. The *gladius* is two-edged ; the edges are straight and nearly parallel for the greater part of their length, and then converge sharply to a point. The blade is about 20 inches long ; examples have been found with blades as long as 30 inches or even more, but some of these may not be genuine *gladii*. There is a tang running the whole length of the hilt, and on this are mounted a guard, a grip and a pommel, all made, as a rule, of bone. The guard is quite small, but thick and solid : the grip is fluted transversely to accommodate the fingers or roughened by spiral grooves ; and the pommel, which is rather large, is generally either circular or semicircular, but may vary a good deal in shape. The *gladius* was worn rather high up on the right side, in a wooden sheath covered with leather or metal. Two types of fitting connected with the sheath are often found : the chape, either in bone or metal, which is a pocket-like object forming the end of the sheath (Fig. 66, *k, l*) and a kind of staple through which the strap for suspension was passed. This is

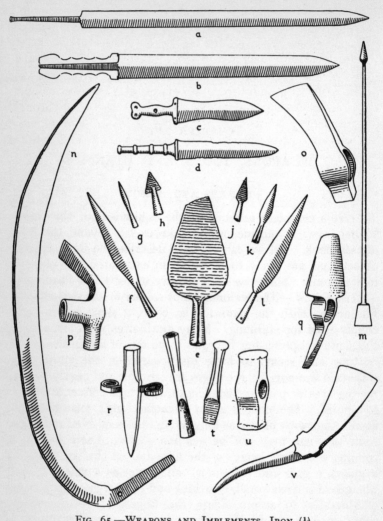

FIG. 65.—WEAPONS AND IMPLEMENTS, IRON ($\frac{1}{8}$).

(a) Long sword (*spatha*); (b) short sword (*gladius*); (c), (d) daggers; (e)-(l) various kinds of spear, lance, and javelin-heads; (m) iron of a *pilum*; (n) scythe-blade; (o) one of the commonest types of axe-head; (p) adze-hammer; (q) combined mattock and pick; (r) mower's anvil; (s) gouge with socket for a wooden handle; (t) mason's chisel; (u) sledge-hammer; (v) *dolabra* or pioneer's axe and pick.

generally of bronze, and is made in two patterns, either dolphin-shaped (Fig. 66 *b-d*) or flat (nos. *e-g*).   The dolphin-shaped type is perhaps the earlier of the two.

The *spatha* or long sword (Fig. 65 *a*), directly descended from the long slashing sword of the La Tène period, was used in the early Empire by some auxiliaries and by most cavalry-men ; as time went on it tended to replace the *gladius* through-out the army.   It was a straight two-edged sword with a point ; a fine example from Cologne has a 29-inch blade and is hilted exactly like a *gladius*.

The Pilum.—*Gladius* and *pilum* were the standard weapons of the early Imperial legion.   The *pilum* was a throwing-spear with a long slender iron (Fig. 65 *m*) and a thick heavy butt, and was 6 or 7 feet long over all.   The iron, which varied in length from a foot to two feet, consisted of a soft rod about the thickness of an ordinary pencil, expanding at one end into a socket to receive the wooden butt, and at the other into a slender head, pointed and hardened.   Details of design varied a good deal, but the purpose was always the same : to provide a weapon of high penetrating power, which would bend by its own weight after striking and therefore could not be thrown back.

The Dagger.—A short dagger with a very broad and some-what leaf-shaped blade, rather like a miniature *gladius*, was in regular use, but is not often found (Fig. 65 *c, d*).

The Spear (*pikes, lances, javelins*).—Spear-heads of various kinds are very commonly found on Roman sites—far more commonly than swords or *pila*—and fall roughly into three classes.   The pike, or spear proper (*hasta*), is an infantry weapon and was in common use among the auxiliaries.   To this weapon must be assigned the commonest large types of spear-head (Fig. 65 *f, l*).   The lance is a cavalry weapon requiring a strong but light head (Fig. 65 *g*).   The javelin or throwing-spear is a pike in miniature, and its head is simply a small spear-head (Fig. 65 *h, j*), with a tendency to show some of the character-istics of an arrow (*cf.* the barbs in *h*).   A very large type of spear-head (Fig. 65 *e*) looks like an artillery projectile ; it would be very clumsy for hand-to-hand fighting.

It will be seen from these examples that the normal Roman spear-head is leaf-shaped and socketed ; the socket is made by bending the iron round into a tube which is generally left open down one side and pierced with a nail-hole in the other. Normally the blade is strengthened with a mid-rib, but sometimes this is entirely absent.

Small Arms.—Theoretically the Roman army had special corps of archers and slingers. But although this theory, in part at any rate, still held the field in the Imperial age, so that one of the regiments on Hadrian's Wall, for instance, consisted of archers officially described as such (*Cohors I Hamiorum sagittariorum*, from Hamath in Syria), in practice it is certain that these small arms were widely used in other units. When we find numerous sling-bullets at Burnswark or a large hoard of arrow-heads at Housesteads, we need not ascribe them to Balearic slingers or a cohort of special archers.

Roman arrow-heads are of various forms. They may be socketed or tanged, and they may be triangular in section or leaf-shaped. Probably the leaf-shape is later than the other. They were used with the ordinary short bow, but the crossbow was also in use.

Leaden sling-bullets (*glandes*), about 1 to 1½ inch long and roughly acorn-shaped, have been found in considerable numbers at Burnswark, Ambleside, and elsewhere. It is thought that they were replaced about the end of the first century by baked clay bullets or pebbles ; and certainly they are not found in, for instance, the second-century excavated sites on the Hadrianic and Antonine Walls.

Artillery.—Ancient artillery consisted of weapons belonging to two types. The first was the two-armed (catapult or ballista) type. This was like a magnified crossbow, except that the propulsive force was generated not by the elasticity of a bow, but by the torsion of twisted gut or horsehair cords. There were two bundles of such cords, in each of which a rigid arm was inserted : the bowstring, connecting the ends of these arms, was drawn back by a windlass and released by withdrawing a catch. The bundles of cord were mounted vertically in a square frame which might be defended by a metal shield, the weapon firing through an aperture in the middle of this shield.

This two-armed engine might throw either a stone or an arrow, but naturally the details of its design varied according

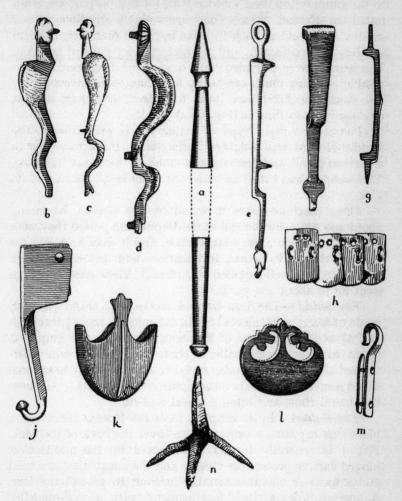

FIG. 66.—EXAMPLES OF SMALL OBJECTS IN MILITARY USE ($\frac{1}{2}$).

(a) Head and butt of heavy arrow or bolt for artillery (Newstead);
(b)-(g) Bronze scabbard fittings: (b) Kirkby Thore (Chesters Museum),
(c) (Brough-under-Stainmore), (d) (Corbridge), dolphin-shaped, (e)
(Caerleon), (f) (Newstead), (g) (Corbridge), plain; (h) Scale-armour
(Ham Hill); (j) *Dolabra*-sheath hook (Wroxeter); (k) Chape (Kirkby
Thore); (l) Another (Corbridge); (m) Cuirass-hook (Chesters Museum);
(n) Calthrop (Wroxeter).

to the ammunition used. Stone balls for this purpose are often found on Roman sites. They are roughly divisible into a smaller size, from an inch to three inches in diameter, for field artillery (*carroballistae*), and a larger size, for guns of position. The arrows were provided with a socketed iron head, recognisable by being much too heavy for a hand-shot arrow : they also had a socketed iron butt to protect the shaft against damage in propelling it (Fig. 66 *a*).

The second main type of artillery was one-armed. The bundle of cord was mounted horizontally, the arm swung in a vertical plane, and discharged a stone at the top of its swing. This weapon was called an *onager* or " donkey," because of its kick.

These machines were invented by the Greeks, beginning about 400 B.C. ; by the end of the Republican period they were already in use on a very large scale, and it may be taken for granted that any Roman fortification, and any considerable field force, was well supplied with them. Their effective range went up to about 400 yards.[1]

The Shield.—The bow-fronted rectangular shield (*scutum*) made of wood, with metal boss in the middle, was 4½ feet high and 2½ wide in the time of Polybius, but under the Empire it seems to have been smaller. There was also an oval bow-fronted shield with a similar metal boss ; and a flat hexagonal shield sometimes appears on sculptured monuments. All these had metal rims, and often a metal mid-rib.

The Helmet.—In its simplest form the Roman helmet is a plain iron cap with a projection to cover the back of the neck. But it is generally further complicated by the addition of hinged flaps to protect the cheeks, and there may also be a crest and a fixed or movable member in front to protect the face. A special type is the " face-helmet," with a well-modelled human mask covering the wearer's face. It is disputed whether this was merely a parade helmet or a piece of genuine armour.

The Cuirass.—Of this there are four main types : (*a*) the leather cuirass, terminating in a kilt of flaps. This was the commonest type, but few remains of it are found except its

[1] Schramm, *Die antiken Geschütze der Saalburg* (1918), is the most important work ; but the subject is well outlined in Stuart Jones, *Companion to Roman History*, 215-223.

fastenings (Fig. 66 *m*) ; (*b*) the so-called *lorica segmentata* (a modern name) made of a number of metal hoops passing round the trunk and others passing over the shoulders ; (*c*) the *lorica hamata* or chain-mail ; (*d*) the *lorica squamata* or scale-armour. Portions of types (*c*) and (*d*), especially the latter, are often found on Roman sites. Scale armour, made of small and very thin bronze plates linked together with bronze wire, seems to have come increasingly into favour as time went on (Fig. 66 *h*).

The body was also protected by a stout belt, covered with metal plates, from the front of which hung a group of metal-studded straps forming a kind of apron.

Decorations.—Of these (for which see Stuart Jones, *Companion to Roman History*, 202-205) the only one commonly found is the *phalera*. This is a metal disc with a head in relief upon it, provided with holes for attachment to the cuirass (Fig. 67 *a*).[1]

§ 2. TOOLS

The implements, mostly of iron, which are briefly described in this section, do not, as a rule, call for close study. For the most part they are very like their modern counterparts, and their purpose is in these cases obvious ; nothing is known about changes in their shape during the Roman period, so that they cannot be used as chronological evidence ; and in a handbook like this the only difficult problem connected with them—the problem, namely, of explaining the various " iron implements of uncertain use " which figure in many excavation reports—must necessarily be left untouched. We can deal here only with the ordinary standard types.

Agriculture.—Model or toy implements in bronze have been found at several different places (collections may be seen, *e.g.* in the British Museum, and at Cologne, Bonn, Mainz, etc. ; *cf.* B.M. Guide, *Roman Britain*, p. 42) ; these include complete models of ploughs, harrows, rakes, etc., which show that on the whole the Roman forms resembled the traditional modern forms.

[1] References for this section : Daremberg-Saglio, articles on the names of the various objects. Couissin, *Les Armes romaines*. Cagnat-Chapot, *Manuel d'Archéologie romaine*, book iii, ch. viii. Lindenschmit, *Tracht und Bewaffnung d. röm. Heeres*. *Newstead*. British Museum Guides to *Roman Britain* and *Greek and Roman Life*. Stuart Jones, *Companion to Roman History*, ch. iii. *O.R.L.* contains numerous illustrations and descriptions.

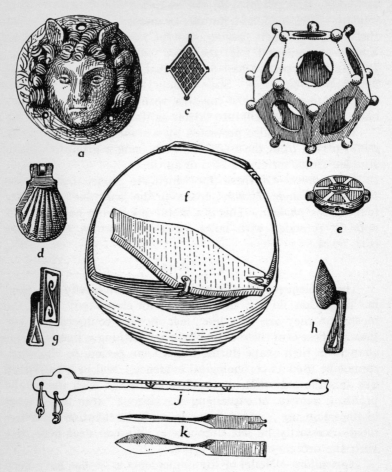

FIG. 67.—EXAMPLES OF SMALL BRONZE OBJECTS (b, $\frac{1}{3}$; *all the rest*, $\frac{1}{2}$).

(a) Phalera (military decoration) with winged head of Mercury; (b) Dodeca-
hedron, with holes of different sizes in each side; (c) Enamelled lid of
seal-box; (d) Seal-box with shell in relief; (e) Seal-box with enamelled
lid; (f) Wrist-purse; (g), (h) Dress-fasteners; (j) Beam of steelyard;
the pan hangs from the left-hand end; the weight slides along the
beam; the instrument may be used either way up, being provided
with two points of suspension and two scales; (k) Handle of surgical
knife.

In the case of simpler objects we can rely on complete specimens, lacking only their wooden handles. The Roman scythe
(Fig. 65 *n*) has a less uniform curve than the modern scythe ;
it is sharply curved near the hafted end and almost straight
towards the tip. In connection with the scythe must be mentioned the mower's anvil (Fig. 65 *r*), with a point below to stick
into the ground, and a flat top, like a hammer-head, on which
the scythe may be hammered to a new edge when it has been
turned against a stone or the like. The sickle, bill-hook,
pruning-hook, and hedging-bill resemble modern forms.

The spade and shovel are found in two patterns—all iron,
as to-day, or of wood with a mere edge of iron to protect the
wooden blade. Picks are found of various sizes and weights.
The mattock is a commoner implement at this period than it is
in England nowadays ; it may be a reversible tool with a pick
or a two-pronged fork at its other end (Fig. 65 *q*). The fork,
whether as a digging fork (either in line with its handle or at
right angles to it), or as a hay-fork, is common ; and other
digging tools, such as a spud and a semicircular turf-cutter,
are found.

Carpentering and Woodworking.—The axe is the commonest
tool in this category. The illustration (Fig. 65 *o*) shows the
most usual pattern, but other patterns are found. In size,
naturally, they vary from a full-sized felling-axe to a small
hatchet.

The hammer is found in a great variety of sizes and shapes,
and in combination with many other tools. Thus we have the
sledge-hammer (Fig. 65 *u*), the ordinary joiner's hammer, the
axe-hammer, the adze-hammer, the claw-hammer, and the
mason's pick. Wooden mallets have also been found.

The adze is one of the commonest tools, and is often
combined with others, forming an axe-adze or hammer-adze
(Fig. 65 *p*).

Chisels (Fig. 65 *t*) and gouges (Fig. 65 *s*) are generally not
tanged, like the modern tools, but socketed. When they are
of iron throughout, handle and all, they are presumably mason's
tools.

The standard boring tools are the brace and bit—bits of
various shapes and sizes are common—the auger and the
gimlet.

Planes and plane-irons of various types are found. They include the ordinary short plane, the jack plane, the rabbeting plane, and the moulding plane.

Paring-knives, with a handle at each end, are fairly common.

Among the kinds of saw, a miniature model in the British Museum shows that the frame-saw (in which a flexible blade is mounted under tension in a wooden frame) was included.

Pincers and claws for extracting nails are just like those in use to-day.

Nails, hinges and various kinds of clamps, bolts and so forth are of common occurrence.

Blacksmith's Tools.—The sledge-hammer has already been mentioned, and the Roman blacksmiths' tongs are of the ordinary pattern. The same is in general true of the Roman anvil. Files are also found.

Cobbling.—The only implement calling for special mention is the last, which resembles the modern last.

Masons' Tools.—The mason's trowel is exactly like its modern counterpart. Chisels and gouges for masons' work, of solid iron, have already been mentioned ; also the masons' pick, a light hammer with the back of its head drawn out into a long sharp point.

The Pioneer's Axe.—A special and characteristic tool is the *dolabra* or military pioneer's axe (Fig. 65 *v*). It is a large heavy implement combining an axe and a pick. Its cutting edge when not in use was protected by a sheath with a metal hook (Fig. 66 *j*) at each end. A cord or thong, passed through these hooks, held the sheath firmly on the axe-head.

Horsemanship.—The ordinary bit was a plain ring-and-bar pattern, but the curb was also in use. The Romans rode on a saddle which had certain iron parts, and wore plain prick spurs, but did not use stirrups. Their horse-shoes were flatter and more plate-like than modern horse-shoes, *i.e.* they covered a larger part of the hoof's under surface. A special type of horse-shoe was the so-called hippo-sandal, an iron plate with cheeks on either side and (as a rule) a hook behind and a loop in front. Their exact purpose is not known, but it is certain that they were attached to the hoofs of horses.[1]

[1] References for this section : Ward, *R.E.B.* ; *Newstead ;* Silchester reports in *A.*, liv, lvii ; B.M. Guides, *R.B.* and *Greek and Roman Life.*

§ 3. Miscellaneous Utensils

It would be easy to fill a book with descriptions and illustrations of the things that excavators call " small objects," but all that can be done here is to mention a few things used in spinning and weaving, in cooking and at meals, and certain writing materials and lighting appliances.

Spinning was done by hand, using a spindle (*i.e.* a stick of wood about the size of a penholder) which was fitted with a spindle-whorl to act as a fly-wheel. A spindle-whorl is a disc, generally about 1½ inch in diameter, with a hole through the middle for the insertion of the spindle. Spindle-whorls made of broken potsherds, chipped and ground into a disc, are extremely common.

Weaving was done on a hand-loom, few of whose parts were so made as to survive to the present day. Loom-weights consisting of stones with a hole through them or a groove round them, or made of baked clay, are, however, not rare.

Needles, generally of bone, are very common; and metal thimbles of Roman date have been found.

Netting-shuttles, consisting of a bronze rod forked at either end, are fairly common.

Cooking was done for the most part at an open hearth (apart from the baking of bread, which was done in a circular domed bread-oven) and generally in earthenware pots. But certain metal appliances may be mentioned.

Pot-hangers, consisting of an iron chain which divides into branches each having a hook at the end, are fairly common. They supported an iron cauldron. Various kinds of metal bowls, etc., were used in cooking, and notably the vessels called *patellae*, *i.e.* bronze saucepan-shaped vessels with a more or less hemispherical body and a flat handle pierced with a round hole at the end. These *patellae* were largely made in the first century A.D. in Campania, and examples from the factory of Cipius Polybius at Capua are widely distributed in Europe. Later the manufacture spread to Gaul. A hoard of such vessels, probably from the camp-kitchen of a cavalry unit, is published in detail in the *Northumberland County History*, vol. xii.

Knives of the most varied patterns are, naturally, among the commonest of all implements. They include types ranging from a large butcher's knife to the smallest folding pocket-knife. As a rule, Roman knives have a pointed blade and a tang to insert in the handle ; folding pocket-knives have a handle of wood, bone, or horn.

In this connection whetstones may be mentioned. The Romans were acquainted with the use of a steel for sharpening knives, but as a rule they used whetstones, and, as their knives were of softer metal than ours, they used them very freely. Pieces of slaty stone that have been used in this way are very common objects on Roman sites ; in the forum at Wroxeter a whole packing-case of unused whetstones was found in a shop.

Spoons occur in three chief types. One has a circular bowl, another an oval bowl connected with the handle by a neck that drops from the handle ; the third has a very long thin bowl like a marrow-spoon, but this is intended for extracting unguents or drugs from small bottles and is a toilet article (or, as its butt-end shaped like a probe often betrays, a surgical instrument) rather than a table-spoon. Spoons intended for table use generally taper at the butt end to a long slender point ; this was used for extracting shell-fish from their shells.

Table-forks were not used.

The commonest method of writing was with a stilus on a tablet. Tablets were made of small pieces of wood with raised edges : commonly two such were hinged together, wax was spread on their inner surface, and the writing done with a pointed instrument, generally of metal or bone (*stilus*), with a flattened butt-end for erasing. Short letters and memoranda of all kinds such as receipts, I.O.U.'s, and so forth, were commonly written in this way. When the writer pressed too hard, the *stilus* penetrated the wax and scored the wood, and this is why tablets are found bearing legible inscriptions (Fig. 68). The tablets could then be folded up, tied with string, and sealed. When it was thought necessary, a seal could be protected by means of a seal-box (Fig. 67 *c-e*), a little box resembling a locket, with holes at each side for the string to pass through ; one hole can be seen in Fig. 67 *e*.

Writing was also done on paper and parchment, with pen and ink. The pen was originally a reed pen, but metal pens have been found, with a small spoon at the butt-end for stirring the

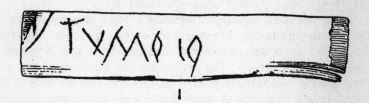

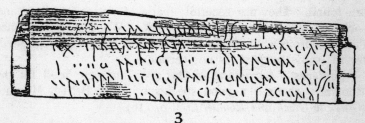

FIG. 68.—WOODEN WRITING-TABLETS FROM LONDON (⅔).

No. 1.—*[per Iov]em optimum maximum et per genium Imp. Domitiani Cesaris Aug. Germanici et per deos patrios.* . . .

No. 2.—*Quam pecuniam petisionis item scriptis solvere mihi debebit Crescens isve ad quem ea res pertinebit.* . . .

No. 3.—*. . . . rem vendidisse . . . ex taberna sua . . . navem faciendam et permissionem dedisse . . . clavi faciendi.*

ink. Ink-pots of metal or pottery (Fig. 50, Ritt. 13) are not uncommon ; sometimes they are double, to hold red and black ink. Compasses are found, made of iron and bronze ; the pin on which the arms turn sometimes projects and is pierced for the insertion of a wedge-shaped cotter-pin, which when tapped home holds the arms rigid in any required position. Proportional compasses were also used, with a definite ratio between the longer and shorter arms—generally 2 : 1.

The ordinary method of lighting a room was by means of small olive-oil lamps, in general about 3 or 4 inches long, consisting of a round container with a nozzle at one side and a handle at the other. The wick rested in a hole in the top of the nozzle, and oil was poured in through another hole in the top of the container. A lamp might have two or more nozzles. Such lamps required constant trimming and refilling, and a large number would be needed to light a large room properly. The earliest type of Roman lamp during the Empire has the sides of its nozzle formed of two volutes ; these disappear towards the end of the first century.

Open lamps, resembling the foregoing in shape but open at the top, may have been used for burning tallow, run into them when hot. Objects of this shape seem sometimes to have been used as lamp-stands : one with three legs was found in London actually containing an earthenware lamp (Ward, *Roman Era*, p. 213).

Candles were used, and candlesticks of various shapes are found. They are generally made of pottery or iron, and socketed like a modern candlestick. Whether the bronze dodecahedrons (Fig. 67 *b*) were used, as has been suggested, for the same purpose, is not certain.

Lanterns for carrying in the open air were used by the Romans : there is a good specimen in the British Museum (*Guide to Greek and Roman Life*, p. 116).[1]

[1] The material briefly reviewed in this section is dealt with in a fuller way in, *e.g.* Ward, *R.E.B.* ; British Museum Guides, *Roman Britain* and *Greek and Roman Life* ; Walters, *Catalogue of Lamps in the British Museum* ; and perhaps the most useful general collection will be the promised fifth part of *Germania Romana*[1], when it appears. Since the above was printed, a very valuable collection has been published in *London in Roman Times* (London Museum Catalogues, No. 3 ; 1930).

PLATE IV

1. AUGUSTUS	5. GERMANICUS	11. OTHO
2. TIBERIUS	6. GAIUS (CALIGULA)	12. VITELLIUS
3. DRUSUS JUNIOR	7. CLAUDIUS	13. VESPASIAN
4. DIVUS AUGUSTUS	8. ANTONIA	14. TITUS
(REIGN OF TIBE-	9. NERO	
RIUS)	10. GALBA	

APPENDIX

UNDER each emperor is given : (a) his full name, either in its only or in its commonest form, as found in inscriptions—variations in form are as a rule ignored ; (b) the dates at which his reign began and ended ; (c) data for calculating the year of any given tribunician power (this is omitted in the case of the later emperors) ; (d) consulships ; (e) members of his family, including such as are mentioned on coins or in inscriptions, but omitting those who attained the rank of emperor.

Emperors marked with an asterisk (*) received the title *divus* after death ; the names of those marked with an obelus (†) were sometimes or always erased from their inscriptions after their death.

Further details about the dates of Imperial reigns can be found in (*e.g.*) Liebenam, *Fasti consulares Imperii Romani*, Bonn, 1909.

In order to facilitate the identification of coins by the beginners for whom this book is chiefly written, five plates of imperial portraits are here added. I am indebted to the kindness of the Department of Coins and Medals at the British Museum for the casts from which the photographs were taken, and particularly to Mr. H. Mattingly for choosing the coins, which are selected not as " show " specimens but as good average examples.

*AUGUSTUS (Imp. Caesar Aug.), 23 B.C.-A.D. 14 (Aug. 14).
> *Trib. pot.* begins about July 1, 23 B.C.
> *Cos.* xi, 23 B.C. ; xii, 5 B.C. ; xiii, 2 B.C.
> *Family :* m. (i) Scribonia ; (ii) Livia ; M. Vipsanius Agrippa, C. Caesar, L. Caesar, Agrippa Iulius Caesar, Nero Claudius Drusus Gernanicus (adopted ss.) ; Iulia (d.).

TIBERIUS (Ti. Caesar Aug.). 14-37 (March 16).
> *Trib. pot.* begins about July 1, 6 B.C. ; *trib. pot.* vi begins July 1, A.D. 4, and so on.
> *Cos.* ii, 7 B.C. ; iii, A.D. 18 ; iv, 21 ; v, 31.
> *Family :* Drusus Caesar and his son Tiberius Caesar ; Germanicus (adopted s.) and Agrippina his wife ; their children Nero Caesar, Drusus Caesar, Iulia Drusilla.

†GAIUS (called CALIGULA ; Gaius Caesar Aug. Germanicus). 37-41 (Jan. 14).
> *Trib. pot.* begins March 18, 37.
> *Cos.* 37 ; ii, 39 ; iii, 40 ; iv, 41.

*CLAUDIUS (Ti. Claudius Caesar Aug. Germanicus). 41-54 (Oct. 13).
> *Trib. pot.* begins Jan. 25, 41.
> *Cos.* 37 ; ii, 42 ; iii, 43 ; iv, 47 ; v, 51.
> *Family :* m. (i) Messalina ; (ii) Agrippina. s. Britannicus ; dd. Octavia, Antonia.

†NERO (Nero Claudius Caesar Aug. Germanicus).   54-68 (June 9).
   Trib. pot. begins October 13 or December 4, 54 ; but *Trib. pot.* vii
    seems to begin December 10, 59 ; viii, December 10, 60 ; and
    so on.
   Cos. 55 ; ii, 57 ; iii, 58 ; iv, 60 ; v, 68.
   Family : m. (i) Claudia Octavia ; (ii) Poppaea Sabina.
GALBA (Ser. Sulpicius Galba), 68 (June 9)-69 (Jan. 15).
OTHO (M. Salvius Otho).   69 (Jan. 15-April 25).
VITELLIUS (A. Vitellius).   69 (Jan. 2)-70 (Dec. 20 ?).
*VESPASIAN (Imp. Caesar Vespasianus Aug.).   69-79 (June 23).
   Trib. pot. begins July 1, 69.
   Cos. 51 ; ii, 70 ; iii, 71 ; iv, 72 ; v-viii, 74-77 ; ix, 79.
   Family : m. Flavia Domitilla.
*TITUS (Imp. T. Caesar Vespasianus Aug.).   71-81 (Sept. 13).
   Trib. pot. begins July 1, 71.
   Cos. 70 ; ii, 72 ; iii, 74 ; iv, 75 ; v, 76 ; vi, 77 ; vii, 79 ; viii, 80.
   Family : d. Iulia.
†DOMITIAN (Imp. Domitianus Caesar Aug.).   81-96 (Sept. 18).
   Trib. pot. begins Sept. 14, 81.
   Cos. vii, 80 ; viii, 82 ; ix, 83 ; x, 84 ; xi, 85 ; xii, 86 ; xiii, 87 ;
    xiv, 88 ; xv, 90 ; xvi, 92 ; xvii, 95.
   Family : m. Domitia Longina.
*NERVA (Imp. Nerva Caesar Aug.).   96-98 (Jan. 25).
   Trib. pot. begins Sept. 18, 96 ; iii seems to begin December 10, 97.
   Cos. iii, 97 ; iv, 98.
*TRAJAN (Imp. Caesar Nerva Traianus Aug.).[1]   97-117 (Aug. 10 ?).
   Trib. pot. begins October 27, and ii begins December 10, 97.
   Cos. 91 ; ii, 98 ; iii, 100 ; iv, 101 ; v, 103 ; vi, 112.
   Family · m. Pompeia Plotina ; sister Marciana, niece Matidia.
*HADRIAN (Traianus Hadrianus).   117-138 (July 10).
   Trip. pot. begins August 11, ii begins December 10, 117.
   Cos. 108 ; ii, 118 ; iii, 119.
   Family : m. Vibia Sabina ; sister Domitia Paulina ; Matidia, d.
    of elder Matidia ; L. Aelius, adop. s.
*ANTONINUS PIUS (T. Aelius Hadrianus Antoninus Pius).   138-161
   (March 7).
   Trib. pot. begins February 25, ii begins December 10, 138.
   Cos. 120 ; ii, 139 ; iii, 140 ; iv, 145.
   Family : m. Faustina I (*d.* 140) ; ss. M. Aurelius Fulvus Anto-
    ninus, M. Galerius Aurelius Antoninus ; d. Aurelia Fadilla.
*MARCUS AURELIUS (M. Aurelius Antoninus).   161-180 (March 17).
   Trib. pot. begins December 10, 146.
   Cos. ii, 140 ; iii, 161.
   Family : m. Faustina II (*d.* 175) ; s. M. Annius Verus.

---

[1] Henceforth all emperors habitually begin their designation with the
titles *Imp. Caesar*, and end with *Augustus ;* after Diocletian, *D.N.* for
Dominus Noster is commonly substituted for *Imp. Caesar.*

PLATE V

15. DOMITIAN	21. ANTONINUS PIUS	26. LUCILLA
16. NERVA	22. FAUSTINA SENIOR	27. COMMODUS
17. TRAJAN	23. MARCUS AURELIUS	28. CRISPINA
18. HADRIAN	24. FAUSTINA JUNIOR	29. SEPTIMIUS
19. SABINA	25. VERUS	SEVERUS
20. AELIUS		

*VERUS (L. Aurelius Verus). 161-169 (winter).
> *Trib. pot.* begins March 7, ii begins December 10, 161.
> *Cos.* ii, 161 ; iii, 167.
> *Family :* m. Lucilla.

†*COMMODUS (L. Aelius Aurelius Commodus, L. Aurelius Commodus Caesar, M. Aurelius Commodus Antoninus Aug., L. Aelius Aurelius Commodus Aug., successively). 176-192 (Dec. 31).
> *Trib. pot.* begins November 27, ii begins December 10, 176.
> *Cos.* 177 ; ii, 179 ; iii, 181 ; iv, 183 ; v, 186 ; vi, 190 ; vii, 192.
> *Family :* m. Crispina.

*PERTINAX (P. Helvius Pertinax). 193 (March 28).
> *Trib. pot.* 193.
> *Cos.* ii, 192.

DIDIUS JULIANUS. 193 (June 1).
> *Trib. pot.* 193.
> *Cos.* 175 ?
> *Family :* m. Manlia Scantilla.

*SEVERUS (L. Septimius Severus Pertinax). 193-211 (Feb. 4).
> *Trib. pot.* begins May (?) 193, ii begins December 10, 193.
> *Cos.* 189 ? ; ii, 194 ; iii, 202.
> *Family :* m. (i) Paccia Marciana ; (ii) Iulia Domna.

†ALBINUS (D. Clodius Septimius Albinus). 193-197.
> *Caesar,* 193 ; *Augustus,* 196 ; *cos.* ? ; ii, 194.

PESCENNIUS NIGER (C. Pescennius Niger Iustus). 193-194.
> *Cos.* ?, ii, 193.

*CARACALLA (M. Aurelius Antoninus). 198-217 (April 8).
> *Trib. pot.* begins autumn, 198 ; ii begins December 10, 198.
> *Cos.* 202 ; ii, 205 ; iii, 208 ; iv, 213.
> *Caesar,* autumn, 196 ; *Augustus,* in the first half of 198.
> *Family :* m. Fulvia Plautilla.

†*GETA (P. (in youth, L.) Septimius Geta). 209-212 (Feb. 26).
> *Trib. pot.* begins 209 ; ii begins December 10, 209.
> *Cos.* ii, 209.
> *Caesar,* June 2 ? 198 ; *Augustus,* 209.

†MACRINUS (M. Opellius Macrinus). 217-218 (June 8).
> *Trib. pot.* April 11, 217 ; ii begins December 10, 217.
> *Cos.* 218.
> *Family :* s. Diadumenianus.

†ELAGABALUS (M. Aurelius Antoninus). 218-222 (March 11).
> *Trib. pot.* May 16, 218 ; ii begins December 10, 218.
> *Cos.* 218 ; ii, 219 ; iii, 220 ; iv, 222.
> *Family :* Iulia Soaemias (mother), Iulia Maesa (grandmother) ;
> m. (i) Cornelia Paula ; (ii) Aquilia Severa ; (iii) Annia Faustina.

†*SEVERUS ALEXANDER (M. Aurelius Severus Alexander). 222-235 (Jan.-March).
> *Trib. pot.* March 11, 222 ; ii begins December 10, 222.
> *Cos.* 222 ; ii, 226 ; iii, 229.
> *Family :* mother, Iulia Mammaea ; m. Orbiana.

†Maximin (called Thrax ; C. Iulius Verus Maximinus). 235-238 (May-June).
   Trib. pot. early in 235 ; ii begins December 10, 235.
   Cos. 236.
   Family : s. C. Iulius Verus Maximus.
Pupienus (Imp. Caes. M. Clodius Pupienus Aug.). 238 (March-June).
Balbinus (D. Caelius Calvinus Balbinus). 238 (March-June).
*Gordian I (M. Antonius Gordianus Sempronianus Romanus Africanus Senior). 238 (reigned 20 days from the middle of February).
*Gordian II (Imp. Caes. M. Antonius Gordianus Sempronianus Africanus Iunior Aug.). 238, as Gordian I.
†*Gordian III (M. Antonius Gordianus). 238-244 (Feb.-March).
   Trib. pot. June 1, 238 ; ii begins December 10, 238.
   Cos. 239 ; ii, 241.
   Family : m. Tranquillina.
†*Philip I (M. Iulius Philippus). 244-249 (Aug.-Oct.).
   Trib. pot. March 244 ; ii begins December 10, 244.
   Cos. 245 ; ii, 247 ; iii, 248.
   Family : m. Otacilia Severa.
†*Philip II (M. Iulius Philippus). 244-249 (Aug.-Oct.).
   Caesar, March (?) 244, and *trib. pot.* begins then, ii beginning December 10 ; *Augustus*, Aug. (?) 246, and a new series of *trib. pot.* dates begins that year on December 10 ; *Cos.* 247 ; ii, 248.
Iulius Aurelius Sulpicius Uranius Antoninus. 248-253.
P. Carvilius Marinus Pacatianus. 248.
Jotapianus. 249.
†*Decius (C. Messius Quintus Decius Traianus). 249-251 (May).
   Trib. pot. begins either in 248 or 249.
   Cos. ii, 250 ; iii, 251.
   Family : m. Herennia Etruscilla.
†*Q. Herennius Etruscus Messius Decius. 250-251 (May).
   Caesar and *trib. pot.* 250, *Augustus*, 251.
†C. Valens Hostilianus Messius Quintus. 250-251 (Nov.).
   Caesar and *trib. pot.* 250 ; *Augustus*, November, 251.
Gallus (C. Vibius Trebonianus Gallus). 251-253 (Sept. ?).
   Trib. pot., November, 251 ; ii, December 10 ; iv, December 10, 252.
   Cos. ii, 252.
Volusian (C. Vibius Afinius Gallus Veldumnianus Volusianus). 251-253.
   As Gallus, but *cos.* 252 ; *cos.* ii, 253.
†M. Aemilius Aemilianus. 253.
   m. Cornelia Supera.
*Valerian (P. Licinius Valerianus). 253-259 (taken prisoner by the Parthians between August 29, 259, and August 28, 260).
   Trib. pot. October 22, 253 ; ii begins December 10, 253.
   Cos. ii, 254 ; iii, 255 ; iv, 257.
   Family : m. Mariniana.

PLATE VI

30. JULIA DOMNA
31. CARACALLA
32. GETA
33. MACRINUS
34. ELAGABALUS
35. JULIA SOAEMIAS

36. JULIA MAESA
37. SEVERUS ALEX-
    ANDER
38. JULIA MAMAEA
39. MAXIMIN

40. BALBINUS
41. PUPIENUS
42. GORDIAN III
43. PHILIP I
44. OTACILIA SEVERA

†*GALLIENUS (P. Licinius Egnatius Gallienus).   253-268 (March 20).
   Trib. pot. August, 253 ; ii begins December 10, 253.
   Cos. 254 ; ii, 255 ; iii, 257 ; iv, 261 ; v, 262 ; vi, 264 ; vii, 266.
   Family : m. Salonina ; ss. Valerian junior, Saloninus.
POSTUMUS (M. Cassianius Latinius Postumus).   258-267 (Dec.).
   Trib. pot. December, 258 ; ii begins December 10, 259.
   Cos. i, 258 ; ii, 259 ; iii, 260 ; iv, 265 ; v, 267.
MACRIANUS.   260.
REGALIANUS.   261.
AUREOLUS.   267-268.
LAELIANUS.   268.
MARIUS.   268.
*VICTORINUS (M. Piavonius Victorinus).   268-270.
   Trib. pot. 268 ; ii, December 10, 268.
TETRICUS (C. Pius Esuvius Tetricus).   270-273.
   Trib. pot. 270 ; ii, December 10, 270.
   Cos. 271 ; ii, 272 ; iii, 273.
   Family : s. Tetricus junior, *Caesar*, 270.
*CLAUDIUS II. (called GOTHICUS ; M. Aurelius Claudius).   268-270.
   Trib. pot. 268 ; ii, December 10, 268.
   Cos. 269.
M. Aurelius Claudius QUINTILLUS.   270.
†*AURELIAN (Domitius Aurelianus).   270-275.
   Trib. pot. 270 ; ii begins December 10, 270.
   Cos. 271 ; ii, 274 ; iii, 275.
   Family : m. Ulpia Severina.
DOMITIAN II.   During the years 270-275.
VABALLATHUS.   270-271.
   Family : Zenobia, mother.
TACITUS (M. Claudius Tacitus).   275-276.
   Trib. pot. 275 ; ii begins December 10, 275.
   Cos. 275 ; ii, 276.
M. Annius FLORIANUS.   276 (2 months 20 days, *c.* April-July).
†*PROBUS (M. Aurelius Probus).   276-282 (Sept.).
   Trib. pot. July, 276 ; ii begins December 10, 276.
   Cos. 277 ; ii, 278 ; iii, 279 ; iv, 281 ; v, 282.
SATURNINUS.   280.
†*CARUS (M. Aurelius Carus).   282-283 (Aug.).
   Trib. pot. 282 ; ii begins December 10, 282.
   Cos. 282 ; ii, 283.
JULIAN (M. Aurelius Iulianus).   283.
†CARINUS (M. Aurelius Carinus).   283-285.
   Trib. pot. 283 ; ii begins December 10, 283.
   Cos. 283 ; ii, 284 ; iii, 285.
   Family : m. Magnia Urbica ; s. Nigrinianus.
†*NUMERIAN (M. Aurelius Numerius Numerianus).   283-284.
   Trib. pot. 283 ; ii begins December 10, 283.
   Cos. 284.

†*DIOCLETIAN (C. (or M.) Aurelius Valerius Diocletianus). 284-305
(abdicated May 1).

Trib. pot. begins September 17, 284 ; ii begins January 1, 285.

Cos. ii, 285 ; iii, 287 ; iv, 290 ; v, 293 ; vi, 296 ; vii, 299 ; viii, 303 ;
ix, 304 ; x, 308.

†*MAXIMIAN (called HERCULIUS ; M. Aurelius Valerius Maximianus, *or*
Herculius). 286-305 (abdicated May 1 ; seized power again
Feb. 307-April, 308).

Trib. pot. 285.

Cos. 287 ; ii, 288 ; iii, 290 ; iv, 293 ; v, 297 ; vi, 299 ; vii, 303 ;
viii, 304 ; ix, 307.

Caesar, April 1, 285 ; *Augustus*, April 1, 286.

*CONSTANTIUS (called CHLORUS ; M. (or C.) Flavius Valerius Constantius),
293-306 (July 25).

Cos. 294 ; ii, 296 ; iii, 300 ; iv, 302 ; v, 305 ; vi, 306.

Caesar, March 1, 293 ; *Augustus*, May 1, 305.

Family : m. Helena.

†*GALERIUS (C. Galerius Valerius Maximianus). 293-311 (May).

Cos. 294 ; ii, 297 ; iii, 300 ; iv, 302 ; v, 305 ; vi, 306 ; vii, 307.

Caesar, March 1, 293 ; *Augustus*, May 1, 305.

CARAUSIUS (M. Aurelius Mausaeus Valerius Carausius). 287-293.

ALLECTUS. 293-296.

ACHILLES. 296.

†FLAVIUS SEVERUS. 305-307 (April).

Caesar, May 1, 305 ; *Augustus*, July 25, 306.

†MAXIMIN DAIA (Galerius Valerius Maximinus). 305-313.

Caesar, May 1, 305 ; *Augustus*, May, 309.

Cos. 307 ; ii, 311 ; iii, 313.

†MAXENTIUS (M. Aurelius Valerius Maxentius). 306-312 (Oct. 28).

Caesar, October 28, 306 ; *Augustus*, 307 (308 ?).

Cos. 308 ; ii, 309 ; iii, 310 ; iv, 312.

Family : m. Maximilla ; s. Romulus.

ALEXANDER. 308-311, in Africa.

†LICINIUS (Valerius Licinianus Licinius). 308-324 (abdicated Sept. 18).

Augustus, November 11, 308.

Cos. 309 ; ii, 312 ; iii, 313 ; iv, 315 ; v, 318 ; vii, 322.

Family : m. Constantia ; s. Licinius junior, *Caesar* 317.

*CONSTANTINE I (C. or L. or M. Flavius Valerius Constantinus). 306-
337 (May 22).

Caesar, July 25, 306 ; *Augustus*, March 31 (?), 307.

Cos. 307 or 309 ; ii, 312 ; iii, 313 ; iv, 315 ; v, 319 ; vi, 320 ; vii,
326 ; viii, 329.

Family : M. Fausta ; ss. Crispus (*Caesar* 317) ; Delmatius (*Caesar* 335);
Hannibalianus (*Caesar* 335).

VALENS. 314.

†CONSTANTINE II (Flavius Claudius Constantinus Iunior). 317-340.

Caesar, March 1, 317 (in infancy) ; *Augustus*, September 9, 337.

Cos. 320 ; ii, 321 ; iii, 324 ; iv, 329.

PLATE VII

45. PHILIP II	53. SALONINA	61. TACITUS
46. DECIUS	54. CLAUDIUS	62. PROBUS
47. HERENNIA ETRUS-	GOTHICUS	63. CARUS
CILLA	55. POSTUMUS	64. CARINUS
48. GALLUS	56. VICTORINUS	65. NUMERIAN
49. VOLUSIAN	57. TETRICUS	66. DIOCLETIAN
50. AEMILIAN	58. TETRICUS JUNIOR	67. MAXIMIAN
51. VALERIAN	59. QUINTILLUS	68. CONSTANTIUS
52. GALLIENUS	60. AURELIAN	CHLORUS

Martinianus. 323.

†*Constans (Flavius Iulius Constans). 333-350 (Jan. 18).
 Caesar, December 25, 333 ; *Augustus*, September 9, 337.
 Cos. 339 ; ii, 342 ; iii, 346.

*Constantius II (Flavius Iulius Constantius). 324-361 (Nov. 3).
 Caesar, November 8, 324 ; *Augustus*, September 9, 337.
 Cos. 326 ; ii, 339 ; iii, 342 ; iv, 346 ; v, 352 ; vi, 353 ; vii, 354 ;
  viii, 356 ; ix, 357 ; x, 360.

Nepotianus. 350.

Vetranio. 350.

†Magnentius (Flavius Magnus Magnentius). 350-353 (Aug. 11).
 Augustus, January 18, 350.
 Cos. 351 ; ii, 353.
 Family : brother, Decentius (*Caesar*, 351) ; s. of Constantius,
  Constantius Gallus (*Caesar*, 351).

Claudius Silvanus. 355.

*Julian (" the Apostate " ; Flavius Claudius Iulianus). 355-363
 (June 26).
 Caesar, November 6, 355 ; *Augustus*, 360.
 Cos. 356 ; ii, 357 ; iii, 360 ; iv, 363.

*Jovian (Flavius Iovianus). 363-364 (Feb. 16).
 Augustus, June 27, 363.
 Cos. 364.

*Valentinian I (Flavius Valentinianus). 364-375 (Nov. 17).
 Augustus, February 26, 364.
 Cos. 365 ; ii, 368 ; iii, 370 ; iv, 373.

*Valens (Flavius Valens). 364-378 (Aug. 9).
 Augustus, March 28, 364.
 Cos. 365 ; ii, 368 ; iii, 370 ; iv, 373 ; v, 376 ; vi, 378.

*Gratian (Flavius Gratianus). 367-383 (Aug. 25).
 Augustus, August 24, 367.
 Cos. 366 ; ii, 371 ; iii, 374 ; iv, 377 ; v, 380.

Procopius. 365-366.

*Valentinian II (Flavius Valentinianus Iunior). 375-392 (May 15).
 Augustus, November 22, 373.
 Cos. 376 ; ii, 378.

†Maximus (Magnus Maximus). 383-388 (July 28).
 Cos. 384 ; ii, 388.

Flavius Victor. 384-388 ; *Augustus*, 384.

Eugenius. 392-394 (Sept. 6).
 Augustus, 392.
 Cos. 393.

*Theodosius I (Flavius Theodosius). 379-395 (Jan. 17).
 Augustus, January 19, 379.
 Cos. 380 ; ii, 388 ; iii, 393.
 Family : m. Flaccilla ; d. Galla Placidia.

*Honorius.　395-423 (Aug.).

　Augustus, November 20, 393.

　Cos. 386 ; ii, 394 ; iii, 396 ; iv, 398 ; v, 402 ; vi, 404 ; vii, 407 ;
　　viii, 409 ; ix, 412 ; x, 415 ; xi, 417 ; xii, 418 ; xiii, 422.

*Arcadius.　395-408.

　Augustus. 383.

　Cos. 385 ; ii, 392 ; iii, 394 ; iv, 396 ; v, 402 ; vi, 406.

Constantine III.　407-411.

PLATE VIII

69. GALERIUS	78. CRISPUS	86. VALENTINIAN I
70. FLAVIUS SEVERUS	79. CONSTANTINE II	87. VALENS
71. MAXIMIN DAIA	80. CONSTANTIUS II	88. GRATIAN
72. LICINIUS	81. CONSTANS	89. VALENTINIAN II
73. LICINIUS JUNIOR	82. MAGNENTIUS	90. MAXIMUS
74. CONSTANTINE I	83. DECENTIUS	91. THEODOSIUS I
75. HELENA	84. JULIAN	92. ARCADIUS
76. THEODORA	85. JOVIAN	93. HONORIUS
77. FAUSTA		

INDEX

N.B.—The following are not indexed : subjects whose place in the book is indicated by the table of contents ; tabular matter (abbreviations used in inscriptions, pp. 178-184, index of Samian potters, pp. 213-215, list of emperors, pp. 275-282) ; sites, dates, etc., referred to in the detailed discussion of individual pottery types (chs. xiii, xiv) and brooches (ch. xv) ; and the plates of imperial portraits.